*George Wythe Randolph
and the Confederate Elite*

THE UNIVERSITY OF GEORGIA PRESS
ATHENS AND LONDON

# George Wythe Randolph
# and the Confederate Elite

## GEORGE GREEN SHACKELFORD

© 1988 by the University of Georgia Press
Athens, Georgia 30602
All rights reserved
Set in Galliard

Frontispiece and jacket: The west front of Monticello, ca. 1825. Pictured are Edward P. Petticolas, George Wythe Randolph, Virginia Jefferson Randolph, and Cornelia Jefferson Randolph. (Detail of a watercolor by Jane Petticolas Bradick; courtesy of The Thomas Jefferson Memorial Foundation, Inc., Charlottesville, Va.)

The paper in this book meets the guidelines for permanence and durability of the Committee on Production Guidelines for Book Longevity of the Council on Library Resources.

Printed in the United States of America
92  91  90  89  88    5  4  3  2  1


Library of Congress Cataloging in Publication Data

Shackelford, George Green.
   George Wythe Randolph and the Confederate elite/George Green Shackelford.
   p.   cm.
   Bibliography: p.
   Includes index.
   ISBN 0-8203-0998-2 (alk. paper)
   1. Randolph, George Wythe, 1818–1867. 2. Cabinet officers—Southern States—Biography. 3. Generals—Southern States—Biography. 4. Confederate States of America. War Dept.—Biography. 5. Confederate States of America—History, Military. 6. United States—History—Civil War, 1861–1865—Biography. 7. Richmond (Va.)—Intellectual life. I. Title.
   E467.1.R23S48  1988
   973.7′092′4—dc 19      87-22199      CIP


British Library Cataloging in Publication Data available

# Contents

# Illustrations

# Preface

Because there is no large, single body of official or business correspondence by George Wythe Randolph, no previous attempt has been made to write an extended biography of him. Although he wrote to his wife Mary once a week when they were apart, virtually none of their letters to each other have survived. It is probable that before leaving Richmond in 1864 he deposited his papers in a bank that burned when the city fell in 1865. Considering how careful Randolph was to preserve and secure War Department records, it is ironic that the most important official records of his secretaryship—classified as *Secretary of War, Letters Sent*—disappeared either because a clique in the War Department wished to destroy records of treason in New Orleans or because they were destroyed when the Union army sent Confederate archives to Washington as booty from the War of the Rebellion. Fortunately, enough of George Randolph's official correspondence has survived in other archival groupings to sustain the author's discussion of his secretaryship.

The Jefferson-Randolph family trait of writing and saving letters was strong in him. The voluminous correspondence of George Randolph with his close relatives provides data to reconstruct all aspects of his life except the profound affection between him and his wife, whose account, therefore, must be foreshortened. The most important of these familial manuscript collections are those of Thomas Jefferson Randolph, Ellen Randolph Coolidge, and Mary Buchanan—"Molly"—Randolph, respectively his eldest brother, his "second mother," and his confidante. There is also valuable data in the letters of Benjamin Franklin Randolph, Meriwether Lewis Randolph, Jane Nicholas Randolph Kean, Sarah Nicholas Randolph, Septimia Randolph Meikleham, Virginia Randolph Trist, and their spouses. Although some other writers who have been concerned with either the Randolph family or the Civil

War have used parts of the Edgehill Randolph Papers at the University of Virginia's Alderman Library, I doubt that any has utilized the closely associated collections ranked under the in-law names of Coolidge, Hubard, Kean, Meikleham, and Trist.

I acknowledge with many thanks the courtesy of several of the descendants of General Randolph's protégés in advising me and permitting me to consult their family's muniments. Among these are Messieurs George and Thomas Bayne Denegre, respectively of New Orleans, Louisiana and Whitestone, Virginia, who furnished me valuable material concerning New Orleans on the eve of and during the Civil War; Mr. Edward Trigg Brown of Danville, Virginia, who shared information concerning Colonel J. Thompson Brown, General Randolph's second–in-command in the Richmond Howitzers and his confidant; Mrs. E. Griffith Dodson of Roanoke, Virginia, who provided me information about her great-uncle, Colonel T. M. R. Talcott; Mr. Daniel Ficklin of Kilmarnock, Virginia, and Mr. James S. Ficklin of Greenville, North Carolina, concerning Mr. and Mrs. James Burwell Ficklin; Professor Thomas E. Gilmer, Jr., of Virginia Polytechnic Institute and State University, who helped me puzzle out the intricacies of the Virginia and North Carolina Gilmers; and Mr. McDonald Wellford of Richmond, Virginia, who gave me valuable information concerning Major Edmund Trowbridge Dana Myers's activities as a civil engineer as well as the lore and insights collected in a lifetime of study of Virginia's history during the Civil War.

This book is the outgrowth of a biographical sketch for the first volume of *The Collected Papers of the Monticello Association* (Princeton, 1965) and of my essay, "George Wythe Randolph, U.S.N.," which appeared in *The American Neptune* in 1978. I am much indebted to Archer Jones of Richmond, who wrote his master's thesis at the University of Virginia on George Wythe Randolph as Secretary of War under the direction of our common mentor, Bernard Mayo, and who also has published important essays about Secretary of War Randolph's strategic contributions in both the *Journal of Southern History* and the *Virginia Magazine of History and Biography*. Although our interpretations of General Randolph's character and career differ, Professor Jones has given me much good advice, attempted to steer me away from military blunders, and warned me not to fall into simplistic, anti-Davis traps.

I wish to acknowledge the inspiration of person and concept that Raimondo Luraghi has afforded me in the Piedmonts of Virginia and Italy. His *Storia della guerra civile* will be translated into English, I hope, but until then his brief *Rise and Fall of the Plantation South* will continue to provoke thought concerning reassessment of that society. As both a creator and a product of post-Fascist Italy, Luraghi has led a generation of Americans to see something more important than improvisation in the Confederate government's centralization, ownership of key industries, and regulation of corporations, partnerships, and individuals. While I agree with him in marveling at the Southerners' remarkable accomplishment in creating from a modest prewar system of manufacturing and supply a war economy capable of competing with the North, I believe that Professor Luraghi mistakenly gives to others credit that should be awarded collectively to the elites whom Secretary of War Randolph led and for whom he was the chief spokesman. Where Luraghi is inclined to detect in the Southern republic's war economy a resort to state socialism, I am inclined to see merely latter-day mercantilism or the ordinary measures of a country at war. Until the spring of 1862 the Confederacy's economic policy, if any, was an ad hoc, ill-formed, and optimistic one. Randolph's accession to the Secretaryship of War occurred at about the same time that the Confederate States Congress first provided that department anything like an adequate number of staff billets. It was he who filled these posts with a technocratic elite. His appointees were centralizers. In order to provide capital, materials, and labor for wartime essentials, they were quite willing to limit the civilian economy.

In seeking to apply the methods and standards of elitism and of proposography to mid-nineteenth-century Virginia and to the Confederacy, I am aware that I risk being charged with overemphasizing genealogy. Such is not my purpose. In seeking to identify and characterize some elites of the Southern republic, 1861–1865, I hope to demonstrate that multiple causes and multiple groups effected policy through coincidence and compromise. The ties of kinship, friendship, and association within the milieu of church, preparatory school, college, and profession were not only descriptive of George Randolph's world; they were forces central to his rise to eminence. They were central, also, to the nature of his successful reorganization of the Confederate military apparatus and war economy. Within the general scope of the writings of Vilfredo Pareto, I have attempted to limn the coincidence of the elites to which George Randolph belonged.

Besides those whom I already have mentioned, I am grateful also to many who have aided me by reading portions of the manuscript of this book, or by giving advice on specific matters. Among these are Malcolm Call and Nancy Holmes of the University of Georgia Press; John Melville Jennings, Executive Director Emeritus of the Virginia

Historical Society; Mary Tabb Lancaster Johnston of Blacksburg, Virginia; Philip C. F. Smith of the Peabody Museum; and the late Walter Muir Whitehill of the Boston Athenaeum. Olivia A. Taylor, Mary McIntire Betts Anderson, Cary Ann Randolph Cooper, and James A. Bear, Jr., kindly shared information about General Randolph and his possessions. Since this work involves several fields or varieties of history, I am grateful to my colleagues in the History Department's faculty seminar at Virginia Polytechnic Institute and State University. To all of them I am greatly indebted. To all I give my collective thanks.

I also acknowledge with thanks the aid of many librarians, but especially the staffs of the Alderman Library of the University of Virginia, the Benaki Museum of Athens, Greece, the Museum of the Confederacy at Richmond, the Newman Library of Virginia Polytechnic Institute and State University, the Virginia Historical Society, and the Wilson Library of the University of North Carolina. I wish to thank the Alderman Library, the Museum of the Confederacy, and the Thomas Jefferson Memorial Foundation for permitting me to use illustrative materials from their collections. I render collective thanks to several generations of secretaries who, in assisting me, have learned more than they desired about General Randolph.

My wife Grace has been forbearing of my efforts to find materials about George Wythe Randolph. I thank her for that, as well as for so many other things.

# CHAPTER I

# *Background and Youth,*
## *1818–1832*

Born at Monticello on March 10, 1818, George Wythe Randolph was the youngest of the eleven children of Gov. Thomas Mann and Martha Jefferson Randolph. He was named after George Wythe, who had taught law to the child's grandfather, Thomas Jefferson, and had been his political colleague. The boy divided his earliest years between Monticello and his parents' Edgehill plantation, about four miles distant in Albemarle County, Virginia. Oblivious of the financial debacle that would soon overwhelm the Jefferson-Randolphs, the six-year-old George, in a beaver top hat, prodded hoops with a stick to make them roll on the pleasure grounds of the west front of Monticello for the amusement of his sisters Ellen and Septimia. At about the time of her marriage and departure from Albemarle, Ellen received from Jane Petticoles Bradick a watercolor of this scene as a keepsake. It captured, as have few artists or writers, the fading arcadian, yet cosmopolitan quality of the Jeffersonian republic, already vanishing before the onslaught of the factory materialism of the North and the slavery materialism of the South.[1]

As a Randolph, George inherited a sacred circle of kinship and shared ideals which dominated the commonwealth of Virginia during the two centuries separating the English from the American civil war. The Randolphs of Virginia never disclaimed their prowess as leaders, whether in the aristocratic years before 1776 or in those after independence, when the concept of natural aristocracy and leadership flourished. Some Randolphs accepted upon terms of equality individuals who possessed neither pedigree nor riches, but most Randolphs retained a degree of hauteur, irrespective of whether such an attitude comported well with their economic or intellectual status.[2]

I

Traditions of a family help shape its younger members. Ever since the mid-seventeenth century when the immigrant, William Randolph, acquired his estate at Turkey Island, the Randolphs had been one of the dozen most prominent families of the Old Dominion. They were so prolific and the names William, Thomas and Richard were so often repeated that, in order to distinguish between their branches, one referred to the Randolphs of this or that country estate. Through his father, George Wythe Randolph was a great-great-grandson of Thomas Randolph who had founded the Tuckahoe branch. Through his mother, he was a great-grandson of Isham Randolph, who, after having been a sea captain and London resident, had retired to Virginia to found the Dungeness branch. More immediately, he was the son of Thomas Mann Randolph, Jr., who, after his father's second marriage, had founded the Edgehill branch. Aside from keeping straight the identities and whereabouts of various Randolphs, this system of patronymics created a romantic mystique that enhanced traditional models of deportment.

Martha Jefferson Randolph devoted much time to the instruction of her children. To her youngest, George, she probably gave more of herself than to the others because she needed the child's affection in the 1820s when she became an estranged wife, a bereaved daughter, and an impoverished widow. She probably instilled in him an interest in the sea by telling him how she had crossed the Atlantic to Europe when Mr. Jefferson had been not only famous but rich and how she had recrossed the ocean to experience a whirlwind courtship and happy early married life, when Tom Randolph was affluent and possessed of a future full of promise. In explaining to the lad the relationship he bore to cousinly playmates, she must have told him how his great-great-grandfather, Isham Randolph of Dungeness, unlike other Randolphs, had been a sea captain, lived in London and died solvent. It may have been that George Randolph believed that the salt of the sea was lucky.

In the 1850s the Virginia historian Hugh Blair Grigsby asserted that William Randolph of Turkey Island had been a carpenter in England before amassing a fortune in Virginia. Unlike some of their kin, the Jefferson-Randolphs did not disagree with Grigsby, but merely called his attention to William's accomplishments and descent from English provincial gentry. No one disputed the Randolphs' royalist, cavalier allegiance, which was demonstrated by Charles I's and Henrietta Maria's patronage of William's uncle, Thomas Randolph, the Cavalier poet and protégé of Ben Jonson.[3]

George Randolph was born when Governor and Mrs. Randolph

were respectively fifty and forty-six. It was not because of Governor Randolph's age that George did not know his father very well during the latter's remaining ten years of life. Official duties kept Thomas Mann Randolph away from home for about one-third of those years: as governor, 1819–1821; as a state legislator, 1824–1825; and as a commissioner to fix the border of Florida and Georgia in 1827. In the hard times after the Panic of 1819, Governor Randolph brooded so much on his financial difficulties, those of his son's father-in-law, Wilson Cary Nicholas, and those of Thomas Jefferson that he became despairing. He suffered the delusion that his wife and eldest son plotted to sacrifice his solvency in order to save Jefferson's. Ignoring facts, he berated the fates whom he saw separating him from his family, and especially from little George.[4] Ill and poor, Thomas Mann Randolph became a recluse for most of the four years before his death in 1828.

Needless to say, the Jefferson-Randolphs tried to shelter the boy from these distressing circumstances. The lad was a favorite with all at Monticello, including the trusted and able carpenter, John Hemings. George grew up in an atmosphere dominated by his aged grandfather, Thomas Jefferson, whose family's love approached deification. Taken to his grandfather's bedside for a last adieu, the boy could not believe that the patriarch was dying.

For guidance, young George looked to his sagacious and loving mother and to his eldest brother, Thomas Jefferson Randolph. The latter was twenty-six years older and had married three years before the lad was born. Jefferson Randolph's children eventually numbered thirteen. The first eight were girls—whom George always treated more as playmates or sisters than as nieces. He looked on his much older sister Ellen as a second mother from the time that she carried him about as an infant. The lad came to associate her approval and good humor with good times and her disapproval and bad humor with unhappy ones. Ellen, in turn, displayed maternal love for and possessiveness concerning George throughout her life. From the time that she married Joseph Coolidge, Jr., at Monticello and moved to Boston, the Jefferson-Randolphs suffered such reduced circumstances that even a child would have known that the good times were over.[5]

Martha Jefferson Randolph went to Boston in 1826 to visit Ellen and Joseph Coolidge when their first child was born and as a respite from her financial and personal problems in Albemarle. She took with her the eight-year-old George Wythe Randolph. When she returned to Virginia in June of 1827, the youth remained with the Coolidges in their house near Bowdoin Square. Joseph Coolidge's grandfather and father were prosperous importers. They already had established precedents for generosity to in-laws by helping the Bulfinches after the architect Charles Bulfinch went bankrupt. Their generosity made a lasting impression on young Randolph and provides a key to his character, which otherwise might seem too materialistic and self-seeking. "Money," he said, "in the hands of a good man . . . is an instrument of benevolence." Because Joseph Coolidge's business did not flourish in Boston, he determined to enter the China trade in order "to recoup his fortune" and to provide for his wife and children. Two years after George's long visit with the Coolidges, Joseph sailed for Canton in the autumn of 1833. Because Chinese regulations then forbade the residence of foreign women, Mrs. Coolidge and their six children remained in Boston.[6]

Between his eleventh and thirteenth years, George made himself useful to his sister Ellen in the great, but understaffed, house near Bowdoin Square which Charles Bulfinch had designed for the grandfather and namesake of Joseph Coolidge and into which the younger Joseph moved his wife and children in 1820. Both Ellen and Joseph Coolidge were very fond of George. Throughout his life they provided him a loving and helpful hand, but especially at the great crises of his life: when he was between eight and ten years of age and in need of a good education, when he was between twenty and twenty-two and revaluating his choice of careers, and between 1864 and 1867 when he lost his fortune and health in the wreck of the Confederacy.[7]

Before leaving Albemarle, Mrs. Randolph taught George enough for him to relish what she called "that Queen of Dotards, Mother Hubbard." In the first of his two years in Boston, the lad attended Mrs. Hannah Stearn's school. In the second year, he went to an old house in Cambridge where Mr. William Wells's classical school provided severe drilling in Latin, Greek, geometry, and advanced algebra. Wells required his boys to take part in manly, out-of-doors sports. A strict disciplinarian, he frequently caned his pupils. Among his thirty boarders and a few day students were members of the Dana, Higginson, and Story families. Among these, George Randolph considered his fellow day student James Russell Lowell his best friend, perhaps because Lowell's visit to Washington, Alexandria, and Mount Vernon gave the two a slender common bond.[8]

Because Joseph Coolidge was an austere man of very high standards, the Randolph family was pleased that George met with his approval as "industrious and excellent . . . singularly honest . . . obliging and intelligent." For George, Joseph probably would have been a beloved and respected uncle under any circumstances, but he was so scholarly and steady that he must have stood out as someone who made things happen, in comparison with the Jefferson-Randolph men, who struggled to respond to events that others set in motion. Even though in the 1850s George Wythe Randolph inveighed against Yankee traits of hypocrisy and parsimony, he always took pains to except his brother-in-law Coolidge, who was for him more of a model than either comprehended until the end of the Civil War.

By the time Mrs. Randolph came back to Boston in the late summer of 1830, Governor Randolph had died and Monticello and many of its furnishings had been sold in order to satisfy Thomas Jefferson's creditors. Mrs. Randolph and George journeyed south by streamboat and by stagecoach. She had decided to establish in Washington a common home for her unmarried children and herself with her daughter Virginia and her son-in-law, Nicholas P. Trist. She proposed to share expenses with Trist, whom President Jackson had borrowed from his regular duties at the State Department to serve as his private secretary. The Trist family of four, Mrs. Randolph and her daughters Cornelia and Septimia and her sons Lewis and George moved into a house at the junction of Pennsylvania Avenue, I Street and Twentieth Street.[9]

Young George Wythe Randolph's lack of a conventional home life marred neither his character, which was manly and noble, nor his disposition, which was sunny. Formal schooling in Cambridge had been better than what he would have got in Albemarle, and it reinforced in him his family's cultivated interests. Residence in Albemarle, Boston, and Washington provided hope that he would never be provincial. His relatively cosmopolitan upbringing made it unlikely that the boy would succumb to overindulgence in rural delights.

In Washington George found for a while both the family life he ardently desired and an opportunity to continue his education. He attended first Mr. McCleod's and then Mr. Hughes's school for boys in order to be prepared for entrance either to West Point or to the University of Virginia. By 1831 the Randolphs had to decide what career and what further education would best suit him. If George secretly desired to return to Boston to complete his education under Sister Ellen's care, he did not have the opportunity to do so.[10]

Jefferson Randolph, as the male head of the family, for a while urged their mother to send George to the University of Virginia, but Nicholas Trist dissuaded her by emphasizing how straitened their finances were. He suggested that they wangle for George an appointment to Trist's alma mater, the United States Military Academy, whose curriculum had prepared him for more than an army career. Because

Jefferson Randolph opposed giving George the slightest encouragement to go into the army, Trist then suggested the navy. He brought home his friend William S. Archer, a congressman from Virginia, who "strongly advised" Mrs. Randolph to choose for her son a naval career because it was "more certain" of appointment and promotion, as well as being "more respectable and agreeable." The army, he said, probably would send George to "some fort to the westward to waste his youth in the most detestable manner and always liable to contract bad habits from idleness and bad company, whereas in the navy they were generally in service, and had opportunities of visiting every part of the world." George's next older brother, Lewis, was then a student at the University of Virginia and a dashing beau in Washington, roles that he soon exchanged for a promising career as a planter and land agent while secretary of the Arkansas Territory. Lewis praised the American West and tried to discourage George's interest in the navy. Amid divided family counsel, the youth himself decided to seek appointment as a midshipman.[11]

On March 31, 1831, Trist helped obtain for George a commission as midshipman in the United States Navy. The Randolph family had no compunction in seeking this appointment through Jacksonian patronage. After all, Mr. Jefferson himself had helped his friends' sons gain preferment in the civil, military or naval service, such as when he helped get for the twelve-year-old Samuel F. du Pont President Madison's commission as a midshipman.[12]

In the 1830s midshipmen were required to serve an apprenticeship of six months before drawing a salary of $319 a year. More important was the free, practical education emphasizing, besides navigation and seamanship, such things as geography, modern languages, and mathematics. To get for George the best possible berth, the Jefferson-Randolphs importuned Navy friends, especially the Stewarts, whom they knew as fellow communicants of St. John's Episcopal Church. The intimacy between George's sister Septimia and Delia Stewart gave the family the influence of Delia's father, Como. Charles Stewart, who headed the Naval Commission which then constituted the U.S. Navy's executive branch. The commodore probably helped obtain for young Randolph orders to the Mediterranean,[13] where many young naval officers eagerly sought assignment. The future Rear Adm. John A. Dahlgren had served there on the sloop *Ontario*. According to him,

> The Mediterranean . . . [is] the best school for an officer. The constant activity and habitual experience in handling a ship in close proximity to the shore, the entering and leaving of all kinds of harbors, and the contact

with the finest ships of England and France, give at once a standard for comparison, and one to strive to excel, if possible, while intercourse with the best officers and the service of these nations, as well as the people of so many highly civilized courts, all contribute to stimulate sentiments and cultivate manners which no other naval station can supply.[14]

Jefferson Randolph's in-law, John Nicholas, was a lieutenant in the United States Navy who was about to go in the USS. *John Adams* on a three-year cruise to the Mediterranean. He persuaded the Randolphs to advance the date of George's commencing his service to March 31, 1831, so that George could enjoy his patronage and supervision. He assured Mrs. Randolph that the midshipmen's "education goes on as regularly at sea as ashore, [and that] the attention of morals [is] very strict." He declared that, because a midshipman's expenses were nothing, George could save between $700 and $1,000 a year. Furthermore, he pointed out, by going now, instead of waiting two years until he was fifteen, George would gain more rapid promotion. Mrs. Randolph steeled herself to make the "dreadful sacrifice" of another separation from her youngest. Proudly she wrote of the lad to Ellen Coolidge: "He is developing wonderfully. His mind seems to have taken a spring which shows itself in his manners, though modest, and he really has a degree of general information that surprized me, and has been remarked by strangers."[15]

At the age of thirteen and a little less than one month, George Wythe Randolph accepted his appointment as acting midshipman from John Boyle, acting secretary of the Navy.[16] There was much to do to fit George out for sea.

# CHAPTER 2

# Midshipman Randolph, 1832–1837

According to the autobiographical novel by Adm. David D. Porter, Jr., naval tailors at Norfolk like "Old Camphor" outfitted midshipmen on credit at ten percent interest. Porter's alter ego, thirteen-year-old Midn. Harry Marline, bought in advance suits of dress and undress uniforms for ages thirteen, fifteen, and seventeen. In the 1830s a midshipman's outfit consisted of white pantaloons and a high-collared, single-breasted, blue work jacket and a gold-laced tailcoat for dress occasions. He had both a plain and a gold-laced cocked hat. In addition, a middie wore a diagonal belt called a "hanger" to carry a short, curved ceremonial sword.[1] A touching commentary on his affection for his mother and on the lamentable state of the Randolphs' finances was George's vow to send home to her half of the twenty-dollar-a-month wage he would earn as an apprentice.

Besides Lieutenant Nicholas, another friend of the family promised to provide guidance: William B. Hodgson of Virginia, who was returning to Constantinople, where he held a minor position in the American legation, as a passenger on the *John Adams*. A linguist well acquainted with the peoples and places of the inland sea, he promised to take George along "to swell the suite" of American officials making courtesy calls on such dignitaries as the Sultan and the King of Naples.[2]

Midshipman Randolph reported aboard the United States sloop *John Adams* at Norfolk during the first week of April 1831. A month later her captain took her out from the Virginia capes and set sail for a Mediterranean cruise, which for Randolph lasted a little more than a year. The lad reported his safe arrival at Gibraltar to his mother and to Ellen Wayles Coolidge,[3] but the details that he provided of his experiences

8

were meagre. Admiral Porter's account, however, provides many details
of Midn. Harry Marline's cruise on the "USS *Thunderbum*," a seventy-
four-gun frigate, that can be applied to Randolph's experience, especially as the sobriquet "Captain Marvellous" may have referred to
either of two men who served as George's commanding officers—Captain Voorhees of the *John Adams* in 1831 or Como. Jesse Elliott of the
USS *Constitution* in 1836. Doubtless George Randolph, like Harry
Marline, learned naughty tricks from older midshipmen with hearts of
gold like Ned Reckless, under whose leadership Marline and his fellow
middies tormented their schoolmaster, "Mr. O'Classics." Like Porter,
Midshipman Randolph must have been impressed by the "grandeur" of
the Spanish coastline—its "vine-clad and smiling villages" and "Moor-
ish towers" on rugged promontories behind which was the vista of the
"snow-clad hills" of the Sierra Nevada.[4]

Perhaps it seemed to Randolph, as it did to Porter-Marline, that
midshipmen shared with "the philosopher, the antiquarian, the poet
and the lover" a delight in Naples—"the most interesting city in the
Mediterranean, with all its poverty and tyranny." George wrote to his
sister Ellen that, when he was at Naples, he visited Mount Vesuvius and
"saw the ruins of Pompeii and of Herculanaeum which are very per-
fect. . . . We saw in the streets the ruts the carriages made, and I got one
or two pieces of marble which I had to steal, as there was a soldier with
us to prevent us from taking anything."[5]

Upon entering the Bay of Naples, U.S. naval vessels were met by
bumboats laden with delicious fruit, entertainers putting on Punch-
and-Judy shows, and "the sweetest singing girls" that the middies had
ever encountered. At Naples Marline-Porter even attended in the San
Carlo opera house a performance of *Masaniello*, just as young David
Farragut heard there *Barbe Bleu*. Whether George Randolph had a similar experience, one can only speculate. When Marline and the other
ship's officers accompanied the American minister in making a ceremonial call upon the King of the Two Sicilies, Admiral Porter said that
they toasted King Ferdinand "Bomba" with this noble and confused
sentiment:

> Naples and America
> Always weak and never strong
> Never right and always wrong.[6]

Although the rest of the ship's company was not allowed to go
ashore when the USS *John Adams* anchored at Constantinople in August 1831, Midshipman Randolph and his messmates could not have

failed to marvel at the bustling traffic of the Golden Horn, whose waters reflected the grandeur of the Hagia Sophia of the Byzantines, the tower of the Venetians, and the Topkapi Palace of the Sultan, where once had been the Palace of the Caesars. The crew manned the yardarms, cheered, and fired salutes when the Sultan Mahmoud came close aboard in his "magnificent caique, covered with carving and gilding and pulled by twenty-four herculean Greeks." The Sultan so admired the American warship that he sent a ship's architect to take her measurements before the sloop sailed back to the Aegean.[7]

The *John Adams* sailed next to the Gulf of Smyrna, whence George wrote his family that, because that city at its head was "very unhealthy," his ship anchored off Vourla at its mouth. The log of another Virginia midshipman related how, a few years earlier, his commodore had sailed up and down the gulf between Smyrna and Vourla, exchanging profuse salutes with American and foreign ships. Meanwhile, the officers supervised the crew in painting ship, tarring the rigging, mending sail, provisioning and watering ship, and overhauling bedding and clothes—interspersed by divine services.[8]

When Hodgson returned to America, he gave Mrs. Randolph "very good accounts" of George. She was proud to know that,

> although George is the youngest midshipman on board, the others being 18 and upwards, he is said to be the *best informed* amongst them, and has a character of *undaunted intrepidity* and integrity. I know him better than they do. He has weak nerves and such are always liable to alarm; but he has a pride and quick sensibility of character that would make him rush into the mouth of a cannon rather than disgrace himself. He has a great deal of observation and a desire for information which makes him visit everything worth seeing.[9]

Mrs. Randolph wrote later to her daughter Septimia: "George looks forward with great impatience to our return to Washington; poor fellow, he seems to repeat the word *home* with a pleasure which none but those like us who have seen the home of our childhood broken up, and been in a manner turned adrift upon the world as we have been can conceive."[10]

In May of 1833 George Randolph's apprenticeship was over. He was "warranted" a midshipman and granted twelve months' leave. In July he visited his mother for a fortnight after conducting her from Washington to Edgehill. It may have been because his eldest brother Jeff Randolph exhorted him to earn some money or because Ellen Coolidge did not bid him visit her, but George applied for active duty before the summer was over. Mrs. Randolph said that it was "with an aching heart" that she pressed into service "every child that could hem a sheet" in order to ready his outfit. George hardly noticed that a visitor had stolen his pair of Egyptian idols, and he left his tame crows for the enjoyment of his nieces. Mrs. Randolph disliked the crows, but concluded that, "bad as they are, as George's pets I take an interest in them."[11]

On August 23, 1833, Midshipman Randolph reported at Norfolk to the USS *Vandalia*. This was a six-year-old, eighteen-gun sloop of seven hundred tons which carried a crew of 190 officers and men. With about six other midshipmen, he slung his hammock in the steerage. Assuming the role of a seasoned sailor, Midshipman Randolph wrote his mother that he did not expect to enjoy his duty because the *Vandalia* was a flagship, "remaining in port while the other vessels are cruising." The ship's preparations for a Caribbean cruise kept him so busy that he went ashore only once during six weeks and hardly mourned the ship's departing Norfolk in early October. He was too preoccupied even to lament the miscarriage of a barrel of hams from Edgehill and a box of books from Boston.

The *Vandalia*'s cruise took her to St. Thomas, Havana, and Pensacola. Fortunately, she was not visited by fever.[12] George Randolph had mixed feelings about his service in the *Vandalia*. He wrote in December 1833 that, although "the commodore is an old dotard, who only thought of getting his ship safe to Pensacola, where he goes ashore to live . . . [o]ur captain is very kind, particularly to me." When in December of 1833 George's ship put into Havana, where Trist was now U.S. consul, he discovered that his kin were on vacation in the United States. The following May, however, he spent several days with the Trists at their pleasant country house. To his family he complained that his tutor was only an "apology" for a teacher, "a Corsican who was in France a few months and undertakes to teach the French language. . . . It is with the greatest difficulty that we can get him to hear us a lesson and he is always anxious to put it off for tomorrow, and tomorrow never comes."[13] When there were occasional gala balls on board the *Vandalia,* George was too shy to participate and he even professed to disapprove of women coming aboard warships. At the same time that he worried about the fairer sex, he wrote to his nieces that he soon expected them to introduce him to their girl friends. Meanwhile, he had the pleasure of friendship with another middie from Virginia, Richard Meade. The two young men had gossip to exchange, because George's brother Lewis was the fiancé of Richard's sister. When the engagement was broken off, George opined: "I never thought it would hold and I am glad it is broken off except on one account, that is I suppose she will be worth $80,000 . . . , and a man is a fool . . . that wouldn't marry anybody on earth for that fortune." George Randolph thought often about money, not because he was avaricious or envious, but simply because he was poor. A friend who was a passed midshipman had decided to attend the University of Virginia until he was assigned to a ship. With a salary of $500, he could barely afford it. Randolph could not consider it, however unhappy he might be on *Vandalia,* because he earned only $319 a year.[14]

On August 14, 1834, Midshipman Randolph received one month's leave, before reporting to the Norfolk Navy Yard's school conducted on the USS *Java,* a former forty-four-gun frigate. A few years earlier, Lieutenant Farragut had lived with his wife on board that ship, while improving the navy's general and nautical schooling. Although it does not appear that Randolph ever met Farragut, he was a beneficiary of the future admiral's educational reforms. On board the *Java,* the shy youth enjoyed an especially good tutor, under whom he studied mathematics, ordnance, and French. Although Randolph met the minimum scholastic and sea-duty requirements to be examined for the rank of passed midshipman by 1835, new regulations specified that no middie less than twenty years of age could take the exam. He could have gone home until the time of examination; but, instead, he sought and obtained in February of 1835 assignment to the USS *Constitution* for another cruise in the Mediterranean.[15]

George Randolph went to New York to join the *Constitution,* commanded by the avuncular Como. Jesse D. Elliott, then on his last cruise. Appointed a midshipman in 1804, Elliott had performed both well and badly on the Great Lakes during the War of 1812, after which he four times challenged or was challenged to duel. In one of these, Commodore Perry challenged him as a result of Perry's allegation that Elliott had been dilatory in aiding him during the Battle of Lake Erie. Fortunately, all four duels were averted, but Perry's complaint was partial grounds for Elliott's suspension from active naval duty for two years. Another reason was the charge by some junior officers that Elliott had acted vaingloriously as commander-in-chief of the Mediterranean Squadron. Ultimately, Elliott cleared his name and was reinstated to active service.[16]

When Midshipman Randolph went to join the USS *Constitution* at New York, it is likely that he unconsciously followed the example of John A. Dahlgren, who had entered the navy as a middie five years earlier than he, in lodging either at Bunker's Hotel, not far from the Battery, or at a house just outside the Navy Yard kept by a gunner named Cobb. In New York, George was able to visit his brother-in-law Joseph Coolidge during the latter's vacation from his enterprises in Canton, China, but he was not able to see Ellen Coolidge when she passed through the city on her way to Boston.[17]

As a senior midshipman, George was horrified at the poor condition of *Constitution*. He wrote to his niece Margaret that the ship had arrived from Boston with "only three midshipmen on board when there was duty enough to employ twenty. . . . We were sent to sea [on maneuvers] only half ready, and that in the most stormy month in the year on the Atlantic, and encountered hardships that I hope never to see again. Three or four men died and the rest of the crew and officers were completely worn down. I am the only officer on board who has not been sick, some of them dangerously, but now all hands are plucking up again."

When the *Constitution* set sail for the Mediterranean under Captain Elliott, she was still "only half ready" for sea and had only ten of her complement of twenty midshipmen.[18] Launched in 1797, the forty-four-gun frigate had given good service before and during the War of 1812, when she had become the most famous vessel of the United States Navy as the result of her victories over the HMS *Guerriere* and *Java*. In 1830 the Jackson administration's emphasis on efficiency and reform set in motion a plan to dismantle the USS *Constitution*, rather than to rebuild the thirty-two-year-old vessel. Oliver Wendell Holmes's poem stimulated such a national outcry against breaking up "Old Ironsides" that the ship was refitted.

The *Constitution* sailed to Port Mahon on the island of Minorca, where the Mediterranean Squadron made its winter operating base. Delegating command of the ship to Comdr. William Boerum, Elliott assumed his temporary rank of commodore of the Mediterranean Squadron, which consisted of the frigate, a twenty-four-gun corvette, two eighteen-gun sloops and a twelve-gun schooner. The squadron's frigate usually cruised for two years before returning to America, while its smaller vessels remained on station until used to convey dispatches or high-ranking persons to the United States. During Randolph's two-year tour of duty on the *Constitution,* she called at Madeira, Lisbon, Gibraltar, Port Mahon, Marseilles, Naples, Milos, Paros, Piraeus, and Smyrna. Doubtless, Randolph, like the young Farragut before him, "examined with great interest" the fortifications of Gibraltar.[19]

Midshipman Randolph made the most of his opportunity to visit the classic lands of antiquity only a decade after Lord Byron's death and soon after the accomplishment of Greek independence. As Commodore Rodgers had done several years before, Commodore Elliott probably took the squadron into Nauphlion on the Gulf of Argos, where modernized Venetian forts, curtain walls and bastions frowned down on the first capital of modern Greece. A castello in its harbor improved Nauphlion's fortifications, which must have fascinated young Randolph, even if they may not have come again to his mind until thirty years later, when as a Confederate artillery officer he helped fortify Yorktown.[20]

The aged *Constitution* was not a healthy ship. When Capt. Thomas McDonough had been her commanding officer in the Mediterranean in 1825, he was relieved of duty because he was dying of consumption and smallpox. In the winter of 1826–1827, Commodore Rodgers's Mediterranean Squadron sent ashore to a hospital "many" of his officers and men who fell ill of "catarrhal complaints." Young Randolph was overcome by "influenza" at Smyrna, where he was hospitalized "for some time" in the early months of 1836. Considering the illness prevalent in *Constitution,* it is difficult to avoid the conclusion that his service in "Old Ironsides" was the source of his later tubercular troubles.[21]

When the *Constitution* put into Piraeus in 1836, it was two years since King Otho had made his triumphal entry into the "deplorable" town of Athens, torn down the old fortifications on the Acropolis, laid the cornerstone for his palace, and opened up broad streets. The young king and his entourage came aboard the *Constitution,* but George Randolph's manly regimen and resolute republicanism made the middie contemptuous of Otho, Piraeus, and even Athens. Although the harbor was commodious enough to accommodate four or five American or British frigates and a number of coastal merchant vessels, Randolph dubbed the city of Athens and its satellite Piraeus "the most filthy and execrable hole in the Mediterranean."[22]

One of George Randolph's best friends on board the *Constitution* was Midn. Edward Clifford Anderson of Savannah, who had also studied in the North. Called "Ned," Anderson was described by George as "a born devil, but [a] high-minded and gallant fellow, scorning a mean action and a mean man, and not fearing Satan himself." Another friend was a younger midshipman from Virginia, George Tarry Sinclair, whose family the Jefferson-Randolphs knew. In the 1840s Tarry wrote to one of his kinsmen how George Randolph had made himself a hero to his messmates. This occurred while the American and English squadrons lay in the River Tagus near Lisbon "to help make a noise" over the wedding of Donna Maria, the Queen of Portugal. Both squadrons gave their crews "buncombe," as they referred to festive liberty. As Sinclair put it, "Our relations with the English officers were not friendly as a rule." Sinclair and Randolph were with a party of American midshipmen, sipping champagne in a restaurant, when officers from the HMS *Hastings* entered. A "big, burly" English officer named Dr. Rogers remarked to the American middies:

> "Oh, you belong, I believe, to the *Chesapeake* that met her match in the darling *Shannon*." Quick as lightning Randolph sprang to his feet and replied "You are mistaken a little in your history and have confused names. We belong to the *Constitution*, a name as well known to English as to Americans. Your object, Sir, cannot be mistaken, and you shall hear from me." The other English officers seemed ashamed of their comrade and tried to make excuses for him. Randolph exchanged cards with Dr. Rogers. It was determined that Randolph, the senior of our party, would peremptorily challenge Dr. Rogers, and, if his mess sustained him, our mess would then send a general challenge. I went on board the *Hastings* [as a second]. The object of my visit was at once surmised and Rogers was sent for. After reading the challenge, he remarked that he was extremely sorry for what had occurred, that his messmates condemned him, and [that] he was willing to make a suitable apology such as I might deem satisfactory. . . . Never will I forget George's sparkling eye as he rose from his seat to answer the insult. I knew and loved him well. A nobler fellow never lived.[23]

When Randolph's allotted time reached its end, he returned in a merchant vessel to America and reported in August of 1836 to the Norfolk School that David G. Farragut had instituted. Complaining of physical "apathy" and boredom, he prepared for his examinations to become a passed midshipman. Because of George's emotional dependence on his mother, the news of her death at Edgehill on October 10, 1836, at the age of sixty-four came to him as so great a shock that, as he wrote to Jefferson Randolph, "I could do nothing. Even now I can hardly realize that I am without a mother."

Martha Jefferson Randolph's last will and testament was only eleven lines in length, but it was eloquent of her bad fortune and of her special affection for George. She left to her daughters all her money— $20,000 that Louisiana and South Carolina had given her. As she often had said she would do, she left specific heirlooms to Jefferson Randolph, Joseph Coolidge, and Nicholas Trist. She made careful arrangement for the "liberation" or "time" of the Hemings family and of her house servants. "To my dear George," she wrote, "I have nothing but my love to leave, [but] in any division of my books [and plate], he should have a share."[24]

At less than twenty years of age, George Randolph was below the new minimum age limit instituted for promotion to passed midshipman. A strict enforcement of naval regulations would have prevented him from triennial examination. While he studied at the Norfolk Navy Yard between August of 1836 and May of 1837, the Randolph tribe was busy seeking a favorable interpretation of the age requirement on grounds that it should not be applied retroactively. Even though George's older brother Lewis was the husband of President Jackson's niece Elizabeth Donaldson, he could not secure what was desired. Finally, George acted for himself. He made a special visit to Secretary of the Navy James K. Paulding at Washington to plead his own case, announcing his belief that "when a person is on the spot, he can do a great deal more than by letter." After winning Paulding's consent, the young man took and passed his examination at Baltimore in May of 1837. He received his commission as passed midshipman dated June 15, 1837. Now with rank and salary, he went on leave, saying that he felt like "a galley slave chained to his oar" and must "get out of sight for however short a time of the eternal ships and sailors."[25]

Since he could spend his leave as he chose until he was ordered to sea, he returned to his family's Edgehill estate and entered the University of Virginia. Prudently, he did not resign his commission until July 22, 1839.[26] He continued to draw his annual salary of $500 because his studies were deemed to be in the line of duty. He already had determined to resign his commission because he anticipated slow advancement in the navy and long separations from his family, instead of the cozy home life which was the international ideal of the contemporary Western world. Not only had he not enjoyed such a family life, but he had also heard his father and Joseph Coolidge criticized for not providing such a life for their families. Thus, in deciding to resign his naval commission and to seek a civilian career, Randolph acted on the circumstances of his own case, in the light of the experience of his close relatives and in conformity to the tenor of his times.

The rigors of life at sea and the strictness of naval discipline may have been good for George W. Randolph, but they could not have been altogether pleasing to a young man of his mettle. He was not the sort to seek refuge in routine, profanity, drunkenness, or boorishness. He had inherited some of the independent restlessness that Governor Randolph had attributed to their Indian blood inherited from the Princess Pocahontas.[27] What did he get from the navy?

While a midshipman, George W. Randolph displayed a charismatic power to inspire and lead others. From the United States Navy, he obtained a sound education with emphasis on trigonometry, ordnance, and French. His travels in the classical world helped make him an urbane and cultivated man. He must have been appalled at the many floggings recorded in the log of the USS *Vandalia* during the years of his service. The thought must have occurred to him that slaves who misbehaved in Albemarle were treated with more consideration than were seamen who misbehaved in the United States Navy.[28] His career as a successful criminal lawyer during the 1850s reflected the concern of a young midshipman for both justice and humane punishment and helped Randolph persuade juries with his "sparkling eye." Most importantly, Randolph's experience as a midshipman became the basis for his military career on the eve of and during the Civil War.

Life aboard ship reinforced his capacity for self-discipline as well as his appreciation for discipline and order among those under his command. Because he also learned gunnery on shipboard and in school, he was able to organize the Richmond Howitzers as a "crack" unit in 1859. The combination of classroom drill and practical exercise in Farragut's navy school expanded his esteem for craftsmen to include engineers. His observation of the fortresses, garrisons, and topography as well as the harbors, passages, and dockyards of the Mediterranean world oriented him to a comprehensive view of economics and warfare. This was especially true with regard to Italy, whose wars of liberation fascinated him in 1859–60. In short, Randolph's naval experience and foreign travel were converted into military expertise which shaped his views as Confederate Secretary of War.[29]

## CHAPTER 3

# Student and Lawyer in Albemarle, 1837–1851

In May of 1837, George Wythe Randolph commenced a leave from the United States Navy that lasted until his resignation in July of 1839. At first, he lived at his family's Edgehill estate, where the young man of nineteen enjoyed happy times with the children of his eldest brother, Thomas Jefferson Randolph, who were almost his own age. A dozen miles away lived another older brother, Dr. Benjamin Franklin Randolph, M.D., and his growing family.[1]

George Randolph was determined to enter a profession and achieve a livelihood sufficient to enable him to have a cozy and cultivated family life. To the annoyance of his sister Ellen, he dodged her and Joseph Coolidge's efforts to guide his career. She desired him first to escort her to Europe, then to gain experience as a clerk in Augustine Heard's mercantile house in Canton, China, and finally to join Joseph Coolidge as a partner.[2]

Instead, George followed his eldest brother's advice by enrolling in 1837 in the University of Virginia. At first he "rode in daily" to attend classes, but he soon rented for fifteen dollars a year a room in one of the hotels on the "eastern range" of university buildings. He did not take his meals "in college." At the same time that he matriculated, the University of Virginia adopted distinct curricular requirements for the bachelor of arts and bachelor of law degrees.[3] At the end of his first year, the faculty cited him as one of eight distinguished students in intermediate mathematics and one of fifteen in natural philosophy. William Barton Rogers, later the founder of Massachusetts Institute of Technology, was his professor of natural philosophy. His mathematics professor was J. J. Sylvester, who later became the Savelean Professor of Geometry at Oxford. The school of civil engineering graduated Randolph and four others with proficiency. The next year, he and fifteen others completed the full course in natural philosophy.

On July 3, 1840, George Randolph was not only one of thirteen graduates of the law department but also one of five cited as distinguished law students. Among the latter group was his good friend Henry Coalter Cabell, later of Richmond. Their teacher, John A. G. Davis, taught the whole legal gamut—the law of nature and of nations, the science of government, constitutional law, criminal law, municipal law, common law, statute law, equity, admiralty, and commercial law. For texts, Davis relied on a massive tome of his own compilation, on Blackstone's *Commentaries,* and on the *Federalist Papers.* An effective teacher, whose classes met in the basement of the Rotunda, Professor Davis was both popular with his students and respected by his colleagues. He advocated so strict an interpretation of the federal constitution that he deemed the Kentucky and Virginia Resolutions of 1798 as important as the *Federalist Papers.* Scholars sometimes have pretended that only hostile Northerners attributed the theory of secession to Thomas Jefferson, but in fact professors at the University of Virginia claimed this for him in the 1830s. When George Wythe Randolph later espoused secession, he reflected partly what he had been taught.[4]

He also received instruction from George Tucker, the well-known professor of moral philosophy—a discipline which comprehended economics, history, and political science. Professor Tucker defended slavery and the existing social order, but he also advocated industrialization in forceful lectures and in books such as his *Theory of Money and Banks.* When in 1834 Harriet Martineau, the English author who had just published her popular nine-volume *Illustrations of Political Economy,* visited the University, she described Tucker as "lively, sensible and earnest." Considered a towering intellectual in Charlottesville, Tucker was a great individualist. He rode horseback daily, followed by his dog "Metaphysics." In an eighteen-year period, he published three books on economics and statistics and a biography of Jefferson, besides contributing to journals. George Tucker was a vehement anti-Jackson man, an advocate of a restricted franchise, and a supporter of Henry Clay's American System.[5] Ultimately, Tucker had considerable influence on Randolph's views concerning political economy.

During its first two decades, the University of Virginia suffered not only from growing pains and from the nation-wide depressions following the panics of 1819 and 1837, but also from the national malaise of student riots. Its students successfully protested requirements that they wear uniforms and submit to a rigid dawn-to-dusk regimen with few occasions for recreation. Discontent culminated in 1840 when one student horsewhipped the chairman of the faculty and another shot and killed Professor A. G. Davis in front of his pavilion on the University's Lawn for admonishing and attempting to unmask him. These dastardly acts against popular professors produced a revulsion among students and faculty alike which culminated in the introduction of the student honor system.[6]

From the outset, the University was dogged by exaggerated tales of student drunkenness and gambling. Unfortunately, there was basis for these tales. When Edgar Allan Poe was a student there, the Randolph ladies of Edgehill told the story of a student who supplemented his father's parsimonious allowance by taking ingenious advantage of credit established for him at the tailor's shop. There he "bought twenty-seven coats, not for his own use, but . . . [to pay] gambling debts." The irate father of a young man from Gloucester County denounced the negligence of University authorities in not strictly enforcing injunctions against students buying on credit. His son ran up bills amounting to $443.75 for items, including what he described as alcoholic "poisons." Hounded by creditors who included "a dirty scrub," a bookseller, and a "dirty retailer of Tape & Bobbin," the father complained that students were allowed to neglect their studies at the same time that they were permitted to run up bills for *"wines & sugar . . . fantastical finery, or pretty books for pretty Misses."*[7]

Between 1837 and 1841 George Randolph shed his shyness. His experiences in the navy had purged him of any pomposity and arrogance which sometimes afflicted those of the Randolph family who had fallen more in estate than in self-esteem. No backslapper, George treated townsfolk, farmers, and casual acquaintances with detachment. As George Wythe Randolph later remarked: "We are not amiable. Clever we may be, eccentric we often are, but no one ever said that the Randolphs were amiable." Nonetheless, although a little older than most of his classmates, he laid the basis for several friendships that lasted the rest of his life.[8]

At the University of Virginia, George Randolph took no part in either the riotous events or the establishment of the honor system. He probably followed the advice he later gave to his nephew and future law partner, Lewis Randolph. If so, he was a model student, the worthy grandson of Thomas Jefferson, and son of Martha Jefferson Randolph. He wrote:

> Stick to your books . . . and forget everything else. You will not only acquire knowledge thereby but you will get what is much better, the

power of application, which is the key to knowledge. Don't lose too much time upon matters extraneous to the line of your profession. . . . Debating societies, for instance, when they have accustomed you to the sound of your own voice and given you self-possession, have done all they can do. . . . I would not [urge you to] quit the Jefferson [Debating] Society, but I should allot to it a very small portion of my time. Take up nothing that you can learn as well after you leave college. . . . Let literature go for the present, except as a very brief relaxation from law. Don't devote too much time to the college periodical under the idea that you are forming your style. . . . Eschew party politics for the time. . . .

Let your study be your textbooks *first,* your textbooks *last,* and your textbooks all the time. Or, if your mind reels from too much application to the law, tone it up with fifteen minutes of Milton or Shakespeare.

Exercise, of course, must not be neglected, so far as it is necessary to health. As you are not intended for the ring, I [discourage you from boxing and talking about sports] . . . to the exclusion of more profitable subjects of conversation.

As men generally form their opinions of each other on very short acquaintance, and from externals, deportment therefore is of great importance to one whose calling keeps him in the public view. Modesty and dignity are the crowning ornaments . . . in our profession. Many a sensible man injures his character for intellect by levity. Of course, I wouldn't have you still or oracular, but simply quiet and sensible.[9]

On October 12, 1840, George Wythe Randolph was accepted as a member of the Albemarle bar, after taking oaths of fidelity to the Commonwealth and to the Constitution of the United States. He commenced the practice of law, renting a room and an office in the courthouse town of Charlottesville for $25 a month. He was, however, frequently at Edgehill, where he enjoyed a circle of nieces, nephews, cousins, and the two dozen girls who attended the select finishing school which the Randolph ladies conducted. George developed a close friendship with his high-spirited niece Molly, as everyone called Mary Buchanan Randolph, the fifth of Thomas Jefferson Randolph's nine daughters, only three-and-one-half years younger than he. Never married, she was his sympathetic confidante and regular correspondent after 1851. The wide Jefferson-Randolph circle of kinsfolk and their county and faculty friends provided the social milieu of George Randolph's young manhood.[10]

Among this charmed circle were the Gilmers. In the 1820s Francis Walker Gilmer was an unsuccessful suitor of George's sister Ellen. Thomas Jefferson had so respected his talents that he commissioned him to help recruit in England the first faculty of the University of

Virginia. In the 1840s Thomas Walker Gilmer was secretary of the navy. The Democratic Jefferson-Randolphs and Whig Gilmers remained friends. The former regretted Thomas Walker Gilmer's accidental death in 1844, but they had scoffed at him and his Charlottesville "satellites" who counted on "his being in the White House . . . after Harrison and Tyler."[11]

One of George's fondest friends was the high-spirited Sara Agnes Rice, a kinswoman of the Gilmers. She was so flaxen of hair and classic in profile that she often was cast in charades and theatricals as Rowena, the heroine of Sir Walter Scott's *Ivanhoe*. In Albemarle she was the leader of a smart young social set that was innocent in amusements and unconscious in their elitism. Although George Randolph was neither Agnes's beau nor an avid horseback rider, he did upon occasion serve as her chevalier along the trails at the foot of Monticello Mountain. Mounted on her horse "Phil Duval" and wearing her green riding habit, velvet turban, and long feather with a rhinestone buckle, the beautiful Agnes must have presented a romantic spectacle worthy of the artistic genius of Thomas Cole.

That Albemarle society prized musical and literary accomplishment as much as wealth, good looks, and good horsemanship was shown by the popularity of Maximilian Schele de Vere, the urbane professor of modern languages at the University. Among the girls' visiting beaux was one who initiated them into the mysteries of the polka, "a new dance with picturesque figures." Albemarle society of George Randolph's day was distinctly genteel. Among its belles was the "lovely" Lizzie Gilmer, usually cast in amateur theatrical productions as Sir Walter Scott's Rebecca. Besides the Randolphs, most of Albemarle's young social leaders were "children" either of faculty like the McGuffeys, Tuckers, and Southalls or of county families like the Riveses of Castle Hill and the Carrs of Dunlora. In this set, although a gift of books was an influential token in the game of love, it was the serenade that really won feminine hearts. One of the county's most dashing beaux was Roger Atkinson Pryor, who had come there first as a visitor from Hampden-Sydney College, then as a law student at the University, and finally as a young lawyer at Charlottesville's Court Square. He married Agnes Rice soon after his graduation in 1842.

George Randolph was in 1839 the "discarded" fiancé of Virginia Minor, a seventeen-year-old beauty from a prominent Louisa County family, who sometimes visited relatives near the University. Wearing a low-cut white dress and carrying a guitar on a broad blue ribband, she could transform a sedate party into "an evening of enchantment." According to one of George's nieces, he "took it hard when she broke the engagement" and later married Henry Rawlings.[12] At a houseparty at Dunlora, the seat of his Carr cousins, George, Virginia, and the others took turns performing popular and operatic "gems" of the day. Once, when it was Virginia's turn to sing, George was able to inflict upon her a high-toned revenge by furnishing these lyrics which he had composed:

> Now I have been flung sky-high
>   And more than that
> The girl whose praises I have sung
>   Said no, said no, and I fell flat.
> And if a girl again cheats me
>   Exceeding smart I guess she'll be
> For I have cut my eye teeth now.
>
> Now like the bumblebee I roam
>   Just when and where I please
> Gathering sweets from every grove
>   And humming round each flower I love
> And dancing in each breeze, breeze, breeze
>   And dancing in each breeze.[13]

Interludes of courtly love may momentarily have diverted George Randolph from his impecunious state as a beginning attorney. It was not very remunerative to represent his eldest brother in the latter's capacity as a residuary legatee and executor of Thomas Jefferson's estate. Ordinarily George would have been jubilant when Ellen Coolidge made him the gift of two hundred dollars in the summer of 1841. It arrived when he was fretful and disgruntled because he was quarantined with a case of the mumps. Had he realized that it was this sickness which probably impaired his sexual potency, he would have been saddened beyond measure.[14]

Although Randolph's classmates in 1841 "looked to the South and West as the El Dorado of Lawyers," he contended that "flush times have passed away" from those parts of America. When in 1851 George Randolph moved to Richmond, he wrote Molly that his motive had been "to make money and not to amuse myself." Probably quoting from a newspaper, he penned a bit of doggerel about money:

> Not for to hide it in a hedge
> Not for a train attendant
> But for the glorious privilege
> Of being independent.[15]

# CHAPTER 4

# *Randolph Finds a Wife and Success, 1851–1859*

By 1851 George Randolph concluded that there was not enough business in Albemarle to "support decently the present bar." He turned his attention to Richmond, "the largest and most prosperous city in the state," where "the higher courts" were located and "success brings fortune."[1] To make the move and to get started as a Richmond lawyer, he borrowed three hundred dollars from his doctor brother, Benjamin Franklin Randolph.

In Richmond George Wythe Randolph hung out his shingle before an upstairs office at 38 Main Street, where he engaged two rooms for $125 a month. He slept in one room, received his clients in the other and boarded next door at the City Hotel. He piled his books on the floor until he could afford to buy cheap book presses at auction. When he made his debut before the Virginia Supreme Court of Appeals, the judges commended his maiden speech. Within a few months, he joined the firm of August and Watkins, whose offices were upstairs at 71 Main Street. At the age of thirty-three Randolph contracted to work for a year as a junior partner of the thirty-two-year-old Thomas P. August and the thirty-one-year-old Isaac R. Watkins for a monthly stipend and an equal share in year-end profits amounting to not less than $1,500. Within six months he was able to report to his brother Ben that "so far we have got on swimmingly." Watkins soon left the law firm, which, by 1855, was known as August and Randolph.[2]

Thomas Philip August was an unusual Virginian in background and demeanor. His parents had brought him as a child from the Netherlands West Indies to Fredericksburg, where they lived for a decade before moving to Richmond. Tom's brother, Peter Francis August, became a convert to the Methodist Church and entered its ministry.

Tom August became a protégé of and law clerk for the prominent Richmond barrister James Lyons, in whose office he read law before being called to the bar. According to Judge George L. Christian, August was not only "the most versatile, genial and popular man at the bar," but beloved and "the toast of the town":

> He was a lawyer of ability, a delightful speaker, and not only captivated the juries with his brilliant presentations, but his manner was so persuasive, courteous and kind that he was almost irresistible before any tribunal or any audience. Of course, he had a large following in the city, and could get any office and almost anything else he wanted. He was one of the most noted wits of his day. . . . He was on one occasion defending a criminal on a charge of having killed a man with a walking cane. The commonwealth had proved that the cane when caught up by the prisoner was in a corner of the room opposite to that [claimed] by the . . . defence. . . . August, seeing the effect of this, interposed with the remark that the testimony had shown that the cane was a *walking* cane, and hence the apparent discrepancy was explained amidst the convulsions of the jury, if not to the satisfaction of the court.

During the 1850s he served on the Richmond City Council and in the Virginia State Senate. Membership in the state militia was a popular diversion for young men-about-town in those days. Having served as an adjutant of Virginia's regiment of volunteers during the Mexican War, Tom August was elected major in 1851 and colonel in 1853 of the peacetime First Virginia Regiment of Volunteer Militia.[3]

A bachelor who boarded at Mr. McCreery's Arlington House at the corner of Main and Sixth Street, August was a bluff and good-hearted Dutchman whose appearance harmonized with his reputation as a "prince of wits." According to Cooper De Leon, he was not only a "wag and punster" who "talked in quips," but he specialized in "the over-familiar retort." In a Richmond drugstore, where August was buying a seltzer to cure his hangover, a little old lady mistook him for a clerk. Desirous of buying some ipecac, she asked for it in the then-common slang, saying: "Can I buy a little hippo?" He replied: "No, madame. We give it away to cure the general chondria." When Miss Hallie Haxall, a noted belle, was considering whether to become engaged to marry the Reverend Henry A. Wise, Jr., she still was being courted by a Mr. Morrison. As a friend, August gave Miss Hallie this advice:

> Haste, O sinner, to be Wise,
> Stay not for the Morrison (morrow's sun).

Tom August seems always to have had the last word. As he lay dying on July 31, 1869, someone standing by his bedside remarked, "It is nearly the first of August." The ill man responded: "Yes, and nearly the last of August, too."[4]

George Randolph's classmate Henry Coalter Cabell also came to Richmond to practice law in 1852. He clerked for a year at the state courthouse on Capitol Square, then hung out his shingle at 152 Main Street between Eleventh and Twelfth Streets, and by 1860 took into partnership Johnston H. Sands. Cabell's practice was more business-oriented than Randolph's, and he spent considerably less time in the criminal courts. They both served on the Executive Committee of the Virginia Historical Society and cherished the fact that they continued the friendship which had existed between their families for more than a century.[5]

As a bachelor, George enjoyed Richmond society, finding it intelligent, sociable, given to simplicity of dress and less concerned with form and ceremony than Northern cities. Pleased by the kindly reception of old friends, he at first made General and Mrs. Peyton's house his headquarters. As the escort of Julia Peyton and her friend Pocahontas Bernard to hear an itinerant actor named Vanderhoff read from Sheridan's plays, he commended a reading as a "capital substitute" for mediocre theatre because "there is no bad acting." With John Baldwin he attended a local theatrical company's performance of *Macbeth,* which was so poor that the audience laughed at the witches' scene. He saw General Tom Thumb in his carriage. He was awestruck by Glidden's "magnificent panorama of the Nile," a nine-hundred-foot transparency by the "best European artists," illuminated from behind by rising, noonday, and setting suns and enhanced by two mummies and a "quantity of Egyptian curiosities." He even went to the Hebrew Ball, where he stayed until three o'clock in the morning for the Jewish girls' polkas and schottisches—"the prettiest dancing I ever beheld." In reporting these urban delights to Molly and the Edgehill family, he explained that subscription balls provided "a good chance to make aquaintances. There is no public gathering of people here like those on Court Days in the Country."[6]

Much of George Wythe Randolph's legal practice consisted of arguing criminal cases. His naval career had provided him both empathy for those who had fallen afoul of the law and also a sincere and open manner with which to convince a jury. In the courtroom Randolph displayed charisma. This slight man's mild countenance could display great animation when presenting a cause. To appreciate his "extraordinary ability," said the Richmond *Dispatch* almost a decade later, one must "hear him and see him while speaking." His practice took him as far away as Lynchburg and Norfolk. By 1859, his able pleading assured George Randolph of an "easy competence" of $3,600 a year. He was able not only to repay his loans, but even to aid his sister Septimia Randolph Meikleham after her husband's death. Success was sweet to George Wythe Randolph, who in 1858 confided that his practice had done so well that he was "afraid to expect more." Relishing his new importance within the family, he dogged the Virginia Central Railroad to pay the $2,300 it owed Jefferson Randolph for its right-of-way and for construction of its line through Edgehill. He also represented the Jefferson-Randolphs in obtaining as collateral kin their share of the estate of John Randolph of Roanoke.[7]

George generously brought into his law firm his kinsman, Samuel Carr, but he dismissed him when he proved to be indolent. Randolph readily admitted that he liked to "make the whips crack," but driving himself to overwork led to periodic attacks of "laryngitis." In the fall of 1858, he became alarmed when he found himself "spitting . . . a clot of blood half as large as a pea." At the same time Tom August grew so "fond of his cups" that Randolph threatened to dissolve their partnership. August mended his ways. George was pleased when August took the lead in inviting Randolph's nephew, Lewis Randolph, to enter the firm. He never was disappointed in Lewis, who heeded his formula for a successful career: "a clear head, method and industry."[8]

Most of George Randolph's early practice was defending clients before juries in the criminal courts of Richmond. It is impossible to reconstruct details of this practice because official records of the court were destroyed in April 1865. On the other hand, Randolph was involved in other transactions of which record has survived such as contracts, deeds of trust to buy or sell property, drawing titles, and aiding in the partition or settlement of estates. Their subject matter is humdrum, but their volume attests a large and remunerative practice. More important in terms of social history are the names of those with whom Randolph was involved. A high proportion of his clients and their adversaries were scions of old families of the Virginia Tidewater or Piedmont who, like himself, had come to the new metropolis. Among them were John H. Anderson, John P. Ballard, Austin and Thomas W. Brockenbrough, George M. Carrington, John H. Claiborne, Alfred V. Crenshaw, Burton B. and William W. Crump, Thomas W. Doswell, Thomas C. Epps, Hugh Hagan, William W. Harvie, Bolling W. Haxall, John T. Jackson, George T. Patton, Thomas Robertson, James W.

Shields, A. W. and James M. Taylor, Mann Valentine, A. D. Williams, William S. Wood and Gabriel Wortham. Besides such members of the F.F.V. (First Families of Virginia), Randolph was involved in transactions with others such as Rebecca Kirschmann, Guggenheimer Seligman, J. B. Siginiago and William C. Walthall.[9]

In the early 1850s George Randolph's curly auburn hair fell below his ears, but his "rather sharp" features looked out from a clean-shaven face to give a calm and mild expression. He turned out a mustache around 1856 and a full beard in 1860. Slender and erect, he had a high forehead and a prominent nose, small glistening blue eyes, sunken cheeks, and a narrow chin. By 1861 he bore many signs of ill health. By 1864, his face was a mass of wrinkles. Customarily, he wore a blue coat, white silk waistcoat, white cashmere pantaloons and a linen shirt—civilian attire little different from the uniform of a naval officer.[10]

Early in his stay in Richmond, George Randolph felt the lack of a wife. This deficiency he soon sought to repair. He was attracted to a beautiful and wealthy young widow, Mary Elizabeth Adams Pope, who was a friend of his niece Molly. It was in the autumn of 1850, while she was a young and attractive widow emerging from mourning, that they met. Her "magnificent eyes" entranced him at once. A decade later, Mary Boykin Chesnut observed: "the men rave over [Mary] Randolph's beauty [and] call her a magnificent specimen of the finest, dark-eyed, rich and glowing Southern womankind. Clean brunette she is, with the reddest lips, the whitest teeth, and glowing eyes." George's cousin Constance Cary said that Mary was "oriental-looking." Her wedding daguerreotype confirms the descriptions of her friends of the Civil War years and shows that she was probably about five feet, seven inches in height and of slight figure, that she favored a billowing dress of tartan silk, and that she wore her hair in lightly curled braids over the ears.[11]

Mary Adams's antecedents were Virginians of importance. Both she and George were descended from the seventeenth-century councilor, Miles Cary. Her great-grandfather Colonel Richard Adams had been Richmond's most prominent citizen at the time of the American Revolution, owning much of the city's eastern section. One of his sons, Dr. John Adams, had served as mayor of Richmond between 1819 and 1825. Dr. Adams's second son, Mary Elizabeth Adams Pope's father, was Richard Adams III (1800–1851), whose second wife died when Mary was very young. Besides the Richmond real estate he inherited, Richard Adams had invested profitably in Natchez, Mississippi. When George Randolph began practicing law in Richmond, Adams visited him so frequently on business that some thought that he was encouraging a prospective son-in-law. After Mr. Adams married a third time and fathered a new family, he sent Mary to the Randolphs' Edgehill School, where she became a friend of Molly Randolph. Before 1850 Mary Adams's older half-sister Sarah married George Mayo Carrington and lived quietly with him on Richmond's Church Hill, while her half-brother Samuel went to Mobile, Alabama upon coming of age.[12]

In 1848 after the eighteen-year-old girl's visit to her brother, Mary Elizabeth Adams married William B. Pope of Mobile. William Pope was the youngest of six children of Alexander Pope, a commission merchant whose affairs were extensive enough to require his voyage in 1846 to confer with his factors, Isaac Law and Co., at Liverpool, England. There the senior Pope died unexpectedly. Exclusive of slaves and real estate, he bequeathed $15,000 to each of his children, implying a cash estate alone of more than $100,000, a princely amount in those days.

William and Mary Adams Pope went to Washington, D.C., for their honeymoon and also to seek patronage from the Whig Congressman, John Gayle of Mobile. In June of 1849 the young couple fell ill, perhaps of typhoid fever. William died after writing his last will and testament that his "beloved wife" inherit his entire estate. He specified that it should descend to any children she might have by a "further marriage" and named her his sole executrix. Fortunately for Mary, her uncle Miles Selden was in the city and was able to help the young widow in her moment of distress. She was on such poor terms with her mother-in-law that she did not return to Mobile. When old Mrs. Pope died eighteen months later, she bequeathed nothing to Mary. Instead, she pointedly gave as additional bequests to her other children the portion she once had designated for her "late son William."[13] The death of Mary's father in 1851 left her with no male relatives to whom she felt close. In such a situation, the rich young widow determined to pay a lengthy visit to the famous and fashionable springs of Virginia.

On learning from his niece Molly of Mary Pope's plans, George Randolph hastened to the White Sulphur Springs late in July of 1851. To Molly he confided that his feeling for Mary was a "Fever . . . strong upon me. . . . It is my destiny and I couldn't avoid it," even though he previously had sworn not to marry until he could support a wife in style. Soon after his arrival at the spa, George suffered a sickness that he himself diagnosed as "dyspepsia," although its symptoms were chiefly a "terrible pain just below the chest and great prostration." Excused from the exertions of dancing and sports, George had ample opportunity for a sedate courtship consonant with the "propriety" of Mary Adams Pope

George Wythe Randolph as a bridegroom, ca. 1852
(Courtesy of The Thomas Jefferson Memorial Foundation, Inc.,
Charlottesville, Va.)

Mary Elizabeth Adams Randolph as a bride, ca. 1852.
(Courtesy of The Thomas Jefferson Memorial Foundation, Inc.,
Charlottesville, Va.)

refraining from "all the gaieties." George wrote Molly that, although Mary would not give him an answer to his suit until October, he thought that his chances of being accepted were "fairly prosperous." To his confidante he boasted that Mary was "the prettiest woman at the Springs."[14] Undoubtedly the two nineteenth-century lovers were familiar with Julia Cabell Mayo's tribute to the White Sulphur Springs' ability not only to cure its votaries' physical maladies but also to solace "their cares and enrapture their lives."[15] Unlike Bob Ruly and the heiress Matilda, who were characters in a contemporary comic poem in *The Southern Literary Messenger,* George and Mary did not venture far afield from the spa to pick whortleberries or to provide him an opportunity to show his manly devotion, as did Bob, who

> . . . killed a
> rattlesnake, long as my arm, for Matilda.[16]

George's wooing was, nevertheless, persuasive. Victorian proprieties, more than Mary's indecisiveness, were the cause for their lengthy engagement. In order to claim his bride, George Randolph again borrowed several hundred dollars from his brothers.[17] The Randolph clan was enthusiastic about the impending marriage and proposed calling George's wife "Mary Wythe," because there were so many Mary Randolphs at Edgehill. Because Mary felt little rapport with either her Richmond or Mobile relations, she and George hit upon the romantic notion of marrying at New Orleans on April 20, 1852, and of attending there a concert by the famous Jenny Lind. Both had friends and relatives in Louisiana—especially the brother-in-law of George's sister Virginia, Hore Browse Trist at Donaldsonville, and the Adams family's friend, William C. Nichols at New Orleans. The happy couple made a leisurely return to Virginia by way of Mobile.[18]

In Richmond the Randolphs bought a house on the south side between Seventh and Eighth streets near East Franklin Street. It boasted illuminating gas and required a staff of four servants, including two women and a child whom Mary had inherited from her father. George's slave, Edward, came down from Edgehill to supervise the establishment as butler.[19]

This quarter of Richmond was then its most fashionable. Consisting of a dozen blocks, it had as its southeast corner the classical facade of St. Paul's Episcopal Church, opposite the entrance to Capitol Square. Like the Randolph ladies of Edgehill, Mary Adams Randolph was an Episcopalian. Although George, like his brothers, was an agnostic, the George Wythe Randolphs rented a pew at St. Paul's from their earliest married days. The quarter then was filled with pleasant, redbrick structures of the Federal or Greek Revival style, of which there now remains only the house at 707 East Franklin Street that Gen. Robert E. Lee rented for his wife and daughters during the Civil War. At a house on Franklin Street between Eighth and Ninth streets, George Randolph's friend John Reuben Thompson, the poet and editor of *The Southern Literary Messenger*, lived with his parents. In this neighborhood too lived the Haxall family, who were connected with the Randolphs by kinship, cultural interests, and legal business. Barton Haxall was a son of the greatest flour miller and merchant of Richmond, while his beautiful wife Octavia was a niece of Conway Robinson, the legal scholar and George Randolph's fellow officer at the Virginia Historical Society. Another of Mrs. Haxall's uncles was Moncure Robinson, who married George Randolph's niece and contemporary, Charlotte Bennett Taylor, for whom Octavia Haxall named her daughter, who later married Robert E. Lee, Jr. In the same vicinity lived the doyenne of Richmond society, the widowed Mrs. Robert C. Stanard, who dispensed lavish hospitality at her house at the corner of Grace and Sixth streets.

The beautiful twenty-two-year-old Mary Adams Randolph quickly conquered Richmond society. Few knew or cared about her first husband. Even if Mary had been less wealthy, George had more than enough blood and brains to be a leader of social life. Social Richmond valued her ties with the mercantile and tobacconist families, whose ancestral parish church and quarter had been, like hers, St. John's on Church Hill. Acting for Mary, George Randolph sold to George Carrington the five lots on Church Hill that she had inherited from her father.[20] Agnes Pryor wrote of Richmond society that, although it claimed to be exclusive, "nobody properly introduced could visit . . . without having a dinner or evening party given in his honor." Its entertainments were simple. Besides conversation, one might expect "an occasional song from an obliging guest," infrequent theatricals or tableaux, or a dramatic reading by such as Anna Cora Mowatt Ritchie, the spirited wife of the editor of the Richmond *Enquirer*. Pizzini was the fashionable caterer who provided pyramids of glacé oranges, nonpareils, spun sugar confections, ices, wine jellies, blancmanges, terrapin, pickled oysters, and chicken salad at dinner parties that began "not later than nine," at which Richmond's illuminati remained "as long as it pleased."[21]

Perhaps it was through the Coolidges, and almost certainly it was in emulation of them, that George Wythe and Mary Randolph collected some of their own furnishings. He bought a consignment of more than two hundred Chinese porcelains. He wrote proudly to his Edgehill kin: "It blazes with bright colours and guilding." The chef d'oeuvre of this collection was a "magnificent Peach Bowl," but he was undoubtedly prouder of his silver vegetable dishes, tea table, and globes that he inherited from Monticello out of the wreck of the family fortune.[22]

From time to time George Randolph suffered from dyspepsia and Mary from neuralgia, sick headaches, and influenza. Nonetheless, they led a full, happy life. That they were childless was almost certainly owing to his having contracted mumps as an adult. George Randolph was particularly sensitive to hot weather. In the summer of 1855 he took a month's vacation, which proved to be both bracing and beneficial. At various times he and Mary fled the summer heat of Richmond to visit Old Point Comfort, the Virginia springs, and, frequently, the family's Edgehill estate. Their diversions before the Civil War were dignified and private. That George Wythe Randolph had inherited his grand-father Jefferson's scholarly tastes is attested by his daily reading before breakfast from Greek and Latin texts. Like many of his family, he delighted in French. He was known to quote La Rochefoucauld as well as Bacon, Shakespeare, and the Bible. Members of a financially revivified first family, the George Randolphs lived with more comfort than splash. As members of Richmond's cultural leadership, their position was, for the most part, a concealed eminence, as neither they nor their friends were given to pretense or display.[23]

Of all of George Randolph's friends, none exercised a stronger or more pleasant influence upon him than John Reuben Thompson. As a poet and editor, he was Richmond's greatest man of letters in the 1850s and 1860s. Born in Richmond in 1823, he had close ties with the gentry of the Green Springs section of Louisa County, Virginia, with whom Randolph was a familiar in the 1840s. Like many of his and Randolph's contemporaries, Thompson was a consumptive. Like Randolph, he had been prepared for college by studies in New England. Both were graduates of the University of Virginia, but not classmates along its "white-washed brick arcades," which they thought lovelier than "Europe's Gothic minsters." They had become acquainted when George had been an Albemarle lawyer and John had returned to the University to study law after having served in Richmond for two years as a clerk for James A. Seddon. Graduated a bachelor of law in 1844, Thompson forsook the bar after three years' practice. As the literary panjandrum of Richmond, he had introduced Randolph to the belles of the city, who had made a pet of the poet. Thompson was a man with virile whiskers, Bohemian plaid trousers, and an artist's cloak. Between 1847 and 1860, he edited *The Southern Literary Messenger,* occupying his friend Edgar Allan Poe's chair and winning Lord Tennyson's approval of his own verse. As a kind of poet laureate of Virginia, he composed upon such topics as the 1857 commemoration of the 250th anniversary of the founding of Jamestown. During the Civil War, the Randolphs' friendship with Thompson gave them first call on him for social occasions.[24]

Fortunately, the George W. Randolphs possessed good friends as well as good fortune. To their house came such young belles as Charlotte Haxall, Evelina Triplett, and Fanny Hunter, the young sculptor Edward V. Valentine and the vivacious Agnes Rice and her husband, Roger A. Pryor. The last was first coeditor of the Richmond *Enquirer* and then the editor of the Richmond *South.* The Randolphs' circle was more concerned with cultural pursuits than giddy pleasures. He was much interested in the Virginia Historical Society and served as an officer of that institution until it became inactive in 1861.[25]

His friends respected George Randolph's interest in historical paintings, if not in art. His pride in reporting that the Virginia Historical Society's collection was "increasing" and his declaration that "we have now Peyton Randolph and Edmund Randolph" suggest that he served on a committee to solicit such works of art. Together with his brother Jefferson, George Randolph presented to the Society in 1858 a portrait they had commissioned by L. M. D. Guillaume after the Gilbert Stuart likeness of their grandfather which hung at Edgehill. Since the copy was on canvas instead of a wooden panel, it could not reproduce the mysterious quality of the original that had beguiled the young Randolphs: a crack swelled enough in the summertime to give Mr. Jefferson the appearance of "opening up," as if to speak.[26] When Rembrandt Peale visited Richmond in the spring of 1858, George Randolph called on him and introduced himself as the younger brother of Jefferson Randolph, Peale's boyhood roommate. After Peale recounted some of his and Jeff's "boyish capers" in Philadelphia of 1804, George took "the old fellow" to the Virginia Historical Society's rooms. He reported to Edgehill that Peale "recognized at once the old French portraits and those of Gen[era]l and Mrs. Washington. He said the two last were by his father [Charles Willson Peale] and he thought the others were probably his. The painting of Queen Anne he pronounced a splendid Godfrey Kneller, one of the most beautiful he had ever seen, and very valuable. The Frenchman in purple and gold is the Chevalier La Luzerne, the first French minister to this country. The other two he was not certain about, but promised to enquire."[27]

Richmond honored George Wythe Randolph by naming him a pallbearer for the reinterment of President Monroe in Hollywood Cemetery on July 5, 1858. There was in the mid-nineteenth century an international fad for reinterments at national cemeteries or tombs. The French had brought back Napoleon's ashes from St. Helena in 1840, and the Second Empire took pains after 1851 to reward civic piety of a Bonapartist variety. In England, the Victorians had rediscovered the glory of burial in Westminster Abbey. In America, attention had been drawn to the burying places of the founding fathers, when John Washington complained that he was not able to maintain properly the mansion, grounds, or even the tomb of his great-uncle at Mount Vernon. Soon after the Virginia legislature had rejected the idea of buying the estate, it commissioned for Capitol Square at Richmond an equestrian statue and a mausoleum for the *pater patriae*. This structure was built, even though the Washington family decided not to permit the transfer of George Washington's remains.

At about the same time a mistaken rumor spread that New York City was not caring properly for the grave of James Monroe, who had died there in 1831. Virginia's impetuous Gov. Henry A. Wise began a confused correspondence with the mayor of New York, who offered to return Monroe's remains to the Old Dominion. Virginia's governor and general assembly appropriated $3,576.54 for Monroe's reinterment in a cast-iron, neo-Gothic shrine in Richmond's Hollywood Cemetery. Ceremonies accorded the bier, many attendants, and lavish entertainment combined to make a notable event. Although he was a newly elected member of the Richmond City Council, George W. Randolph persuaded it to appropriate $2,500 for the occasion. In turn, he was named to the three-man committee in charge of arrangements, along with the governor's son Obediah Jennings Wise and Major William Munford, the son of the secretary of the commonwealth.[28]

So that both New York and Richmond could focus their Fourth of July ceremonies about Monroe, the cortege departed from New York on Saturday, July 3d, and arrived in Richmond on Monday, July 5th. The Virginia Steamship Company's *Jamestown* carried the casket, while the New York City Council hired the steamer *Ericsson* to transport the Seventh Cavalry Regiment and its forty-five-man band. Off City Point, near Hopewell, Virginia, the New Yorkers had to transfer to a smaller vessel, the *Glen Cove*. Among the New York delegation were Monroe's grandson, Samuel L. Gouverneur, and Alexander Hamilton's grandson, Lawrence Hamilton.

The relentless schedule for the obsequies was not to be put aside, even though the *Glen Cove* was late in joining the *Jamestown* at Richmond's lower harbor, Rocketts. In these ceremonies, George Wythe Randolph was an indispensible man. He was not only waiting on the dock with Governor Wise, young Wise, Major Munford, and Mayor Joseph Mayo, but he also had "organized" the procession, whose column was led by Col. Thomas P. August, the commander of the First Virginia Volunteer Infantry Regiment. Six white horses, each with a black postillion in white uniform, drew a large hearse. The Richmond Grays relieved the Seventh Regiment's honor guard. The city's church bells tolled. The Seventh Regiment's band played a dirge. The cortege moved between soldiers with reversed arms. The march began at 11:30 and traversed the hilly streets of Richmond, reaching Hollywood Cemetery on schedule at 1:00. A brief shower early on the morning of July 5th undoubtedly saved many from heat prostration and abbreviated the governor's oration. Among Wise's remarks were sentences of unconsciously tragic irony: "Who knows . . . that New York is of the North and Virginia is of the South? They are one, even as all the now proud and eminent *Thirty-two* [States] are one." After lengthy prayers by the Reverend Charles H. Read, D.D., of the United Presbyterian Church, three salvos broke the still air. To a lively tune by the Seventh Regiment band, the soldiers marched back to the center of the city followed by the civilians on foot and in carriages.

Randolph's efforts to "start the ball [rolling]" enjoyed great success. To accommodate the unusually large number of official guests exceeded the ability of Richmond's hotels. The Virginia Committee commandeered and decorated as the site of a sumptuous banquet the newly constructed Warwick and Barksdale flour mill. At 2:30 the Seventh Regiment began to arrive, climbed to the sixth floor, stacked arms, washed, and refreshed themselves from fifty-gallon punch bowls. At 4:00, the guests entered the dining room on the fifth floor for the all-male banquet. After consuming courses of fish, fowl, meat, and innumerable vegetables, they saw the top table cloth removed and champagne set before them. The celebrants made thirteen toasts, beginning with one to "July the 4th, 1776. The birthday of this nation. Its anniversary, the most important in the history of mankind." The next toasts were offered to Washington and Monroe. The fourth toast was, "The Union of the States. May the spirit of liberty, like the rod of Aaron, swallow up the spirit of fanaticism." James Lyons of Richmond proposed as the toast to the honored guests, "New York and Virginia. United in glory, united in interest and united in marriage. Nothing but fanaticism can separate them." The final toast hinted at nocturnal flirtation. It was the simple word "Woman." That night the Richmond Armory band played in Capitol Square, which was lighted by hundreds of Chinese lanterns. Above the gates of the square had been placed illuminated transparency arches which read:

> James Monroe.
> He controlled millions, and died poor.
> This is virtue.

Another triumphal arch had been erected by the Mount Vernon Ladies Association, calling on Virginians to "Open your hearts and your purses" in order to purchase Washington's home and maintain it as a national shrine.

Writing to his niece Molly about this "festive funeral," George Randolph confided:

> I rather flatter myself that the unrivalled success of the entertainment was owing in great measure to me. . . . The New Yorkers went away thoroughly astonished and gratified at V[irgini]a hospitality, and we were equally so at their magnificient regiment which surpasses anything that I ever saw in this country or in Europe. The only drawback was poor [Lawrence] Hamilton's death [by accidental drowning just before the New Yorkers reembarked]. . . . The Council devolved on me the draughting of the resolutions of condolence, and it was somewhat indicative of the dying out of old animosities that a grandson of Hamilton lost his life escorting the remains of Monroe, and received some of his own funeral honors from Jefferson's grandson.

Colonel August and his men of the First Regiment rallied to give to the twenty-five-year-old Hamilton's remains military honors in Capitol Square.[29]

An unexpected and brief by-product of Randolph's participation in the Monroe obsequies was his endorsement of Governor Wise's proposal that the remains of Washington, Jefferson, and Madison be reinterred near Monroe in Hollywood Cemetery. George wrote to his niece Molly that, although at first he was "shocked" by the governor's proposal, he had come to favor it because vandals had broken the stone over his mother's grave and the obelisk over Thomas Jefferson's. But what most influenced him were broadly patriotic considerations and a sailor's pride in the symbols of American nationality. Thomas Jefferson,

George declared, "belong[s] to the country and not exclusively to his family, and . . . [he deserves] a resting place . . . accessible to the thousands and millions who revere his memory. . . . I felt as if it would be selfish in us to detain him and that it was unjust to his memory to seclude his tomb from his countrymen." However, as none of Jefferson's other progeny agreed with George, his remains were left at Monticello.[30]

It is possible to read too much into George Randolph's accepting the notion of moving his grandfather's remains to Richmond. He was certainly willing to break with the past, even with Thomas Jefferson's stated desire. Perhaps George Randolph told himself that, in throwing off the dead hand of the past, he was both Jeffersonian and a modern, self-made man. He never failed to honor his grandfather with words, but his actions often were untraditional, if not un-Jeffersonian in their urban, nationalistic, and belligerent character. George Randolph's investments were in bank and railways stocks, not acres. He was alert to the desirability of Bessemer steel, not just charcoal-smelted iron.[31] Although he was pleased when he took stock of his and Mary's fortune, he did not rest. Implicit in his actions was his favorable comparison between himself and both his father and grandfather. Whatever were the currents carrying George Wythe Randolph away from Monticello, they were definite, but not yet distinct in the mid-1850s.

Another honor which the city of Richmond pressed on George Randolph was membership in the reception committee that greeted the Prince of Wales in 1859. Unimpressed by the future King Edward VII and his entourage, Randolph exclaimed: "There is hardly a Court House Town in Virginia that couldn't produce more of good grace, presence of mind, power of conversation, and quickness of comprehension. . . . They were up on one of our national peculiarities, . . . the custom of shaking hands. This they carried to excess and I had the honour of repeated pump handle shakes from the various members of the party." The only one of the prince's party whom Randolph liked was the Duke of Devonshire. Doubtless George recalled the strained rivalries in which Midshipman Randolph and his messmates engaged their British counterparts.[32]

Many of George's close relatives were frequent visitors at his and Mary Randolph's house on Franklin Street. His brother, Dr. Benjamin Franklin Randolph, resided there between 1854 and 1858 while he attended sessions of the legislature as delegate from Albemarle. Besides his niece Molly, another of his nieces, Jane Randolph, brought her new husband, Robert Garlick Hill Kean, soon after their marriage in 1854.[33]

George encouraged the marriage in 1859 of his niece, Ellen Randolph, with the widower William Byrd Harrison of Upper Brandon. Although George Randolph and Harrison were both descended from Robert "King" Carter and from Isham Randolph of Dungeness, their friendship was nurtured by their mutual friend John R. Thompson, who was a favorite of Harrison's widowed sister-in-law, Isabella Ritchie Harrison. In what some consider Thompson's best poem, he described Mrs. Harrison's Christmas and May parties at Lower Brandon as seen through a window pane on which previous revellers had inscribed their names with a diamond ring. It is probable that George and Mary Randolph were members of the party at Upper and Lower Brandon on the way to the 1857 ceremonies at Jamestown and that Ellen accompanied them. Because the widowed William Byrd Harrison was considerably older than Ellen and was the father of four mature children by his first wife, some at Edgehill frowned on his courtship. Forbearing to mention that Ellen was almost an old maid, Uncle George sarcastically declared that the amiable Mr. Harrison was "quite good enough for us." Besides being a relative and friend, he was a college graduate and the master of a well-managed estate of some 3,000 acres. Admitting to his kinfolk at Edgehill that Mr. Harrison's wealth was an added inducement to the match, George denied any notion of fortune hunting. Thinking of the Coolidge family's generosity to their relatives, he assured his Edgehill kin that "money . . . in the hands of a good man . . . is an instrument of benevolence." When Ellen and William Byrd Harrison married, Randolph's judgment was confirmed by their happiness. Indeed, the Harrisons presented him with a handsome silver cup as a token of their special friendship.[34]

George W. Randolph's ability to view others dispassionately was extended to Henry S. Randall, who published his distinguished three-volume biography of Thomas Jefferson in 1857–58. After a visit from Randall, George commented that the New Yorker "talks of himself and his book without intermission. His egotism, conceit and bad taste are dreadful, and yet there is an appearance of warmth, right feeling and boldness about the man which redisposes me in his favor." Both Roger A. Pryor for *The South* and John R. Thompson for *The Southern Literary Messenger* asked George W. Randolph to review Randall's *Jefferson*. He declined. To Molly he wrote: "I could not panegyrise my own grandfather nor avoid doing so without doing him an injustice." While George was undoubtedly sincere, he left a suspicion that he believed that Randall's praise of Jefferson was too fullsome.[35]

Although George Wythe Randolph conversed freely with Randall, he did not relish being pestered by strangers who sought his opinion about what Thomas Jefferson would do or think about events of the 1850s. To one such inquirer, however, he replied:

> I know of nothing which affords the slightest grounds to suppose that Mr. Jefferson would consider the Fugitive Slave law unconstitutional. . . . The Declaration of Independence . . . is usually relied upon by Northern Abolitionists when they see fit to quote Mr. Jefferson for authority . . . to provide the unconstitutionality of slavery itself. . . . In my judgement it has not the slightest bearing upon either. . . . 'All men are created equal . . . with inalienable rights' if literal, applies to prisoners in jail.[36]

True to his familiar upbringing, George carefully avoided religious "extremes of skepticism and enthusiasm." He engaged in long discussions with his niece Molly on religion, however, and appears to have read often the Bible, New Testament, and various religious commentaries. He attended St. Paul's Episcopal Church with Mary, but he did not make a formal profession of faith until 1864.[37]

Although George and Mary Randolph were drawn ultimately into Roger and Agnes Pryor's group of fire-eaters, their milieu during the first years of their marriage was one of scholarly interests and quiet philanthropy. As John R. Thompson expressed it, they "lived apart from noisy fame" and "the plauditory clamour of the crowd." Randolph's sudden rise to public prominence in the secession crisis and early war years rested in part on such friendships. Besides his fellow members of the Virginia Historical Society like Charles Gorham Barney and Conway Robinson, there were his associates in the Richmond Library Company (and later in the Confederate service) Herbert Augustine Claiborne and Gustavus A. Myers. Rather than restrict the holdings of the library, they merged it with the Virginia Mechanics Institute, the predecessor of today's University of Richmond. In 1858 this move was shaped more to the development of technical than to belletristic ends. Although disposed to retire to his own library for contemplation, George Randolph was a lively conversationalist with intimates, one of whom professed that he "held us captive heart and brain" with his tales of "far lands beyond the sea" and "of gentlest fancies and of wisest lore."[38] He was interested in the economic and political affairs of his own country and of Europe, concerning which he had not only personal recollections but also the teaching of his respected Whiggish professor of university days, George Tucker.

When in 1858 John R. Thompson wrote a poem on the dedication of Crawford's equestrian statue of Washington, he undoubtedly spoke for the majority of Virginians in advocating unity, the Constitution, and the status quo.[39] Just as Thompson was a States-Rights Whig, Randolph was a Whiggish Democrat. The persistent sectional struggle during these years changed all this. Why and how George Wythe Randolph evolved from a private into a public person, from a U.S. patriot into a secessionist will be treated elsewhere, but this change strained personal as well as patriotic ties. The summer of 1858 saw a cooling of relations between George Randolph and Joseph Coolidge. The younger man's consorting with fire-eaters may have made him unnecessarily prickly. When the Coolidges returned to America after a long absence abroad, they invited Ellen's brothers and sisters to visit them at their summer place at Beverley, Massachusetts. Inadvertently, Joseph's letter to George failed to include Mary in the invitation. George took this as a conscious slight until a second letter from Joseph reassured him. More bluntly than he ought, George had replied that, if his wife Mary was meant to be included, they would journey to Beverley; otherwise, they would repair to the Virginia springs. Ultimately, George wrote that his and Mary's recent illnesses forbad their making the long journey to Beverley. All parties were out of humor. Although in August of 1859 George and Mary Randolph made a progress of the White Sulphur, Sweet, and Hot Springs, their dispositions were not much improved. In hope of good company and diversion, they asked his niece Molly to accompany them. Claiming absorption by household affairs, she declined. This was a disappointment to all three, who enjoyed together "a quiet dish of scandal at the expense of . . . friends and relatives." The strained relations between the George Randolphs and the Coolidges were made worse by the gossipy Henry S. Randall, who told Randolph that the Coolidges had led him to believe that Mary Randolph was "uncommonly plain." This infuriated George, who thought that the Coolidges had so many accounts of Mary's beauty that they could not imagine that she was an "ugly woman." To his confidante Molly, he wrote: "Even my brother Coolidge never alleged that against her that I am aware of. Possibly Randall heard something from that quarter about her 'ugliness,' which means in Yankee dialect, bad temper; and [he] understood it as an English word."[40]

Ellen Coolidge made a southern trip in the spring of 1860. Although she enjoyed Charleston and Columbia, South Carolina, her Virginia relatives considered her visit to the Old Dominion a "fiasco." In Richmond, George waited on the dock at Rocketts until eleven o'clock at night for her overdue steamboat. When it arrived more than an hour later, Mrs. Coolidge disembarked at once and went to a hotel unaccompanied, instead of waiting until morning to go ashore. Dutifully, George and Mary called on her the next day before she proceeded to Albemarle, but it was a strained meeting. Ellen still expected to dominate her baby brother, but she had become maddeningly deaf. To Molly, George averred: "I wish neither to run after nor to avoid her, but if we meet I desire to behave as a brother should." Although Mrs. Coolidge enjoyed her stay at Edgehill, she found that, in spite of Nature, mankind had made the Hot Springs a "dismal" place.[41]

In the later 1850s, Attorney Randolph sometimes had to go to Norfolk on business. He enjoyed the sea air and renewing his maritime ties. On one occasion he crossed Hampton Roads to lodge for several days at the famed Hygeia Hotel, where he found about eighty "nice people," beautiful weather, and fine bathing. Recalling the Coolidges at Newport or at Beverley, he exclaimed in tones that would have pleased the most professional Southerner: "There is a purity and a softness about the ocean air in these latitudes which makes it far more delightful than that at the Northern seacoast bathing places."[42]

By the autumn of 1859, George Wythe Randolph had achieved all that he had hoped for in becoming a very successful lawyer. His loving wife was beautiful, charming, and rich. He had expanded upon his circle of college friends to hold an undisputed place in the social and intellectual leadership of Richmond. Although he was well aware that there were within the American union acrimonious disputes on moral and political levels about sectional balance, slavery, culture, and economy, he considered that these were not entirely new and hoped that they would be transient. Only a remarkable thunderbolt could disturb the serenity of his world.

The John Brown raid provided such a thunderbolt for many, not least of whom was George Wythe Randolph.

## CHAPTER 5

# The Emergence of a
# Political Leader, 1859–1861

As Vilfredo Pareto remarked, "Violent movements take place by fits and starts, and effects therefore do not follow immediately on their causes." When in October of 1859 news of the John Brown raid burst upon an amazed country, the reaction of most Americans was not hasty calls for war, but condemnation of Brown and his deeds. Not only did the Richmond press express outrage, but Richmonders became irritated by Northern admonitions to keep cool. George Wythe Randolph was as much infuriated against the Northern minority's apology for Brown as against Brown himself, and he castigated those "low, half-educated Yankees" who posed as beneficent reformers.[1]

George Randolph's worldview reflected that of the several cultural groups among which he was numbered: the F.F.V.s, military officers, graduates of the University of Virginia, Virginia's legal community, the Virginia Militia, and the literary world of John Reuben Thompson. The last was certainly the most unusual and interesting of his formative influences. Besides having subscribed to his friend's magazine, he was also a member of a discussion group led by Thompson that met alternately at Randolph's and *The Southern Literary Messenger*'s offices. The editor secured Professor George F. Holmes of the University of Virginia to review George Fitzhugh's two great works, *Sociology for the South, or the Failure of Free Society* and *Cannibals All! or Slaves Without Masters*. Although Fitzhugh spent much of the Civil War in Richmond, he is not known to have associated with any high Confederate administrative official. Because Thompson and his friends customarily discussed his journal's reviews, there is strong circumstantial evidence that George Randolph knew the main contours of Fitzhugh's thought through Thompson's auspices. After printing a brief review of *Sociology for the South* in the March 1854 number of *The Southern Literary Messenger,* Thompson took the unusual step of publishing in the April number Holmes's extended review of that book and of Du Var Robert's *Histoire de la classe ouvrière jusqu'au prolétaire de nos jours* (4 vols., Paris, Michel, 1845–46).

That Holmes's disagreement with Fitzhugh was only partial and that his adverse criticism was provocatively qualified showed how well Thompson had learned from the examples of Voltaire and the Encyclopedists. The review was in fact covert agreement, intending to stimulate others to concur. Although Holmes admitted that, if the South were to compete "with the North in trade and manufactures, the South will become the North, and slavery will be speedily extinguished . . . , [yet] the aggressions of the North may compel the adoption of this course in self-defence." He showed so much interest in the "initiative" of the British and French governments in trying to ameliorate the lot of their workers and to bring "the agencies of society . . . into harmony" that the editor may well have challenged Randolph, who, he said, inherited "ancestral intellect," to endorse similar programs for his own country. At the same time that Thompson professed to deplore the "error, the inefficiency and the impracticability" of the means suggested by the socialists, he teased his readers by saying that some socialist suggestions "merit approbation. . . . After undergoing slight modifications, they harmonize with the general current of events, and are available for urgent requirements." When editor Thompson apologized for not translating Robert's word, *prolétaire,* he called attention to it and to both its literal and figurative meanings. By conceding that a new order of things would require the "same energy and ability in the management and conservation as in the accumulation of fortune," he hinted at forced capital accumulation for purposes of state expenditures. For Thompson to express regret that Fitzhugh "should have partially identified Socialism with Slavery" was little more than an invitation to his faithful readers to come to such a conclusion, too. All of this stimulated a man like Randolph, who was torn between reverence for the eighteenth-century ideals of his grandfather Jefferson and his own nineteenth-century melange of urban, commercial, and maritime interests which he had developed as a protégé of Joseph Coolidge, in the navy, at the University of Virginia, in Thompson's discussion group, as a lawyer, and as an officer of the Virginia Militia. Holmes's and Thompson's commentary on Fitzhugh's repudiation of the concepts of social contract and equality of man captured George Randolph's interest. The author and the editor allayed the latter's suspicions by excusing Jefferson for having tried to bind together these concepts in the Declaration of Independence on grounds of Jefferson's well-meaning optimism and of his "partiality for Voltaire, Rousseau and their compeers." Fitzhugh declared that the social contract idea was only a mechanical trick of the Enlightenment without much meaning and that the notion of equality of man was a delusory device for subjecting the able as well as the less enterprising to despotism. As we have noted, George Randolph echoed these sentiments, saying that the proposition "'All men are created equal . . . with inalienable rights,' if [accepted] literal[ly], applies to prisoners in jail."[2] Thompson published Professor Holmes's review of *Cannibals All!* in the March 1855 number of *The Southern Literary Messenger,* but his promised extended review never appeared, unless an essay "American Slavery in 1857" in the August number is counted as a partial fulfillment.[3]

If Thompson was to direct the literati of Richmond and the future Confederacy, he had to do a great deal more than invoke old ways, old virtues. He was persistent in his efforts to introduce them to modern works of scholarship. Publication in the 1850s of George Bancroft's volumes in the *History of the United States,* of Charles Campbell's *History of the Colony and Ancient Dominion of Virginia,* and of Hugh Blair Grigsby's *History of the Virginia Convention of 1776* provided splendid opportunities for him to bewitch readers of *The Southern Literary Messenger* by means of his pet device, the extended book review. What better way for him to prepare the literati and leaders of society than to declare, "We are in a transitional state; there is nothing fixed, nothing settled." Using these authors, he set about to demolish outworn arguments. In the controversy over Virginia's aristocratic or plebeian origin, he asserted that Grigsby was "probably right in repudiating the popular idea that this colony was mainly settled by . . . Cavaliers." Building upon the probability that Virginia was settled by "every sort of people in Great Britain," he maintained that Virginia's gentry was a natural aristocracy. Contrary to Bancroft, Thompson believed that the Revolution in Virginia was the creation of the gentry, not of the masses.[4]

When an unusually generous offer briefly lured John R. Thompson away from *The Southern Literary Messenger* in the spring of 1860 to edit the *Southern Field and Fireside* at Augusta, Georgia, twenty-five of his closest friends, representing Richmond's intellectual, professional, and social elites, joined to tender him a testimonial dinner at Zetelle's restaurant. The affair began at 5:00, and it is likely that more than a wee dram o' Randolph's favorite Scotch liquor was consumed before they went to table at six o'clock to feast on eleven entrées, vegetables, fruits, cheeses, French coffee, chartreuse, and cigars until 11:00. Besides Thompson and Randolph there were present William H. MacFarland, the publisher of *The Southern Literary Messenger;* the mayor of Richmond, Maj. William P. Munford; Dr. Robert W. Haxall and his brother, the great flour manufacturer, William H. Haxall; former Judge William W. Crump, who sat on the Richmond City Council and Board of Trustees of the College of William and Mary and who had been an attorney in the John Randolph will case; James Lyons, the States-Rights Whig; Col. R. Milton Cary, who had helped organize the 1857 ceremonies commemorating the 250th anniversary of the settlement at Jamestown; Dr. Charles Gorham Barney and Thomas H. Wynne of the Virginia Historical Society; Capt. John M. Patton, who helped Conway Robinson edit legal tomes; and Joseph R. Anderson, a 1836 graduate of West Point who was head of the Tredegar Iron Works.[5]

Like Thompson, Randolph seems to have been drawn against his will into the political controversies of the 1850s. Randolph had made no secret of his proslavery and prosouthern ideas when he went to Richmond. Even if he and his wife Mary were more moderate in their views than their friends Agnes and Roger A. Pryor who moved to Richmond in 1854, such hotheads and fire-eaters frequented his house. Although he was not active in the Virginia gubernatorial campaign of 1855, which saw Henry A. Wise and the Democrats defeat Thomas S. Flournoy and the Know-Nothings, he undoubtedly applauded Pryor's contributions to Wise's victory. During the drift toward secession, George Wythe Randolph was called from his legal practice, his literary associations, and his domestic life by friends to file for and win election to the Richmond City Council in the mid-1850s. This modest start in politics gave him a geographical base and identity at the critical moment when change and a new face was possible.[6]

If the first effect that the John Brown raid had on George Wythe Randolph was primarily cerebral with overtones of political action, the second was a call for a physical response to the challenge of insurrection. He felt compelled to take up arms, don a uniform, and abandon for the nonce a cozy home life so that he could demonstrate by personal example that the time had come for the South to show that she was "able to protect herself, and what is more *she intends to do it,*" as the Richmond *Whig* expressed it.[7]

George Randolph was not impetuous, but he was never left behind. He became the commander of the new artillery unit that he founded. Clearly he preferred to start afresh. Perhaps there was among his motives the belief that, because he was an old Navy man, he had best avoid the carping of army veterans. At any rate, he raised a new artillery company and armed it by converting naval small-boat guns—howitzers—to land use. These were short guns for the high-angle firing of eight- or twelve-pound shot at low velocities. This company was known as the Richmond Howitzers, and it enjoyed many advantages, over both older and newer units, because of its high degree of preparedness. Beginning in the autumn of 1859 and continuing until the outbreak of war in 1861, Randolph and his officers adapted to their use Dennis Hart Mahan's West Point textbooks on tactics and field fortifications. What the Howitzers did not owe to Randolph's military prescience they owed to his care and thoroughness; and the Howitzers became the "crack" unit he had set out to create. Not only did they have their equipage while others drilled with broomsticks, but their arms and gear were of top-notch quality. In 1861 remarkably little disruption occurred when the Howitzers' one company expanded to a brigade of three companies, totaling 225 men and officers. This expansion was an evolution in which corporals became sergeants and sergeants became lieutenants. In 1859, the Howitzers was able to pick and choose even its privates by appealing to the sentiments and traditions of Richmond bluebloods, who considered themselves the inheritors of Virginia's tradition of patriotism and military prowess. Many youths enlisted in this unit at the age of eighteen and served throughout the war as cannoneers. Not only was there exceptional camaraderie and esprit de corps among the officers and men of the Howitzers, but they were inclined to give these qualities their French inflection by turning out the mustaches and imperial goatees favored by Emperor Napoleon III. Few Howitzer men transferred to other units. Often officers were plucked out to command less august units. The Howitzers were an elite microcosm. Closely knit in terms of place, family, and association, they had good reason to believe that, in addition to their bravery, they had in Randolph a leader whose careful planning enabled them to suffer fewer hardships and less loss of life than did most other units.[8]

The Howitzer Company held its first organizational meeting on November 9, 1859, in the clerk's office of the State Circuit Court. As its organizer, George Randolph was elected captain. The second meeting was held a week later in the Military Hall over the Market at the corner of Main and Seventeenth streets. Other officers were elected, and the company was exercised at its first drill. By November 19, 1859, the Howitzer Company was armed with old muskets by the state and sent to the vicinity of Harper's Ferry to resist threatened attempts to free

John Brown from the Jefferson County jail at Charlestown. Although most of the Howitzer battery were without uniforms, they nonetheless boarded railway cars of the Richmond, Fredericksburg and Potomac Railroad with some other Richmond units, and were led—as the press reported—by the "brave George Randolph." Because the railroad's northern terminus was at Aquia Creek on the Potomac, they had to proceed by boat to Washington. When they disembarked, "an irreverent hack-man" exclaimed to a laughing crowd: "Here's your Revolutionary Ducks!" For a while, this sobriquet became the nickname of the original members of the Howitzer Company. Upon arrival at Charlestown, the Richmond Howitzers were quartered in the basement of the Charlestown Presbyterian Church. Besides serving security purposes, the company profited from the opportunity to drill. It remained at Charlestown until after Brown was tried and hanged on December 2, 1859.[9]

Considering his subsequent ill health after the autumn of 1862, it is remarkable that the hardships of temporary barracks in Jefferson County proved exhilarating to Randolph. To his niece Molly he wrote: "I have always, you know, been taken for an invalid, and my men evidently feared that I could not stand the fatigue of the campaign. To their great astonishment, it turned out that I could endure harder service than any of them." To commemorate their first period of active duty as a unit, George Randolph and some of his friends posed for a photographer. By this time, not only had he acquired a proper uniform, but he had turned out a full beard.[10]

Alarmed by the John Brown raid, the ensuing Virginia General Assembly authorized a three-man Military Commission to renovate the state armory and stock it with $500,000 worth of arms. Governor Letcher appointed Philip St. George Cocke and Francis H. Smith of the Virginia Military Institute and George Wythe Randolph as commissioners. In April they and the governor made a tour of arms manufactories at Harper's Ferry; Wilmington, Delaware; Springfield, Massachusetts; and both West Point and Cold Spring Harbor, New York. Mary Randolph seems to have been the only lady to accompany the commissioners. They received a good reception everywhere. At Wilmington Henry du Pont and his associates extended a cordial reception, due in some degree to the friendship between his and George Randolph's grandfathers. The powdermaker assured his visitors that he would be happy to provide Virginia all the munitions it desired.[11]

At West Point, the commissioners ordered a three-inch rifled Parrott gun and one hundred rounds of ammunition for immediate deliv-

Some members of the Richmond Howitzers at Charlestown, 1859.
George Wythe Randolph is at lower right.
(Courtesy of The Museum of the Confederacy, Richmond, Va.)

ery to the Virginia Military Institute at Lexington in order that it could be tested by Professor Thomas J. Jackson. The commissioners also ordered twelve additional Parrott guns for more leisurely delivery, thus selecting what proved to be one of the Confederacy's best field pieces. At about the same time Randolph secured from U.S. Secretary of War John B. Floyd authorization to buy from the Arsenal at Harper's Ferry 5,000 muskets and 20,000 seasoned gun stocks. Always interested in craftsmen, he undertook to keep master gunsmiths in Virginia and to provide them with challenging work.

In the preceding decade, the Virginia State Arsenal had secured Salomon Adams as its master armorer and Joseph R. Anderson had recruited J. H. Burton from Enfield, England, to be the master armorer of his Tredegar Iron Works at Richmond. For these craftsmen, Randolph secured through Secretary Floyd copies of drawings, tools, machines, and castings used at the Harper's Ferry and Springfield armories. With justifiable pride in the Virginia Military Commissioners' defense preparations, Randolph declared that "when Lincoln takes his seat [as President, Virginia] will be better prepared for Civil War than any state in the Union."[12] Thanks largely to Northern willingness to sell her arms, this probably was true.

On May 25, 1860, the Washington arsenal shipped to Randolph the six guns with which the commonwealth of Virginia would outfit his company—five smooth-bore and one rifled Dahlgren boat howitzers. Because these guns were designed originally to be used by navy gun crews in small craft, the Virginia State Arsenal had to fit them with light carriages drawn by two horses. On July 4, 1860, the Howitzer Company made its first parade with these weapons. By February of 1861 the company had seventy-four officers and men.[13]

Randolph's training as a midshipman, along with both his reading and his friendships, led him to embrace the role of the activist, somewhat in the way that he once had been willing to fight a duel with a British bully in Lisbon to uphold the honor of his ship and his country. When his friends of 1859 spoke of crises and the need for an enhanced militia system, George Randolph did not disappoint them by remaining silent. His law partner, Thomas August, encouraged him to take such a stand. Although not as serious-minded as Randolph, August and Randolph made a good legal and civic team. In his capacity as colonel of the First Virginia Volunteer Regiment of Infantry Militia in the 1850s and brigadier general of the Second Brigade, Fourth Division, of Virginia Militia in 1860, August stimulated Randolph's interest in political and military affairs. After extensive service in the field during the first year of the war, Tom August suffered a physical breakdown, partly from tuberculosis, in the early autumn of 1862. As secretary of war, George Randolph was able to bring him into the War Office to assist Gen. Samuel Cooper in administering conscription.

In the summer and autumn of 1860 the Military Commission so preoccupied George Randolph that he attended only one political meeting. Nor did he have many opportunities to engage in political speculation with Roger A. Pryor about the intense rivalry for the Democratic presidential nomination.[14] He did converse with Henry S. Randall on this subject when the latter passed through Richmond to take part in the Democratic nominating convention at Charleston, South Carolina, but the two talked more of family than of politics. Randolph regarded Lincoln's election to the presidency as "certain" and prophesied that Virginia would not secede immediately because "the western half of the state contains nearly two-thirds of the white population, controls the State Government, has very few slaves and is by no means so sensitive to the attacks of the abolitionists as we of the east." He predicted that she would attempt a role of "armed neutrality" and to deny permission for federal troops to march through her territory to coerce the states south of her. He foresaw that eventually Lincoln would attempt "to force a seceding state back into the Union[, an act that] would lead to general hostilities." He admitted that, in the unlikely event that the North defeated the Southern states, the latter would "be no longer states but conquered provinces, held by force and necessitating large armies to keep them in subjection." He hoped that the cessation of cotton exports would constrict "the imports which nourish northern cities," but the notion that "Cotton is King" never enthralled him. Advocating that Southern leaders move quickly in seceding before apathy seized the general public, he predicted in October that there would be a Southern republic before February. Confident that President Buchanan would "not disturb the quiet of the last days of his administration by a civil war," Randolph believed that Lincoln would commence the irrepressible conflict, but that the South would have a year in which to prepare for a major campaign. During this period of grace, he advocated that Virginia and the Southern states arm themselves so strongly that they could successfully resist subjugation.[15]

In Virginia's secession crisis, Randolph was an able, if partisan, oracle. Deriding those opposed to secession as submissionists, he scorned their indecision and their hopes that the North would be more just and that the South would be less irascible. Insisting that the North would bully and insult the Southern minority until the latter seceded, he demanded that Virginia secede soon enough to do so successfully. If she remained in the Union, he argued that her position would be not only "dishonorable, dangerous and ruinous," but that "she would feel her degradation and be made to feel it. The anti-slavery agitation," said he, would "go on until emancipation is forced upon her."[16] At the same time, Randolph painted a rosy sunrise for Virginia in a Southern republic that was not distracted by disputation over slavery. Echoing his professor at the University of Virginia, George Tucker, he advocated a centralized political economy that had elements of old-fashioned mercantilism and pre-Marxist socialism. Virginia, he said, "could have opportunity to devote her whole attention to the development of her wealth and industry. Her population would give her great influence and her favorable situation for European commerce would make her the greatest manufacturing and commercial state of the Southern Confederacy, and being relieved by a tariff from northern competition. . . . An immense Southern market would exchange raw materials for her manufactures, [and] she would advance in wealth and population with great rapidity."[17] The events of 1862–65 show the accuracy of Randolph's argument in that he was able to staff the Confederate States War Department with men whose technological abilities had led them to propound centralized and elitist solutions for the South's deficiencies in economic and industrial prowess.

On the surface of things, there was little in George Wythe Randolph's experience to explain why he was elected as one of Richmond's three delegates to the Virginia Convention of 1861. Except for service on the City Council, he had had no political involvement or experience during his fifteen mature years in Albemarle and his eight years in Richmond. Most of the principals of the convention had served at least in the Virginia General Assembly, if not in Congress. It is not enough to say of Randolph's election that the man and hour were met under unusual circumstances or to join John R. Thompson in saying that his sense of civic responsibility was so great that he was "to duty vowed" and always "content to do the task, to bear the burden."[18]

Although George Randolph was a Democrat, his position was almost indistinguishable from that of many former Whigs. He was an advocate of moderate tariff protection, of maintaining Virginia's lucrative out-of-state sale of wheat, tobacco, and livestock, of fostering production of coal, iron, and salt for internal and external sale, and of developing new industries. Virginia's political configuration of the 1850s had been chaotic after the demise of the Whig party. In spite of their bitter factional rivalries, both ex-Governor Henry A. Wise and U.S. Senator Robert M. T. Hunter made advocacy of Southern nationalism dogma for Virginia's Democrats. Hunter's faction won most of the Southern nationalists. His organ, the Richmond *Examiner,* and Roger A. Pryor's *South* joined forces in endorsing the candidacies of Southern nationalists in the February 1861 election to the state constitutional convention. In such a moment, George Randolph possessed a winning combination of attributes. No matter how advanced and sophisticated he might be in his private economic and social views, he was perceived as genteel, respectable, and conservative. He was a popular and successful champion of defense preparedness. He managed to make his early advocacy of Southern nationalism appear both the way to peace and the path best justified by the manner in which events were unfolding. As a matter of practical politics, he and his law partner General August could rely on their militia to campaign for him. Both the *Examiner* and the *South* endorsed Randolph for one of Richmond's three seats in the Virginia Constitutional Convention of 1861. In February he won election by a respectable margin, as did also a Unionist and a neutralist. Of the 152 delegates, about 30 were avowed secessionists. That the convention in April named him to the three-man commission to call on President Lincoln was less a recognition of his leadership than it was of the importance of his constituency and its newspapers. It was also a shrewd move by Senator Hunter's friends to outflank Wise, whom they distrusted because of his erratic and precipitous nature, because he had deserted the Democrats to be a Whig in the 1840s, and because of his open challenge to the senior senator's leadership. Thus it was that F.F.V. credentials, a blend of Democratic, Whiggish, and secessionist principles, a personal following in an important constituency, and self-destructive rivalry among seasoned officeholders catapulted Randolph to the forefront of Virginia political life in 1860–61.[19]

George Wythe Randolph bore a doubly honored name. As much as he professed to seek nothing except what he could win on merit, there were plenty ready to lionize him as a Randolph of Virginia, as Jefferson's grandson, and the namesake of the proverbial fount of legal wisdom, George Wythe. The man behind this facade was far more complicated than he appeared to all but a few. It was the combination of the shock of the the John Brown raid and of his hidden economic and social views derived from Tucker's lectures and Thompson's discussion group that made it possible for George Randolph to become a secessionist and for Virginians to accept him as a newfound leader. The likelihood that the crisis of 1860–61 would end in warfare must have influenced many Virginians to place Randolph in a position of leadership as a military expert. On the other hand, it may not be too much to affirm that he demonstrates the truth of Vilfredo Pareto's theorem that it can be easy for a member of a nongoverning elite, such as George Randolph was until 1861, to move into the governing elite by dint of "inheritance" and "wheedling the voters."[20]

Although a combination of Tom August's efforts and his Richmond militia service had gotten Randolph started on the political ladder and the Hunter faction had promoted him to the top, George Wythe Randolph had the respect and support of the quiet leadership of Richmond's economic and social elites. The city's newspapers, with the possible exception of the Richmond *Dispatch* and *Whig,* were edited by his friends or relatives: Ritchie and Pollard of the *Enquirer,* Daniel of the *Examiner,* and Pryor of *The South.*

Even with all these advantages, it was still remarkable that George Randolph should emerge suddenly as the man of the hour. In retrospect, one can perceive that his success did not depend on local specifics, but was borne on a great wave that touched all parts of the continent. America's climate of opinion by February of 1861 had become supercharged with emotion. Paradoxically, Virginians congratulated themselves on being rational at the same time that they engaged in passionate oratory in their constitutional convention, where secessionists, neutralists, and unionists blocked any decision until after events at Fort Sumter brought an end to talking.[21] The pretence of rationality merely concealed the emotional character of a choice which was seen to be between secession or submission. The new editor of *The Southern Literary Messenger,* Dr. George W. Bagby, voiced the impatience of Virginia advocates of secession: "The once proud and noble Old Dominion [seems to be] waiting for coercion, before it does its duty. Monstrous."[22] Randolph was a charismatic leader who rose to the occasion. The midshipman who had risked a duel to defend his country's good name, the midshipman who had been sickened by brutality toward enlisted men, the criminal lawyer who could sway the jury— George Wythe Randolph suddenly was presented with the largest audience and the greatest opportunity that he ever had had. It was an audience which welcomed him as aristocrat and democrat, as loyal Virginian and good secessionist, as man of reasoned words and saber-rattling action.

The Richmond *Dispatch* hailed Randolph's secessionist speech in the first, open session of the convention as "most practical and sensible" and pronounced his arguments that Virginia would be the economic and industrial leader of the Confederacy as "stern facts and irresistible deductions." Remarking that George Randolph's appearance was "calm and mild," the *Dispatch* declared that one must "hear him and see him while speaking" in order to appreciate his "extraordinary ability."[23]

On April 1, 1861, the Virginia Convention in its second, secret session appointed a committee of three to wait upon President Lincoln and ascertain his intentions. These three were William Ballard Preston of Montgomery County, an old Whig and unionist; Alexander Hugh Holmes Stuart of Augusta, an old Whig and neutralist; and George Wythe Randolph of Richmond, a Democrat and a secessionist. Indeed, the Washington *Star* described Randolph as "a poisonous secessionist." Because storms disrupted the rail and steamer traffic of the Richmond, Fredericksburg and Potomac Railroad at its Aquia terminal, the commissioners had to proceed to Washington by way of Norfolk and Baltimore. They met with President Lincoln at 1:00 on April 12, stated their purpose and obtained an appointment for a conference the following morning at nine. When they reassembled, the president reiterated a passage from his inaugural address that he would "hold, occupy and possess the property and places belonging to the Government . . . [and that,] beyond what is necessary for these objects there will be no invasion—no using of force. . . . [But] I shall repel force by force."

The commission's last-minute effort to avoid a provocative incident was futile, because, much as Randolph had predicted, Lincoln had already dispatched a ship to resupply Fort Sumter. By the time that Randolph and his fellow commissioners reported their failure to the convention on April 15, 1861, no doubt remained about Lincoln's intentions. Even if the commissioners had arrived before the attempted strengthening of Fort Sumter, it is improbable that they would have been able to sway President Lincoln from his course.[24]

In the midst of these exciting events, George Randolph's former shipmate Ned Anderson of Savannah visited Virginia in April of 1861. The Georgian described in his diary how the city's excitement increased until "the Confederate flag [was] flying all over Richmond." It was probably he who first told Jefferson Davis of how Randolph could provide strategic help to the Southern republic, offering as proof Randolph's confidential account of the commissioners' meeting with President Lincoln and his conclusion that "the attack on Fort Sumter leaves [Lincoln] at liberty to repossess himself of the Southern forts. . . . He will suspend the mails and means to collect the revenue."[25]

The Virginia Convention reconvened in secret session on April 16, 1861, and continued for more than a week of daily and often evening meetings. The three commissioners declined to repeat President Lincoln's exact words, believing themselves honor-bound by his remarkable request that "his conversation would not be reported." Preston, Randolph, and Stuart did, however, share with their confreres "the impression" that that conversation had made upon them individually.

Randolph declared that the time for debate, for a border-state conference, or for neutrality was over: "we are in the beginning of the greatest war that has ever been waged on this continent." He scotched any notion of divided Northern opinion, saying that the Lincoln administration's war policy would have "the entire support of the Northern people . . . at least, in the beginning of the war," and that the U.S. government would commit its "entire force" to the war. A realist, he brushed aside quibbles about defensive and offensive warfare, urging that Virginia secede speedily in order to throw the responsibility of military operation on the Northern confederacy and denying that the Lincoln administration could confine its policy simply to retake federal installations such as Fort Sumter. Scoffing at the idea of neutrality, he counseled: "You have got to fight—and the question is, which side will you fight with?" He called for immediate action. Otherwise, said he, Virginia would lose the services of many of her best sons, she would be subject to federal taxation to support a war to crush her Southern sisters, and the Northerners would be able to remove vital war goods from the naval dockyard at Norfolk.[26]

There was considerable debate whether or how Virginia should create her own regular army. For the Military Committee, Randolph presented a draught for an ordinance creating and regulating such a force. Concentrating on the creation of a regular army, he reminded everyone that the war "may last for years. Unless you intend to keep men of business—farmers, merchants and mechanics in the field for years, you must have regular troops to take their places. Unless you intend, when the Confederate Government calls on you for your quota, to send your very best men to stand and fight along side of regular soldiers, you must organize a regular army." How many generals to appoint, what would be their precedence relative to generals of the old, volunteer militia and whether rank could be guaranteed if Virginia's army were mustered into Confederate service were questions Randolph left to others to argue. He concerned himself with few details, but they were significant ones. Although the Virginia ordinance copied closely the U.S. articles of war in most respects, Randolph saw to it that it forbade any corporal punishment "by stripes or lashes." He interested himself, also, in conferring power on the governor of Virginia to construct a state-owned telegraph system between Alexandria and Winchester and between Fredericksburg and Baltimore. And, finally, he took umbrage at the suggestion that Virginia entered the crisis unprepared.[27] Not so, he declared.

> This State is far better prepared than any Northern State. . . . She has an army . . . [of] 25,000 men with arms now in her arsenals and in the hands of her troops . . . , the worst of them equal to the arms used by the United States in Mexico. . . . She has powder for at least two campaigns for a train of artillery. . . . I have been informed by the agent for the du Pont Mills that any time powder is needed, they can supply us to an unlimited extent. . . . The arms that our troops have, are precisely the arms that will be brought against us . . . and are not at all inferior to those which the 75,000 men called for by the President [Lincoln] will have, if they come here; and, so far as drill is concerned, the State has several thousand men in drill since the Harper's Ferry affair.[28]

Before the Virginia Convention rose, the Richmond Howitzers on April 19, 1861, went into quarters in the basement of the Spotswood Hotel at the corner of Eighth and Main streets in Richmond. Two days later, the company was mustered into State service for one year's duration.[29]

Civil War had come. Randolph the man, Randolph the secessionist, and Randolph the artillerist was ready.

## CHAPTER 6

# From a Captaincy to the Cabinet, March 1861–May 1862

Having been a spokesman for Virginia's secession and espousal of Southern liberty, George Wythe Randolph reasonably could aspire to a role in state or Confederate government. Although his part in Virginia's secession movement had been prominent and honorable, it was not, however, sufficient to move him immediately into high levels of Confederate leadership.

Ever since 1859 George Randolph's military reputation coincided and grew with that of the Richmond Howitzers. On April 21, 1861, he commanded, with the rank of major, the Howitzers—now a battalion composed of three companies. At the beginning of the war, the Howitzers' first company remained at Richmond to help V.M.I. cadets train recruits, while Major Randolph led the second and third companies, under Capt. J. Thompson Brown, Jr., and Capt. Robert C. Stanard, to join Col. John Bankhead Magruder's army between the York and James rivers.[1]

Magruder had attended the University of Virginia in 1825–26 before going to West Point, from which he graduated in 1830. He had commanded a battery in the Battle of Chapultepec in the Mexican War and was so popular a host on U.S. Army posts that he was called "Prince John." George Randolph, however, followed the Magruder family's custom in calling him "Bankhead." Contradicting gossip that Magruder was "very dissipated," Randolph declared that "since his appointment as a brigadier general, [Magruder] has not used intoxicating liquors of any sort and has been . . . [a] rigid temperance man."[2] Although Randolph admitted that no two men were "less alike" than he and Magruder, they got along so well that Randolph was reputed to have "more influence at Headquarters than any officer in the Peninsula"

59

because of his ability to get guns out of the bureaucrats at Richmond. When George Randolph's acquaintance Louis D. Guillaume came to Yorktown to paint a full-length likeness of Magruder, Randolph jokingly asked if the artist could capture the general's "very large" and "intensely red face." He suggested disbelief that Guillaume could portray accurately his commanding officer's bellicosity because Magruder spoke with a pronounced lisp. According to Randolph, Magruder had won confidence and popularity with his men "by his devotion to his business." Bankhead and Randolph seem to have discussed only martial matters, never the marital disaster of almost fifty years earlier, when George's eldest sister Anne had married Magruder's relative, the alcoholic Charles Lewis Bankhead.[3]

When Magruder became a major general and reorganized his forces into the Army of the Peninsula, he secured Randolph's promotion to colonel in charge of all artillery. George Randolph was well acquainted with many of the officers with whom he was to serve. He had known his second-in-command J. Thompson Brown, Jr., for several years before the Civil War. As a Petersburg youth, Brown had attended the University of Virginia where he had met and married in 1858 Mary Martha Southall, a friend of the Randolph family. Brown had practiced law in Richmond before being commissioned a lieutenant in the Howitzers on April 21, 1862, at the age of twenty-six. George's friend, classmate, and fellow barrister of Richmond, Henry Coalter Cabell, commanded another artillery company under Randolph.[4]

Randolph complained that failure to oppose Union amphibious landings, such as at Port Royal, South Carolina, had prejudiced the Confederate States War Department against making serious efforts to stop Union landings elsewhere. The reason for failure, said he, was insufficient artillery practice. Southerners aimed their cannon so high that the shells went not only over the Union landing forces, but over the mastheads of the Union fleet. His insistence on rigorous drills carried with it a penalty of sorts: General Magruder required that Randolph be on a constant alert to direct the employment of the batteries at the Yorktown forts against invasion by Union forces.[5] As a former navy man, Randolph participated in consultations on fortifying Yorktown against land and naval attack. He was drawn into strategic as well as tactical decisions, partly because of his role, since the fall of 1860, as one member of Virginia's three-man military commission. It is not clear how long or seriously Confederate authorities planned to defend Yorktown. Until midspring of 1862, Randolph was not alone in thinking highly of its log and dirt fortifications, armed both with deadly metal guns and with their wooden replicas, called Quaker guns. Hoping for a water-borne attack, he was ready to use against a Union armada hot shot, which Guillaume called *bullets rouges*. Randolph did not, however, advocate a last-ditch defense of the town.

Randolph played a prominent part in the opening skirmishes of the war. In April of 1861, he borrowed the Parrott gun he had left for testing at V.M.I. a year earlier. On May 14, 1861, he used it at Gloucester Point, Virginia, to beat off the USS *Yankee*'s probe of the York River, the first use of field artillery in the Civil War.[6] On June 10, his two companies of Howitzers provided decisive firepower in winning the Battle of Big Bethel, between Yorktown and Fort Monroe. He placed his guns in a wood behind "two snug little homesteads," which its human inhabitants had abandoned. Randolph was proud of the fact that his men had not depredated upon the farms, as did the New York Zouaves, who, "resplendent in red trousers and fancy work," were so busy chasing the farmers' pigs that they did not realize until too late that the Howitzers were about to blow them to kingdom come. Although the vital statistics (eighteen killed and fifty-three wounded Yankees; one killed and three wounded Rebels) did not justify the extent of Confederate jubilation which ensued, the engagement was not without significance. Randolph had chosen the site for his guns and his men were ready. Sometimes called the first battle of the war, Big Bethel proved once again that superiority of firepower will prevail: the Confederates had one three-inch rifled Parrott gun and four twelve-pounders; the Union forces had two six-pounders and one twelve-pounder. Not only did the two Howitzer companies overwhelm the regular U.S. Army battery opposite them, but they helped 1,200 Confederate infantry under Colonel D. H. Hill rout 2,500 Northerners. Privately, Colonel Randolph remarked after Big Bethel that "these are the scenes that render invasions so terrible."[7]

In his official report Randolph lauded his men, acknowledged the "useful suggestions" of D. H. Hill, a former artillerist, and pointed out deficiencies of his gun carriages and ammunition. Magruder's report acclaimed the "skill and gallantry" of the Howitzers' "most acomplished" commander, saying: "He has no superior as an artillerist in any country, and his men displayed the utmost skill and coolness." The encomiums that Randolph received for his part in the Battle of Big Bethel were a tribute, not just to his training as a midshipman, but also to his having learned much since 1859, to his having added to the amphibious art of gunnery solutions to terrestrial problems of terrain, targeting, concealment, and movement. In recognition of this victory,

Magruder was promoted to brigadier general. Magruder chose Randolph as his chief of artillery in the "pestilent marshes of the Peninsula" and to superintend ordnance and quartermaster stores with the rank of colonel.[8] John B. Magruder went into eclipse after the summer of 1862, but he then was probably Virginia's greatest war hero. George Wythe Randolph enjoyed a somewhat similar acclaim. President Davis wrote to Gov. John Letcher of Virginia that General Magruder's "commendation of Major Randolph . . . accords with all I have previously heard of him."[9]

Still basking in the acclaim for their action at Big Bethel, the Yorktown garrison greeted the news that the Confederates had defeated the Union Army at Manassas with "shouts and the roar of our big guns." Soon, however, Randolph wrote that he and his fellow officers had concluded that the victory was not "so complete as it is reported."[10]

In the early autumn of 1861, Randolph became so ill of "bronchitis" that he could hardly "put pen to paper." He went on sick leave in order to recuperate at his family's estate in Albemarle County.[11] Election to the first, prewar session of the Virginia Constitutional Convention had qualified him for membership in its "secret" November, 1861 session. Along with the majority of the members, he failed to answer the first roll call on Wednesday, November 13th. He was present the next day, when there also was no quorum. There were tempting diversions for those weary of arduous duties before taking up newer burdens. Since George and Mary Randolph enjoyed good music, they may have attended the November 1, 1861, concert of the Richmond Philharmonic Association in Franklin Hall to hear selections from *Norma, I Puritani,* and *Le nozze di Figaro.*

On its third day, the second session of the Constitutional Convention mustered a quorum. In the first order of business, Thomas Jefferson Randolph was elected to chair the convention, while George continued to chair the military committee. His work was so important that it provides the best reason for his appointment as Secretary of War a year later. He played the major role in perfecting the Commonwealth's militia ordinance, basing it on that of Prussia. The ordinance required service in an active militia of all males from eighteen to thirty years of age who were not engaged in essential occupations or were not conscientious objectors. The ordinance also provided for a reserve of all other men and a system of providing substitutes. Randolph was proud to claim that Virginia's system was not excelled by France or Prussia.[12]

Civil War historians have not paid much attention to Yorktown, but in January of 1862 George Randolph considered it an important post, "incessantly threatened by land and sea. . . . The naval expeditions of the enemy . . . pass in sight of our batteries. Of course, we are on the qui vive whenever one is fitting out, as we never know whether we may not be its object. We have seen three [expeditions] get ready under our noses and put to sea. . . . We had constant alarms and were ordered up at night to man the batteries and heat shot until the furnaces were well nigh worn out." Because of respiratory trouble, Randolph did not look forward to wintering on the Peninsula, where Magruder insisted that tents were adequate winter quarters for his army. Another consideration governing Randolph's future was the fact that his regiment was about to be mustered out. He repeated to his wife and to his niece Molly that:

> I am not robust enough to discharge the duties of Chief of Artillery and Colonel of a Regiment. . . . I could not continue to do so even if I were reelected again. Nor do I have the least idea of offering myself as a candidate for election by the men or of petitioning the Governor for a commission. If they choose to commission me for the purpose of serving as Chief of Artillery or of performing any other duties not involving the command of a corps, I will serve them. If not, I will go home and endeavor to repair the damage to my private fortune caused by my employment in the public's service. I have raised and instructed one corps of artillerists and I think that that is as much as ought to be expected from me now.[13]

A possible alternative presented itself when former President Tyler's death created a vacancy in the Confederate States House of Representatives. Randolph announced his candidacy. Unknown to him, there was a law forbidding military officers running for civil office. Embarrassed when this was pointed out to him, Randolph did not campaign and withdrew his name from consideration. Meanwhile, he prepared for Confederate States Secretary of State R. M. T. Hunter a report on the defense of the Bay Shores of Virginia. This was the second time in as many years that Virginia's elder statesman had showed his appreciation of Randolph's expert abilities. It likely due to Hunter's influence that Randolph's naval service was seen to have fitted him to interpret the relationship of land and naval forces between the Potomac River and Albemarle Sound.[14]

At the base of the peninsula between the James and York rivers, the Union Army in 1861 had expanded its control beyond Fort Monroe's crenelated walls to include the town of Hampton, the blame for whose burning Confederate and Union officials disputed.[15] For as large a campaign as Gen. George B. McClellan planned for the spring of 1862, he needed an advanced base closer to Richmond. An important requirement for such a forward base was that it be capable of rail communication with Richmond. Either Yorktown or Portsmouth satisfied this condition. During the American Revolution, the British had demonstrated that both were ideal for an invader with superior seapower.

In his memoirs, Gen. Joseph E. Johnston praised Magruder for his enterprise and "boldness" in entrenching Yorktown during the autumn of 1861 and in perfecting its defensive fortifications during the spring of 1862. Even with a tenfold numerical superiority, General McClellan felt compelled to lay siege to the town, rather than attempt to bypass it. Johnston credited Magruder with delaying McClellan long enough to enable the Confederate government to assemble sufficient troops to save Richmond.[16] While the Confederates piled high the sandbags at Yorktown, they also created a strong force south of the James River at Suffolk, whence a mobile defense force could move by ships, railways, or turnpikes towards Norfolk, Portsmouth, Petersburg, Richmond, or even Yorktown. As a land-and-sea expert, George W. Randolph was posted to this new command with the rank of brigadier general. Subordinate to him was Brig. Gen. Howell Cobb, the tactical commander of six regiments of infantry.

While both the Rebels and Yankees built up their forces, stockpiled supplies, and improved their defensive positions, they delayed committing their armies to serious action. During this period, General Randolph formed the nucleus of the staff he was to take with him to the War Department a few months later: Maj. Isaac M. St. John headed his engineer detachment and Capt. Robert Garlick Hill Kean was his assistant adjutant general. St. John was a Mobile nephew of Mrs. Randolph's first husband. He and his wife had visited the Randolphs in Richmond in the 1850s.[17] Kean was the husband of George Randolph's niece Jane Randolph. After having been the outstanding law student of his class at the University of Virginia, he had practiced law in Lynchburg. Because General Randolph knew that he could count on these two men professionally and personally, he ignored the possibility of being accused of nepotism.

The question of whether areas of command should correspond to geographic or political boundaries has plagued wartime leaders throughout history. Because it was later to be an important factor in the greatest crisis of Randolph's secretaryship, it is significant both that the question arose early in his career and that he provided a pragmatic solution. Because North Carolina authorities were loath to acknowledge that Brigadier General Randolph's writ extended as far south as the Chowan River in their state, it was with reluctance that they furnished him North Carolina troops when a concentration of forces was required in March of 1862. After he became secretary of war, he solved the problem of North Carolina's and Virginia's cooperation satisfactorily by endorsing the petition of W. T. Dortch and O. R. Kenan that Brig. Gen. J. J. Pettigrew, a North Carolinian, exercise from Suffolk the command of southside Virginia and eastern North Carolina forces so that he would be able to "concentrate a larger force in a shorter time than [if there were a] divided command."[18]

When George Wythe Randolph received his promotion to brigadier general, the commonwealth of Virginia presented him a handsome dress sword. It was a fine example of the armorer's craft, wrought by C. M. Kinsel for the L. Halman and Brother Company in Columbus, Georgia. Its silvered blade bears the inscription: "Brig. Gen. G. W. Randolph, Bethel, June 10th 1861." Its handguard is made of three intersecting arcs of ormolu. Its elaborate hilt bears a topaz. Two seals decorate its sides, one seal inscribed "Deo Vindice" and the other "C.S.A." In the top of the hilt is set an amethyst carbuncle.[19]

Many of the leading members of the Confederate government felt frustration in the months after the First Battle of Manassas. *The Southern Literary Messenger's* fulminations were typical of the Richmond press. In its February–March 1862 number appeared a pseudonymous poem which complained that the Southerners' "great realm" had "not one noble leader at the helm." Dr. George W. Bagby, who had succeeded John R. Thompson as editor, wrote the poem as well as an irate editorial, which reveals how the Richmond literati were ready to make radical experiments in government in order to win the war. He asserted that the initial mistake was made in Montgomery, by modeling too closely the Confederate upon the Federal Constitution, saying that, "the old system is . . . too narrow and cumbersome." Consequently, it was not an accident that the Confederacy had "such a President, such a Cabinet, such a Congress, such Generals and such disasters." Bagby's solution was to make "organic changes [in the government,] by which the Executive shall be charged with less power and the Cabinet with more responsibility."[20]

There long had been dissatisfaction with the conduct of the Confederate War Office. The first Confederate secretary of war, Leroy Pope Walker (1817–84), had resigned in September 1861. Walker had been educated at the universities of Alabama and Virginia before practicing law in Huntsville, Alabama. He had advocated secession before he became a delegate to the Democratic National Convention of 1860. Although lacking military training or experience, he had been appointed a brigadier general of Alabama militia before accepting in March of 1861 President Davis's invitation to join the Confederate cabinet. Surprised at the outbreak of war, Walker had sent only two purchasing agents to Europe and had haggled over prices in the belief that "the supply of shot and shell was ample." He was more than tardy in buying war supplies and calling on the states to equip and train their full quotas of troops. Mary Boykin Chesnut remarked that Secretary Walker had "ruined us almost before we were under way."[21] Even more inhibiting of the department's direction of the war was its extreme understaffing. Walker's health had broken under "incessant labors" and "want of adequate assistance."

The second man to serve as secretary of war was Judah P. Benjamin (1811–84). He had studied briefly at Yale College before moving to New Orleans where he had read law before his brilliant antebellum career in the federal courts. He had served as U.S. senator from Louisiana between 1852 and 1861. Originally a Whig, he had declared himself a Democrat in 1856. In 1861 he had advocated secession and resigned from the Senate. President Davis had appointed him attorney general in March of 1861. When in September of that year Walker had resigned as secretary of war, the President had named Benjamin acting secretary of war in addition to his regular post. On November 15, 1861, Benjamin had ceased being attorney general and become full-time secretary of war. His personality and manner made enemies among military officers.[22]

In different ways both Walker and Benjamin had lacked a good temperament to head the War Department and the ability to select and direct good subordinates. Both, however, had recognized that their staffs were far too small. Benjamin had gained President Davis's support for its expansion, but he filled few of the new billets. Benjamin paved the way for his successor to reform the War Department, and he does not appear to have meddled in its affairs after moving to the State Department. Benjamin was so maladroit in his relations with army officers and congressmen that he became unpopular with the very leaders who otherwise might have welcomed him as a kind of Disraeli among Confederate tories. Right or wrong, Benajmin's refusal in February of 1862 to send to Roanoke Island the reinforcements requested by Gen. Henry A. Wise had contributed to the capitulation of that fort built upon the sand for the purpose of dominating North Carolina's shallow sounds. Wise was not a lucky man, as the former Virginia governor's role in the John Brown affair had shown in 1859.[23] Although Wise had been insubordinate in leaving Roanoke Island to lobby legislators for reinforcements, most congressmen, newspapers, and Richmonders so blamed Benjamin for the disaster that it became expedient for the President to replace him as secretary of war.

The fortuitous resignation of the Virginian R. M. T. Hunter as secretary of state provided Davis with a suitable berth for Benjamin, from which he could still advise the president on foreign affairs and other matters about which the president desired advice. Politically it became almost obligatory that Davis name a Virginian to the War Office. It may be presumed that the President sought the advice of Hunter, who had been impressed by Randolph's defense report. Magruder's army was then the toast of Richmond. Publication of Magruder's report of the Battle of Big Bethel had shown that Randolph had proved himself in the field. As a heroic brigadier and as one of Richmond's cultural, economic and social elite, Randolph was a good, if not an ideal, nominee. On March 17, 1862, President Davis sent to the Senate his nominations of Judah P. Benjamin for secretary of state and George Wythe Randolph for secretary of war.[24]

One of the first to congratulate George Randolph on his promotion to the secretaryship was D. H. Hill, who hoped that, with Randolph at the helm, greater attention would be paid to the virtues of "concentration." He reminisced that "we have often conversed . . . [on] the scattering of our forces and batteries. It seems to have been the policy of Mr. Benjamin (if he had any policy at all) to have a small detachment and a weak battery at every point where the enemy might land. The consequence is that we have been beat in detail." Another of Randolph's well-wishers was Joseph R. Anderson, a former member of the Thompson-Randolph discussion group and now a brigadier in eastern North Carolina. To his congratulations he added polite advocacy of improved river defenses. The two had had ample opportunity to ponder the consequences to river and harbor defense resulting from the construction of CSS *Virginia,* whose plates Anderson's Tredegar Iron Works had rolled. Still another who felicitated Randolph was Thomas H. Wynne, also a member of the Richmond literati and an amateur historian with whom Randolph had shared the direction of the Virginia Historical Society. Wynne now was chief engineer of the defenses of Richmond. Anderson, Randolph and Wynne generated a number of documents advocating the blockage of the Chowan River near Warrenton, North Carolina, and the James River below Richmond, as the only effective means of defense against ironclad warships. Presumably, these documents helped the secretary obtain President Davis's endorsement of these defense measures in spite of cries of anguish from those who desired business as usual and others who wanted troops at every river ford.[25]

Editorial comment on Randolph's appointment in the Richmond press was uniformly favorable. Telling readers that Randolph's "talents are of a very superior order," the *Enquirer* remarked that he possessed accomplishments in addition to his "signal service at Bethel" and his promotion to brigadier of the Suffolk command: "A fine scholar, of military education and experience, of excellent abilities, of a reputation without a blemish, of pleasant manner and easy approach, and of indefatigable industry, General Randolph will doubtless fill his post with credit to himself and his State and with justice to the important interests entrusted to him." The *Dispatch* contented itself with remarking that he was a "distinguished son of Virginia . . . [with] high military attainments."[26]

Randolph's experience had provided him strengths with which to put aside both perfunctory emulation of the U.S. War Department and the drifting of his predecessors, Walker and Benjamin. In what turned out to be a nine-month tenure, Randolph reorganized his department, whose powers and functions were expanded so greatly that there was hidden meaning in its becoming known as the War Office. As author of Virginia's Conscription Act of 1861, there was none better than he to direct the formulation of a Confederate counterpart. He was a model civilian-soldier, a recent military hero who had naval training as a youth. Appreciative of education, of craftsmanship, and of civil liberties, he was recognized as an able lawyer with diversified business interests. All these qualities enabled him to deal intelligently with both civilian and military leaders.[27]

The War Department staff that Randolph inherited from Secretary Benjamin was essentially the same that had accumulated since Walker's appointment. It was divided into six "appropriate" bureaus, headed by the following officers: the Adjutant and Inspector General's Bureau under Brig. Samuel Cooper, the Engineering Bureau under Maj. Josiah Gorgas, the Quartermaster General's Bureau under Lt. Col. Abraham C. Myers, the Commissary General of Subsistence's Bureau under Lt. Col. Lucius B. Northrop, the Surgeon General's Bureau under Surgeon Samuel P. Moore, and the Indian Affairs' Bureau under the Honorable David Hubbard.[28] It is possible only to estimate the number of clerks in the War Department in 1861. In April, Walker had requested an expansion from thirty-eight to forty-one officers. Of the latter, there were seven existing surgeons and six new ones. Presumably, Walker got the three new billets.[29]

Since the Western world adopted the use of gunpowder, all countries quickly have discovered that their supply was insufficient. Seeking desperately to meet its need for gunpowder, the War Department, through President Davis, sought and, on April 11, 1862, obtained congressional authority to appoint a corps of thirteen officers to procure nitre, a basic ingredient of powder. Maj. Isaac St. John was Randolph's first Chief of the Nitre and Mining Bureau in the War Department. When St. John was promoted to Commissary General of Subsistence, he was succeeded by Capt. Richard Morton.[30]

While it may be praiseworthy that Benjamin had not appointed additional staff before he had legislative authority to do so, it is surprising that so brilliant a lawyer had not devised some cloak or pretext to get a staff large enough to correct the "arrears" in which he had found the Department in September of 1861. In February he requested through the President legislative authority to hire for the seven bureaus of the Department twenty more clerks at salaries graduated from $1,000 to $1,500 a year. To prove the "absolute necessity for an augmentation," he recounted how he "and the chiefs of bureaus are compelled to extend their labors beyond reasonable limits; the clerks have been directed to attend their desks two additional hours in the evening, and yet the details of business have accumulated with such rapidity that the accounts of disbursing officers to the extent of many hundreds remain unsettled, and correspondence in arrears in all bureaus." In December, Benjamin had requested an increase in the Army Engineer Corps from twelve to between fifty or sixty billets. Presumably, all were in the field and none in the War Department. On the staff that Benjamin had inherited from Walker, there was one pro tempore high-ranking official, Assistant Secretary of War Col. Albert T. Bledsoe, whose position Congress authorized in December.[31]

When Randolph came into office, there were two assistant secretaries of war, Bledsoe and Robert Ould. A grandson of a Virginia Baptist minister, Bledsoe was himself at various times a clergyman of two different denominations and had published two theological books. Fifty-three years old when Randolph became secretary, Bledsoe had had several careers before the war. A West Point schoolmate of Robert E. Lee and Jefferson Davis, he soon left the U.S. Army for study and teaching at Kenyon College before practicing law at Springfield, Illinois, from 1838 to 1848. Professor of Mathematics at the universities of Mississippi and Virginia in a day when oratory often passed for intellect, the eloquent Bledsoe frequently contributed to journals, especially ephemeral southern magazines. A restless man, he already was fretful in his job before Randolph's advent. Despite his undoubted abilities as a polemicist, preacher, and professor of law, he lacked the technocratic expertise that Secretary Randolph was looking for in the Department of War. Since Bledsoe once had denounced Thomas Jefferson as "the source of the South's woes," Bledsoe was a minor embarrassment until President Davis sent him to London to investigate precedents for neutrality during civil wars and "perhaps to influence English public opinion." To replace him, Randolph created within the War Department the Bureau of War and named Garlick Kean with the rank of captain to be its head. The secretary was well satisfied that he would continue the able and loyal staff work of which he had shown himself so capable while on General Randolph's staff at Suffolk.[32]

Ould was a "plump, mild-looking" native of Washington, D.C., who had studied law at the College of William and Mary before becoming district attorney of his native city, a post which he held from the Pierce Administration until after Lincoln's inauguration. Three years younger than Randolph, Ould at the age of forty-two was compatible with the secretary for many reasons, but especially because of their mutual interest in criminal law. Ould's most celebrated law case was his unsuccessful prosecution in 1859 of Con. Daniel E. Sickles on charges of having killed Philip Barton Key in a duel arising from Key's adultery. (Edwin M. Stanton, soon to be Lincoln's secretary of war, got Sickles off on grounds of temporary insanity.) After Randolph became secretary of war, he made this honest and capable lawyer commissioner of exchange and his position, assistant secretary, lapsed. Colonel and Mrs. Ould were not so intimate with the Randolphs as was their beautiful daughter, Mattie.[33]

Several officials in Randolph's War Department were carryovers from Benjamin's tenure. Gen. Samuel Cooper was one of these, serving as adjutant and inspector general. Sixty-four years old in 1862, he was the ranking officer of the Confederate States Army. He could have been very powerful, had he been younger or had he possessed the temperament to exert himself more aggressively. As it was, Garlick Kean commented that Cooper was "uniformly courteous and uniformly noncommittal"; he never decided anything and was usually "out" of his office. Among his assigned duties were the details of enforcing conscription, a thankless but vital part of the Confederacy's effort to gather sufficient manpower and a problem to which Secretary Randolph himself devoted increasing attention in the autumn of 1862. A West Point graduate in 1815, Cooper had enjoyed an admirable career in the field before serving as adjutant general of the U.S. army from 1848 to 1861. The son of a Revolutionary War major from New Jersey, he had unimpeachable credentials among the F.F.V. elite as the husband of a granddaughter of George Mason of Gunston Hall. Having been an ally of Jefferson Davis when the latter, as U.S. secretary of war, had feuded with Gen. Winfield Scott, General Cooper had great prestige.[34]

The offices of Surgeon General and of Indian Affairs were not controversial posts and they were filled by little-known men. Samuel P. Moore served throughout the war as Surgeon General. There were two successive Indian Commissioners: David P. Hubbard and S. S. Scott.[35]

Perhaps it was more because he poorly advised than because of his own overoptimism, but Benjamin perpetuated in his reports to Davis the overconfidence that George W. Randolph had to fight against throughout his service as secretary of war. As late as December of 1861, Benjamin reported that "cessation of foreign commerce" had so stimulated domestic production that "with the single exception of small arms . . . the Confederate States have . . . since June 1st . . . evinced the capacity of providing all that is necessary to the maintenance of their independence. . . . It will . . . be in the power of the Department [of War] to furnish all that is required, not only from supplies of blankets, cloth and shoes already imported from Europe, but from the productions of manufacturing establishments at home. . . . It is admitted [however] that there has been a deficiency in certain articles in the rations."[36]

# CHAPTER 7

# Randolph Assumes the Secretaryship, May 1862

When George W. Randolph took control in May 1862, the War Office was lodged in the former Mechanic's Hall. Thus, he found himself in quarters which he had helped found a decade before. His staff was so undermanned that, in spite of his efforts to enlarge his office, Randolph had to devote much time to picayune chores at the same time that he was actively reforming the office and redefining its mission.[1]

One of his first problems was how to reply to Brig. Gen. Henry A. Wise's request for a new command at a time when there was still much public controversy about whether it had been Wise's or Secretary Benjamin's fault that Roanoke Island had fallen with only Wise and a few others making an escape. Looking more to the future than to the past, Randolph informed Wise in a formal interview that, because no brigade was then without a commander, there could be no immediate place for him. Indignantly, Wise declared to those of his staff who had been able to join him after escaping capture at Roanoke Island: "There is no Secretary of War. He is merely a *clerk*, an underling and cannot hold up his head in his humiliating position" of subservience to President Davis. Harsh words such as these often stick, even when uttered by a man of such "insatiable ambition" as Wise. In this case they usually have prevented scholars from recognizing Randolph's special abilities and goals. So far as the Wise affair itself was concerned, most except Wise have always thought that Randolph dealt judiciously with the volatile political general.[2]

Seclusion had been a major complaint against Randolph's predecessors. It is not surprising that Secretary Randolph announced that ordinarily he would be available for discussion of public business between ten o'clock in the morning and one in the afternoon. For a while, a respectably clad country gentleman like Dr. Benjamin R. Fleet could complain in person to the secretary that the army had impressed his horse irregularly, receive a personal apology, and obtain quick monetary satisfaction.[3]

Heads of old Virginia families constantly importuned Secretary Randolph for the preferment of their scions, among whom were grandsons of Patrick Henry, General Everard Meade "of Revolutionary fame," and the like. In place of hastily improvised military training camps, Randolph instituted a comprehensive system under distinct rules for military education—perhaps the first regular military camps to train civilians to become soldiers in the United or Confederate States since Baron von Steuben's during the American Revolution. The secretary was able to fit into his plans for basic military training underemployed college faculty such as Green Peyton and Arthur H. Gooch of the University of Virginia.[4]

As secretary of war, Randolph also had to suffer much amateur military advice from congressmen and other prominent persons. When his nephew-in-law, Captain Kean, attempted to shield him from time-consuming busybodies, war clerk John B. Jones smelled aristocratic exclusiveness. Not all of this advice was gratuitous or foolish; in some of it lay the background for important decisions. Separate proposals by Randolph's distant kinsman, Alexander H. H. Stuart, and by Rep. Albert S. Boteler asked that the Confederate high command devote more attention to western Virginia. Stuart endorsed the merit of forming a semi-independent partisan corps, while Boteler insisted that it would be best to commission a prominent Wheeling graduate of the Virginia Military Institute to organize a brigade of regulars from the northwestern counties of Virginia. Randolph adopted Boteler's argument that the regulars could make better use of able young men loyal to the Old Dominion than an irregular partisan corps, particularly if they as regulars were directed to garner supplies from the area for other Confederate forces to draw upon.[5] Randolph's friendship with the literati of his day was not always a boon. Hugh Blair Grigsby, whose works on the Virginia Conventions of 1776, 1788, 1830, and 1850 are classic examples of nineteenth-century historiography, pressed a lengthy epistle on Randolph as "the only member of the administration to whom I am known personally." Grigsby's advice was a fine-tuned historical and constitutional argument intended to persuade Great Britain to recognize Southern independence. Not only was this far afield for Randolph, but he received it on the eve of his resignation from the Confederate cabinet.[6]

The most urgent problem which Secretary Randolph inherited was one that he shared with President Davis and General Lee: how to cope with General McClellan's large and well-supplied force threatening to march up the peninsula between the York and James rivers into Richmond. There were, of course, other Federal and counterbalancing Confederate forces in Virginia and North Carolina whose activities were mainly dependent on what McClellan did. These forces were in the vicinity of Winchester, Fairfax, Fredericksburg and Roanoke Island. Since it was clear that the threat to Richmond was more than Magruder's Army of the Peninsula could handle, Gen. Joseph E. Johnston, who had been in overall command in Virginia, superseded Magruder. After General McClellan got all his forces ashore on April 1, 1862, the Union general commenced to lay a methodical siege to Yorktown on April 5th. The real or imagined strength of Confederate fortifications at Yorktown delayed the Union army for more than a month before President Lincoln called on his general to "break the enemy's line" from Yorktown to the James River at once.

At this juncture, Gen. T. J. Jackson was a district commander at Winchester, Gen. James Longstreet was an area commander at Fredericksburg, and Gen. R. E. Lee was in charge of military operations, reporting directly to President Davis. To meet the critical problem of the moment, the President convened on May 1st an unusual eleven-hour council of war at Richmond with Johnston, Longstreet, Lee, and Randolph. Johnston advocated evacuating Yorktown at once, making a Fabian retreat from the lower peninsula, bringing regiments and supply depots to full-strength, inflicting the greatest possible damage on the enemy without risking a major engagement, and choosing a field of battle close to Richmond, where McClellan's line of supply would be attenuated. At first Lee and Randolph counseled that the Confederates should not abandon the lower peninsula precipitately but that they should not insist on making a last-ditch defense there. Proud of the defensive works at Yorktown, Randolph knew that they had served their purpose. General Lee contended that there would be sites nearer to Williamsburg more favorable for the Confederates to make a stand than at Yorktown. President Davis pronounced in favor of Lee's and Randolph's proposal. Secretary of the Navy Stephen R. Mallory added weight to this decision by stressing that delay in withdrawing might avoid "tremendous losses" of public property on the peninsula and at Norfolk. General Johnston accepted this—apparently with the mental reservation that circumstances probably would render the president's instructions meaningless and confirm his own wisdom.[7]

On May 2, while the secretaries of war and of the navy were conferring with the Confederate officials at Norfolk, Johnston's order for Norfolk's immediate evacuation arrived. Randolph countermanded it on the spot. He and Secretary Mallory secured a week's delay for the removal of matériel. Although in May he did point out the disadvantages of abandoning Norfolk as a naval base, he was more concerned over the impending loss of war matériel in the port's storehouses and marshaling yards. He made a similar effort to save the war supplies at Pensacola before the Confederates evacuated that Florida naval base. Strange to say, such intervention was unusual. Too often Confederate authorities made little effort to avert needless abandonment or destruction of valuable matériel. At Norfolk Randolph was frustrated in his attempt to salvage war goods by the desertion to the Yankees of the skipper and crew of the principal steamer designated to bring guns, munitions, and other supplies to Richmond.[8]

As McClellan and Johnston girded for great battles, the Confederate government became so absorbed in contingency plans for evacuating Richmond that it could have touched off a panic. Secretary of War Randolph was more careful to set a good example of fortitude than was Secretary of the Treasury Memminger. The latter could not conceal from the apprehensive public that he "had a special locomotive and cars, constantly with steam up, in readiness to fly with the [government's] treasure." Although the Secretary of War warned his staff that "tomorrow the enemy will be here," he meant at, instead of inside, the city's gates. Maintaining an outward calm, he contented himself with setting his clerks to packing records in trunks which he sent secretly by canal boat to Albemarle. Privately, he instructed Captain Kean to take Mrs. Randolph "into the country" if the Yankees should get into the city.

President Davis and members of his cabinet do not seem to have recalled their scorn of Washington officials who made a junket to northern Virginia on the eve of the first Battle of Manassas. Until General Lee stopped Confederate officials, they flocked out of their capital to observe troop dispositions during the fighting outside of Richmond between the end of May and the first of July 1862. When General Randolph found his colleague John H. Reagan wandering about in search of Hood's Texan brigade, he took him in tow, saying: "You had better go back with me; Yankee bullets have no respect for Postmaster-Generals."[9]

It is remarkable that Johnston was able to avoid pressure to take a stand before McClellan reached the outskirts of Richmond. Doubtless this can be best explained by the magnitude of the contest for the Confederate capital, in the first part of which Johnston played so able a role until he was wounded in the Battle of Seven Pines.

When in March of 1862 George Randolph first assumed his duties as secretary of war, his position differed from that of almost all U.S. secretaries of war in that the president's military advisor, Gen. Robert E. Lee, was designated his superior in strategic matters. Although Randolph was an amateur military strategist compared to Davis and Lee, he understood their views and was in general agreement with them on military matters. It was only after General Lee was ordered to assume a field command in the place of the wounded Gen. Joseph E. Johnston that Randolph became President Davis's chief military advisor. The preceding months had laid the basis for a good working relationship between the secretary and the president. Now that Lee had his hands full reorganizing what had become the Army of Northern Virginia and setting its goals, Randolph did not always have to give ground to him or to share the president's ear with another military leader. The way was open for Davis and Randolph to collaborate in the evolution of policy for other portions of the Southern republic, especially those which lay west and south of the Appalachian mountain ranges.

Before Randolph took office as secretary of war, the Confederacy's loss of Forts Donelson and Henry had created reverberations through the Mississippi delta from Tennessee to the Gulf of Mexico that led to the fall of Memphis. A month after Randolph began his duties at the War Office, the surrender of New Orleans to the Union made a mockery of Confederate military organization west and south of the Appalachians. Except for a stretch of river north and south of Vicksburg, the Union navy ruled the Mississippi River. The Union army's possession of the western terminus of the Memphis and Charleston Railroad gave it the potential to threaten Middle Tennessee and even Atlanta.[10]

These disasters required President Davis and Secretary Randolph to revamp the Confederate command structure between the Alleghenies and the Gulf of Mexico. In the process, one of their major concerns was to prepare for a campaign to rewin New Orleans. It and the new departments they created will be discussed in chapter 11.

When Gen. Joseph E. Johnston reported to the War Office early in November that he had recovered from wounds suffered six months before and that he desired a new command, Secretary Randolph told him informally that the President and he expected to give him supreme command in the West. It would have been strange, indeed, if Randolph and Johnston had not discussed options available to the Confederacy along the Mississippi. Randolph was, of course, quite capable of making up his own mind in such matters, for all that he valued and respected Johnston's expertise. The two were in thorough agreement in calling for a major buildup to restore Confederate control of Tennessee and open up activities in Kentucky and even Missouri. If Randolph spoke to Johnston about schemes to liberate New Orleans, he did so only incidentally.[11] President Davis and Secretary Randolph were in general agreement concerning strategic goals for the West and the identity of its new supreme commander. Although Davis and Randolph may have felt irritation toward one another, they were harmonious collaborators until November of 1862.

Since Randolph was in general agreement with the strategic views of Davis and Lee,[12] he came to have increasing influence with the President as he grew more accustomed to and competent in his job. In the early summer of 1862, while General Lee confined himself strictly to conventional military affairs in Virginia, Randolph proposed in his almost daily conferences with the President several unconventional plans concerning maintaining military manpower, selling cotton to obtain foreign capital, exchanging cotton for enemy bacon and other supplies, sponsoring fifth-column activities, and liberating New Orleans.

President Davis had not been accustomed to the introduction of such disturbing, perplexing problems by secretaries of war Walker or Benjamin. Less than six months earlier, Secretary Benjamin formally had reported to him in such optimistic terms that Randolph's proposals must have surprised and confounded Davis. Outwardly it seemed that, as Randolph came to master the routine of the War Office, President Davis granted, and the secretary assumed, increasing authority.[13]

# CHAPTER 8

# *The Randolphs in Wartime Richmond*

While George W. Randolph was on active duty near Hampton, Yorktown, and Suffolk, he took little part in the life of Richmond. During his service as secretary of war, he had little time for any except official business, which, of course, included official entertainments. After he resigned from the cabinet, Randolph resumed his role as a leader in Richmond's civic and social life. On the other hand, Mary Randolph was one of the city's foremost civic and social leaders from the beginning of the war until she accompanied her husband abroad in 1864. General and Mrs. George Wythe Randolph played a prominent part in the desperate whirl of Richmond's wartime society. If he had done nothing else during the war, he still would deserve a worthy place in its annals for briefly accepting the leadership of reserves in May of 1863 when the capital was threatened by Stoneman's Raid and for comforting or defending strikers, dissidents, and prisoners. Similarly, Mary Randolph deserves a degree of fame for her leadership in hospital work.

In November of 1862, tiring of the conflicts of his job as secretary of war, George Randolph told friends that he was too ill for a field command and that he desired a staff job. After procrastination, the Davis administration offered him the choice of three unpalatable jobs: to displace two men he had appointed or to carve a field command out of an already undermanned brigade. None comported with his principles and practice. Concluding with disgust that the Davis administration was plotting to "get [him] out of commission," he resigned his active Confederate commission without surrendering his reserve status.[1]

On Sunday, May 3, 1863, Richmonders were worrying about the

Battle of Chancellorsville seventy miles away. Mary Boykin Chesnut, the South Carolinian, penned a dramatic description of what she heard and saw from the Randolphs' pew at St. Paul's Church: "The rattling of the ammunition wagons, the tramp of the soldiers, the everlasting slamming of those iron gates of the Capitol Square just opposite the church, all made it hard to attend to the service. There began a scene calculated to make the stoutest heart quail: the sexton quietly waking up persons, members of whose families had been brought home wounded, dying or dead; and the pale-faced people following the sexton out."[2] Suddenly news came that Major General Stoneman was leading a Union cavalry raid toward the capital. There were no regular troops to block his path. Richmond momentarily fell into such despair that there was reason to fear that the city was lost before it was actually assaulted. A spontaneous meeting gathered at the Richmond City Hall, a block from St. Paul's. At the request of the mayor, Josiah Gorgas, and some other prominent citizens, General Randolph agreed to organize volunteers to defend the city. He mustered citizens, senators, and cabinet officers into ranks, collected all sorts of arms and marshaled the batteries in anticipation of Stoneman making an early morning attack on Monday. General Randolph succeeded in getting his motley force in place by 11:00, only to discover that the artillery pieces lacked powder and primers. Gen. Arnold Elzey, who was officially responsible for the city's defense, declared that "he wished he was dead [because] the Yankee cavalry would certainly take the city." Even Randolph privately admitted "tomorrow the enemy will be here," but he set such a good public example of fortitude, confidence, and order that he restored calm.

In fact, Stoneman and his troopers were turned back fifteen miles from the capital. Not wishing to advertise its unpreparedness, the government expressed no gratitude to Randolph. The acidulous war department clerk, J. B. Jones, averred that his former boss was "very busy organizing the second class militia . . . under the supposition that he would command them" and was gleeful when President Davis eliminated the reserves by requisitioning eight thousand of that class for Confederate frontline duty.[3]

Of all the foreigners who served in Confederate forces, none was more glamorous than the Prussian soldier of fortune Heros Von Borcke. When in June of 1862 he had come to Richmond to enlist in the Southern cause, Secretary of War Randolph had given him a horse, a letter to Gen. J. E. B. Stuart, and the "advice to lose not a moment if he desired to see something of the impending battles." The three became firm friends. When Von Borcke delivered to Randolph Stuart's report of his famous ride around McClellan's army, the secretary commissioned the Prussian a captain on the spot. On June 5, 1862, George Randolph was a special observer of the greatest military review of the war, organized by J. E. B. Stuart, who, as Von Borcke said, had a "weakness for the vanities of military parade." Von Borcke met Randolph at Gordonsville, Virginia, to escort him by special train to Culpeper "with all honours, our battle-flag floating from the locomotive." The night before the review there was at the court house a ball which was described in perfervid terms as a "gay and dazzling scene, illumined by . . . numerous chandeliers" and followed by refreshments on the moonlit verandah of the old tavern next door. The fifth of June was a "bright and beautiful" day. Stuart, his staff and guests were "gay and gallant" as they rode from the town along a route where smiling girls strewed flowers. Bugles sounded as the entourage came onto the reviewing field. "Every man in the army could be seen at one view. The neighing of steeds, the glitter of arms, the dancing of plumes, the waving of . . . red battle flags and the grand swell of martial music" united to make a "magnificent sight." The cavalry corps was drawn out in a line a mile and a half long, more than 12,000 horsemen, who cheered as twenty-four guns of horse artillery thundered a salute. Gathered about the reviewing area were "hundreds of spectators, mostly ladies . . . in ambulances and on horseback." The corps passed twice in review, first by squadrons at a walk and finally in a sham charge by regiments at a gallop, concluded by a rapid-fire volley directed at an imaginary enemy. The day concluded with an open-air ball on the greensward, illumined by bonfires, whose ruddy glare gave "a wild and romantic effect."[4]

Alas! Such rousing spectacles could not be repeated after July of 1863.

General Randolph's alternation between respiratory illness and periods of good spirits misled him and many of his friends. Neither he nor they realized how much his tuberculosis had weakened him. After his departure from the War Office, friends suggested that he allow them to press his candidacy for the governorship of Virginia. Due to the war, election was by the General Assembly, which was unlikely to view Randolph's war record, no matter how distinguished, as a complete substitute for legislative service. Randolph dissuaded his friends, saying that he preferred "the gentlemanly ease of private life to the careworn existence of the Politician."[5]

Not long after abjuring a gubernatorial campaign, Randolph accepted election to the Richmond City Council, on which he had served before the war. Instead of considering this an ignominious comedown, he probably was inspired by John Moncure Daniel's contemporaneous comments in the *Examiner* on how important to the Confederacy Richmond's contributions were. When he took his seat on April 4, 1863, Randolph's chief concerns were to seek improvement of "relief for the meritorious poor" and to quiet labor unrest. He got committees created for these purposes and chaired them. In his conscription acts, Randolph already had shown his appreciation of the importance of civilian enterprise and industry in wartime. As an old navy man, he could communicate with artificers and craftsmen. During Richmond's Bread Riots in the spring of 1863, it was more natural than strange for him to invite "mechanics" to hold a protest meeting and "instruct" demands that the City Council institute price controls, "or else resign."[6]

Just as Randolph was willing to sit on the Richmond City Council from a sense of enlightened social responsibility, so he consented to seek election to the Virginia State Senate. His elitist sense of responsibility required him to do what he could for society when the able-bodied men were in the field. His legislative service was cut short when doctors advised him to seek the advice of London lung specialists.[7] Even while hoping to repair his health in Europe, his sense of duty led him to accept the responsibilities of a Confederate purchasing agent.

Although after November of 1862 Randolph was far more than a genteel placeman, he must have reflected that even functionaries can be useful. In May of 1863, he served as chief marshal for Gen. Stonewall Jackson's funeral. This ceremony was one of the most solemn public events during the Confederacy. John R. Thompson described it as

> . . . a lull,
> With victory, in the conflict's stormy closes,
> When the glad spring, all flushed and beautiful,
> First mocked us with her roses,
> With dirge and minute-gun and bell we paid
> Some few poor rites, and inexpressive token
> Of a great people's pain, to Jackson's shade,
> In agony unspoken.

Almost a year later Randolph was a pallbearer in the funeral at St. James's Church for J. E. B. Stuart, whose rites were simpler than Jackson's, both by the request of the widow and because of the realization of the deepening crisis of the Confederacy. Again, Thompson commemorated the man and the occasion:

> . . . The doubtful strife went on, . . .
> We could but lay our dear, dumb warrior down
> And gird us for the morrow.
>
> No wailing trumpet and no tolling bell,
> No cannon, save the battle's boom receding,
> When Stuart to the grave we bore, might tell
> Of hearts all crushed and bleeding.
>
> The crisis suited not with pomp . . .
> Only the maidens came sweet flow'rs to twine
> Above his form so cold and painless
> Whose deeds upon our brightest records shine,
> Whose life and sword were stainless. . . .[8]

Ceremonies were not Randolph's sole preoccupation in 1863. Although he managed to avoid considering the moral problems of slavery until late in the Civil War, George Randolph had considered the ethics and practicalities of human and civil rights since he had been a midshipman. As the architect of the Virginia and Confederate conscription acts, he was superbly equipped to defend clients who were not liable to conscription because of occupations or technical loopholes. While secretary of war, he had resisted pressure to jail such well-known pacifists and Unionists as Alexander Rives of Albemarle and former Congressman John Minor Botts of Richmond. Instead, he simply paroled them to their farms. For humanitarian reasons, if not to protect rights, he had interceded to gain less onerous treatment of some prisoners of war whom the Confederate government had isolated in retaliation for Union mistreatment of prisoners.[9]

After resuming his law practice at his home, George Wythe Randolph soon entered into partnership with Gustavus A. Meyers. Confident that he could make a lot of money as a lawyer, he told any and all that he and Mary needed it because of a heavy loss she had suffered in her Mobile investments. There were, however, some who unjustly said that Randolph was selling his birthright by defending flour-hoarders, speculators, draft-dodgers, "Jews and extortioners." In fact, the docket of the Virginia Supreme Court of Appeals shows that he was an attorney in four of twelve cases it heard in its May 1863 term and that these cases were unexceptional in both subject matter and clients.[10]

The most notorious trial in which George Wythe Randolph ever participated was his defense in the autumn and early winter of 1863 of Mrs. Genevieve Allan on charges of espionage and treason. He seems to have felt no qualm in defending this silly, gossipy, and woefully indiscreet lady. Because her civil rights had been violated and because she was an in-law of the cadet line of the Tuckahoe Randolphs, he probably thought that to defend her was his duty. Finally, he took pleasure in investing in a $1,000 Confederate bond, the fee his talented and name-worthy representation deserved. Perhaps he saw Mrs. Allan's predicament as much the same kind of chivalric challenge that had prompted his grandfather Jefferson to procure for Mrs. Mary Willing Byrd of Westover forgiveness for her too "willing" hospitality to Benedict Arnold almost a century earlier.

Genevieve Allan was the wife of Patterson Allan, whose father had been Edgar Allan Poe's wealthy foster father. After Patterson Allan's graduation from the University of Virginia, his widowed mother, née Louisa Gabriella Patterson of New York knickerbocker antecedents, had taken him to Italy in the course of a European grand tour. While in Rome, he fell in love with and married Genevieve, a lady from Cincinnati who had a "special talent for music and art," even though the match was "not congenial" to his mother. This was the age of Jenny Lind, and the younger Mrs. Allan vainly had sought, through several years of Italian voice lessons, to emulate the Swedish Nightingale. In social circles there may have been real or pretended confusion between her and the Anglo-Italian diva, Madame Caradori-Allan. Although the latter had sung in the United States in 1837, Americans knew of her mainly for her operatic and concert reputation in England and for her musical compositions, some of which even found their way into port-folios in Virginia.

During the Civil War Genevieve's husband and his two brothers served the Confederacy honorably, but the lively war widow lacked oc-cupation or diversion. She alternated her residence between the Allans' country estate near Sabot in Goochland County and Richmond, where she visited friends, especially the wife of the Reverend Dr. Moses Hoge, one of the most prominent Presbyterian clergymen of his time. In July 1863 Mrs. Allan attempted to send by covert means a letter to the Rever-end Mr. Dix of Trinity Episcopal Church in New York City. Because they had been friends in Italy, she addressed him as "Caro Signore." A conduit for such underground communications was the proprietor of a Richmond gambling casino, who turned Mrs. Allan's letter over to Confederate authorities. Suspicions were increased because the Rever-end Mr. Dix was the brother of the Union general John A. Dix, then stationed in eastern Virginia. Worse yet, Mrs. Allan frivolously had sug-gested that when Dr. Hoge returned to New York from Europe, where he had gotten Bibles to distribute to Confederate soldiers, he ought to be arrested for having spread Confederate propaganda abroad. In a gossipy and indiscreet vein, she had remarked how close Stoneman's Raid had come to the plantations near the Allan estate in Goochland and how richly their secessionist owners would deserve to have their houses burned and their possessions looted.

In spite of high wartime spirits and adverse publicity, Randolph and his associate Peter Lyons persuaded the jury to doubt the authenticity of Mrs. Allan's letter and the seriousness of its contents. So far as treason was concerned, they got their client off with a hung jury. Convicted on lesser charges, Mrs. Allan was freed on $100,000 bail and confined to the Hospital and Asylum of St. Francis de Sales at Richmond.[11]

While George Wythe Randolph moved from one activity to another between 1861 and 1865, Mary Randolph devoted most of her time and energies to hospital work. Her emergence from a sheltered privacy had much the same exhilarating effect upon her as it did on her husband. While George was fighting for his country on the peninsula between the James and York rivers, she was thrown upon her own resources. These proved to be considerable. Mary Randolph's days were full of good works, whether her husband was in the field, in the War Office, on the hustings, or trying a case in court. To avoid being "quite alone" and to help in organizing her hospital volunteers, she invited George's niece Sarah Nicholas Randolph to live with her as a kind of social secretary. Sarah's presence made George's periodic illness easier on Mary, who usually carried him to Albemarle to convalesce.[12]

When the war began in 1861, Mary Adams Randolph was a native Richmonder, a young married lady of thirty-seven years of age without children whose husband was a colonel of artillery on the Hampton front. She was thus unusually well qualified to head a city-wide committee to organize and supervise volunteer help for Richmond's hospitals. She was elected president of the Ladies Aid Association of Richmond, whose internecine battles were almost as furious, if not as bloody and mortal, as those on the field of combat. According to the South Carolinian Mary Boykin Chesnut, whose husband Col. James Chesnut was an aide-de-camp to President Davis, Mary Randolph could hold her ground under feminine fire:

> Mrs. Randolph presided in all her beautiful majesty at an aid association. The ladies were old ones, and all wanted their own way. They were cross grained and contradictory, and the blood would mount rebelliously into Mrs. Randolph's clear-cut cheek, but she held her own with dignity and grace. One of the causes of disturbance was that Mrs. Randolph pro-

posed to divide everything equally with the Yankee wounded and sick prisoners. Some were enthusiastic from a Christian point of view; some shouted in wrath at the bare idea of putting our noble soldiers on a par with Yankees, living, dying or dead. Shrill and loud it was; fierce dames, some of them; august, severe matrons who evidently had not been accustomed to hear the other side of any argument from anybody, and who were just old enough to find the last pleasure in life in power—the power to make their claws felt. These old ladies each had philanthropic schemes, but they held to their own and would listen to no other. Maybe such warmth will hurry on the good work.[13]

Mary Randolph persuaded Mary Chesnut to beg from friends in South Carolina and Florida arrowroot and tannic acid for hospital use at Winchester, Culpeper, and Richmond. Mary Randolph once took Mary Chesnut with her to visit one of Richmond's fifty improvised hospitals before the construction of the centralized complex of Chimborazo's 150 one-story buildings commenced to serve its wartime total of 76,000 patients. Mrs. Chesnut left a gruesome account of this incident:

Long rows of ill men on cots; ill of typhoid fever, of every human ailment; wounds being dressed; all horrors taken in at one glance. At the Alms house, Dr. Gibson is in charge. The Sisters of Charity are his nurses. That makes all the difference in the world. . . . We went to the St. Charles [Hospital]. Horror upon horrors again. Want of organization, long rows of men dead and dying; awful smiles and awful sights. A boy from home had sent for me. He was lying on a cot, ill of fever. Next to him a man died in convulsions while we stood there. I was making arrangements with a nurse, hiring him to take care of this lad. I do not remember any more, for I fainted.[14]

The Randolphs' intimate friend, Agnes Rice Pryor, had a similar experience later when in May of 1862 she went to Kent and Paine's warehouse which had been converted into a hospital. The matron in charge of nursing tried without success to discourage Agnes from this "very exacting" work. Mrs. Pryor described the incident thus: "As I passed by the rows of occupied cots, I saw a nurse kneeling beside one of them, holding a pan for a surgeon. The red stump of an amputated arm was held over it. The next thing I knew I was falling over my face. I had fainted. Opening my eyes, I found the matron standing over me [saying]: 'You see it is as I thought. You are unfit for this work.'" Unlike the more spirituelle Mary Chesnut, Agnes Pryor persisted in her determination to help and several days later persuaded the matron to accept her services on condition that she work near the door. So great were the needs of the wounded after the Seven Days Battles in June of

1862 that she wrote: "Every linen garment I possessed, except one change, every garment of cotton fabric, all my table linen, all my bed linen, even the chintz covers for furniture,—all were torn into strips and rolled for bandages for the soldiers' wounds."[15]

Among those to whom Mary Randolph ministered were two Union prisoners—grandsons of Paul Revere—who were friends of her husband's Boston kin: Paul Joseph and Edward Hutchinson Robins Revere. The former was a major of the Twentieth Massachusetts Volunteer Infantry and the latter was its assistant surgeon. Both had been captured in the Battle of Ball's Bluff in Loudoun County, Virginia on October 21, 1861. Declining parole, they had been among 514 men and fifteen officers who had been marched to Richmond in three days' time. Another Massachusetts prisoner whom the Randolphs befriended was William R. Lee, who wrote in a postwar memoir that two Richmond ladies were so "true to their womanly instincts" that they sought out and relieved the Bostonians with "generous and timely beneficence." Once was Elizabeth Van Lew, the notorious Union spy. The other was Mary Randolph. The Bostonians' predicament appealed to George Randolph's chivalrous sense of justice, and he succeeded in arranging their parole and exchange in the early months of 1862.[16]

Housing was so short in wartime Richmond that few found comfort there. As Mary Chesnut put it: "Richmond was crowded to suffocation, with hardly standing room left." The government did nothing to alleviate the housing shortage it had created by commandeering buildings for offices and by bringing in more clerks in mufti or in uniform to man the Confederate bureaucracy. There was much doubling up, as residents took in relatives. Because of the shortage and inflated cost of foodstuffs, some refugees could hardly keep body and soul together.[17] All the same, Richmond took pride in affording asylum to such old families as the Carys. At the outbreak of the war, Hetty and Jennie Cary lived in Baltimore, where the younger, Jennie, had set John Randall's poem "Maryland" to the music *Lauriger Horatius*. They joined their aunt, Mrs. Monimia Fairfax Cary, and her daughter Constance in Virginia after the latter were displaced from the Fairfax estate on the Potomac. Shortly before the First Battle of Manassas, Jennie and Connie made the most of a glorious opportunity by singing "Maryland, My Maryland" to Confederate troops from the Old Line State. The three girls took pride in being among those who claimed to have made the first official Confederate battle flag. After a while in Culpeper and Orange counties, Connie led the way to Richmond in the early winter of 1862 and the other Carys followed. Because Constance's grand-mother had been brought up by George Randolph's mother, the Cary ladies looked on him as their special protector, a role he enjoyed, since these heroines never seemed to be in distress.[18]

Civil War Richmond delighted to honor George and Mary Randolph. All Richmond society knew their ancestry and snickered when he innocently discomfited self-important and bombastic politicos by casual reference to what his grandfather used to say on such-and-such a subject. Any young lady as beautiful, stylish, intelligent, well-mannered and rich as Mary Adams Randolph, all Richmond society took to their hearts, congratulating themselves on having produced such a paragon. Richmond has never been a city to despise new money, much less to look down on scions who have won the means to revivify ancestral greatness. Public eminence cost George and Mary Randolph their pre-war privacy as much because of her volunteer hospital activities as because of his position as a sometime general or secretary. It has been said that her wealth enabled the Randolphs to entertain on a "lavish" scale.[17] No doubt it helped. It is, however, a fact both that George Randolph earned wealth as a lawyer and that the best known of their parties took place after she had lost a large part of her fortune.

The Randolphs found that national independence required of them, as it had of New York and Philadelphia society in the Washington administration, that they accept into their circle people from other states. George Randolph joked about his lack of "amiability" and gregariousness at the same time that he welcomed new friends like the Gorgases into the company of relatives and intimate friends. Besides their numerous Cary, Harrison, Kean, Randolph, Ruffin, and Talcott kin, George and Mary Randolph had close friends among his legal associates such as the Henry Coalter Cabells, Gustavus and Mattie Paul Meyers, and the J. Thompson Browns; and among such members of the Virginia Historical Society as Herbert Augustine Claiborne and Conway and John Moncure Robinson. There were also those whom George Randolph had known at the University, such as Cabell and Pryor. Of course, there were neighbors and fellow parishioners of St. Paul's such as Mrs. Robert C. Stanard, who entertained so bountifully and often that she had to sell her large house at the corner of Sixth and Grace streets and move into a smaller one at Eighth and Franklin streets. Not far from the Randolphs' house, their respected but not intimate neighbor, Mrs. Robert E. Lee, lived in a rented house at 707 East Franklin Street. Mrs. Lee was so crippled by arthritis that she did not move about in society. When he was in the city, General Lee often paid social calls on the Randolphs, but it was the Lees' unmarried daughter, Mary, whom the Randolphs encountered most socially.[20]

When George W. Randolph became secretary of war, he and Mary had to put on something of a "show." According to Colonel Chesnut, Mrs. Stanard and Mrs. Randolph shared top honors as hostesses, at whose "delightful teas statesmen and warriors" feasted. Because Mrs. Stanard boasted that "she never read a book," while one could rely on finding at Mrs. Randolph's "what few literate" people there were in town (including Richmond's literary panjandrum, John Reuben Thompson), Mary Boykin Chesnut preferred the latter's soirées to the prosperous widow's parties. Thompson's literary repute made Mary Randolph's parlor as close to a salon as Civil War Richmond could boast.[21]

The artistic leader of the Randolphs' set was William Dickinson Washington. He was lame and moody, reticent, and devoted to the wild and gloomy aspects of nature which he observed and painted in now-lost canvases depicting the mountainous regions of the Potomac and New rivers in western Virginia. He had studied under Emmanuel Leutze at Dusseldorf and was a protégé of the banker and philanthropist William W. Corcoran, who gave him some popularity in the District of Columbia before the war. In order to earn a living, Washington had painted portraits at Warrenton, Virginia, during the heyday of the Fauquier White Sulphur Springs. He moved to Richmond early in the war and he became famous when his painting *The Burial of Latané* caused a sensation when it was exhibited in Richmond.[22]

Entertainments helped integrate into Richmond society Confederate officials who lacked close ties to the Old Dominion. Shared experience in the crowded capital dramatically expanded the Randolphs' circle to include Secretary of the Navy and Mrs. Stephen R. Mallory, Postmaster General and Mrs. John H. Reagan, Brig. Gen. and Mrs. John Smith Preston and their daughters from Columbia, South Carolina, and Senator and Mrs. Louis Trezevant Wigfall of Texas. Army families such as those of Gen. and Mrs. Robert E. Lee, Gen. and Mrs. Joseph E. Johnston, and Gens. Simon Bolivar Buckner, John B. Hood, and J. E. B. Stuart became intimates, too. The Randolphs (and, indeed, the Lees and many others) were far from acting like condescending grandees toward newcomers. They sincerely welcomed Jefferson and Varina Davis to Richmond, and all parties discovered that they shared standards of Victorian deportment. Because the presidential family did not accept social invitations, few Richmonders became social intimates with the Davises. Thus the social relations between the Davises and Randolphs were formal and correct. Mrs. Davis listed General Randolph as one of her "particular favorites" and Mrs. Randolph was concerned about the Davises' plight after Appomattox.[23]

As early as the summer of 1862 Mary Randolph wrote to her in-laws in Albemarle about the increasing scarcity of food and fuel and the escalation of their prices. It was, she averred, no time to have as wasteful a cook as she did. Her domestic arrangements were so vexing that she concluded that their four servants under the direction of Edward the butler were "unsatisfactory," even before her husband's secretaryship made far greater demands on their life and larder.[24] She canvassed her Albemarle in-laws for bacon, hams, pork, butter, and general produce, for which she exchanged "not very white or nice" sugar from what her husband had secured from a fifty-barrel consignment captured after the First Battle of Manassas. By August of 1862 she wrote: "Times are getting so hard I commence to tremble for the winter. Coal is scarce and provisions are dear." When winter came, butter and cabbages each cost a dollar a pound and eggs cost a dollar apiece. By January of 1863, George Randolph remarked that Richmond's social advantages had become "few and far between." Hoping that "this wretched war will wear itself out, and that our old Richmond society may flourish as of old," he assured his friend Thompson Brown that he could still provide him with "genuine tea and coffee and a wee drop of liquor," if he came to call.[25]

Social life in wartime Richmond provided the Confederate bureaucrats with a reprieve from the dispiriting ennui of discovering new shortages of everything. It provided army officers a respite from their arduous profession for which few were as well suited as they pretended. Caught up in the toils of an epic that by the fall of 1863 they realized held less and less hope of a tolerable solution, city folk, refugees, civilian and military officials, belles and beaux amused themselves for the nonce. As someone should have said, and probably did, all that was lacking was a Duchess of Richmond to give a ball. Instead, the Confederates played at charades. According to Mary Chesnut, Mary Randolph gave the best such soirées, to which the gallant Prussian, Heros Von Borcke, gave an international touch.[26]

On the steps of St. Paul's Church, "the beautiful, oriental-looking" Mary Randolph appealed to Constance Cary "to arrange for her the entertainment for an evening party that she felt that she had to give to "social and official Richmond" on Wednesday, January 20, 1864. This party set the pattern of entertainment for the remaining evenings when

Richmond was capital of the Confederacy. Constance Cary "'thought up' a series of charades in pantomine [and] called in the players." Frank Vizitelly, the English war correspondent and artist, helped Connie by painting a backdrop and "the faces of all the actors." Mary Randolph's niece Jennie Pollard and the gossipy Cooper De Leon served as prompters and state managers. John Reuben Thompson helped by writing "a set of verses" to be narrated by the beauteous Mary Buchanan Preston costumed as a Greek goddess. She was supposed to pronounce the word that was to be the theme of first a brief verse and then of a tableau. "Knighthood" was the first subject. This was intended to be a flattering allusion to Gen. John Bell Hood who was not only in the audience but was known to be Miss Preston's suitor. It brought down the house. The performance could not continue until the embarrassed Hood acknowledged his accolade.[27] Another of the words acted out in charades was "Penitent." Its first syllable was portrayed by a scene from Dickens's *Nicholas Nickleby,* in which Miss Josephine Chesney acted the role of Fanny Squeers while sharpening quill pens for Capt. Gordon McCabe as the infamous Master of Dotheboys School. The last syllable was to be inferred from the cast's representation of a lush tented feast suggested by Byron's "The Corsair" and involving a large number of ladies as beauties of the harem with men puffing at hookahs. Still another tableau was enacted by Mrs. Phoebe Levy Pember, who, like Mary Randolph, was deeply immersed in hospital work. She acted out the three syllables of "Ingratiate." Clad entirely in gray, she ate ravenously of hardtack and bacon. The tableaux vivantes featured the beauties of the Randolphs' set: Constance Cary as "Hermione" from Shakespeare's *The Winter's Tale;* Hetty Cary as "Simplicity"; Mattie Paul Meyers as a "Venetian Lady"; Mrs. John Moncure Robinson as Goethe's "Mignon"; Josephine Chesney as a "Syrian Girl" serenaded by Capt. Joseph Denegre; and Betty Brander as "The Flower of the Family," emerging from a flour barrel. Other scenes included bits from *The School for Scandal* and "Coming Through the Rye." The charades came to an unexpected, but highly satisfactory, conclusion when the unruly volunteer stagehands, J. E. B. Stuart and Fitzhugh Lee, threatened to strike "if Hetty Cary wouldn't sit and talk with them." At this point the props and scenery collapsed.[28]

Mary Chesnut mused over the contrast of the gay parties and the terrible times: "Hope and fear are both gone, and it is distraction or death with us. I do not see how sadness or despondency would help us. If it would do any good, we could be sad enough."[29] Richmonders, whether natives or sojourners, also took refuge in routine—snoozing in church and the men paying New Year's calls on their wives' best friends.

When Mary Chesnut and Mary Randolph attended the parade and civil reception honoring the Kentucky partisan leader, John Hunt Morgan, after his escape from a Union prison, they were contemptuous of how politicians sought by vain oratory to enhance their own repute. Mrs. Randolph led her companions in departing before the end of the ceremonies, saying, "We came only for soldiers."[30]

Richmond had taken pride in having withstood the menace of the Seven Days Battle in the spring of 1862 without experiencing real panic or disruption. In comparison, it did better than did Paris in 1870 or 1940. But the long walls of gray-clad Southern warriors were fewer and thinner each succeeding year. George Wythe and Mary Randolph belonged to a patriotic and proud stratum of society which felt only slight concern about invading their material and spiritual capital in a great and just cause. Even after Mary's investments in Mobile ceased to provide income and the Randolphs were less affluent, they did not reck the cost of the occasional and rather simple pleasures with which they briefly brightened the increasingly bleak lives of their coterie. Theirs was not the peasant cunning of hoarding, nor the hedonists' cry, "Eat, drink, and be merry, for tomorrow we die." It was instead a sharing of the last of the wine. It is difficult to establish when Confederate leaders did face up to the increasing omens of defeat. By January of 1863, George Wythe Randolph seems to have despaired of a victory on the battlefield or of a victory of diplomacy, and he took refuge in the "hope that this wretched war will soon wear itself out." He could only hope that his Northern counterparts were equally war-weary. Otherwise, Randolph and his friends had little choice but to "die game," as Raimondo Luraghi has said so well.[31] The Randolphs and their friends had freighted all their aspirations and possessions on the frail barque of Southern independence, and they seem to have known from the beginning how fragile a ship it was.

# CHAPTER 9

# *The F. F. V. and the Technocrats*

Many who have written of the Civil War have been so concerned with military events or slavery that they have paid little attention to the conceptual nature of Confederate administration. In 1861, because of the euphoria of independence and of commencing hostilities, few realized the implications of moving the capital of the Confederacy from Montgomery to Richmond. Defeat in 1865 precluded an answer to the question whether Virginia's Richmond ever really became the Confederacy's Richmond.[1]

Graciously, the city on the James welcomed an influx of able, energetic and brainy men, but her acceptance of outsiders was upon terms. Although Richmond took pride in becoming more cosmopolitan, the old ways of the Old Dominion ran strong and deep. There was a muted insistence that in accomplishments Virginians be recognized as *primi inter pares*. Many Virginians believed that, in moving its capital to Richmond, the Confederacy recognized Virginia's leadership in the evolution of Southern culture since 1607. They expected others to accept Virginia's primacy within the Southern republic.[2]

This expectation exhilarated Virginians such as George Wythe Randolph. Very conscious of his grandfather Jefferson's part in the American Revolution, he evinced a desire to emulate Jefferson's concern for the dignity of liberty and freedom. George Randolph had little interest in or concern for those unwilling to work hard to enjoy their fruits. He does not appear to have quoted Thomas Jefferson's opinions concerning the right of revolution or the durability of constitutions. Most of what he did comported well with his grandfather's adage that the earth belongs to the living and that the present generation should not be bound by the dead hand of the past. Randolph had foreseen the separation of the old union. He had helped call forth the new nation from what he saw was the tomb of the old. Secession had fired him and

others of Richmond's different circles of leadership with energies they
had not shown previously—a phenomenon true of many other Southerners in both civil and military life.

Suddenly what had been no more self-conscious than informal
coteries became transformed into self-conscious elites, which, although
at first nongovernmental in nature, aspired to shape national policy.
Because George W. Randolph was a member of several of these, his
appointment as secretary of war in 1862 provided an opportunity to
give effect to their goals. Even though his tenure at the War Office
lasted only nine months, his reorganization proved to be so important
that it set the department on a course for the rest of the war. In his
reformation he gave emphasis to elitist recruitment of personnel and
innovative and elitist administration.

Vilfredo Pareto in the early years of the twentieth century commenced the first serious study of elites by saying that "every people is
governed by an elite, by a chosen element in the population. . . . The
remainder of the population follow[s] the impulse given by it." Since
Pareto, scholars have directed their attention to elites most often with
special application to the twentieth century.[3] After World War II, scholars observed that usually it has been a combination or plurality of elites,
rather than only one, that in congruence or alliance has set their country's course in shaping society and government. Although the author
recognizes that an effort to apply such concepts to the Confederate
States of America is limited by that country's four-year effort to establish its independence, he proposes to discuss three elites which for a
while and to a degree directed the Confederacy, to call attention to
some of the administrative stresses of the Confederacy, and to note
some causes for successes and failures. These three were the F.F.V. elite,
the cultural elite, and the technocratic elite. The first was the largest in
numbers and was epitomized by Robert E. Lee and George Wythe
Randolph. The second was fugitive and revolved about the person of
John R. Thompson. The third, represented by Josiah Gorgas, advocated management of the country's slight industrial resources by experts
for the good of the whole community. The three elites usually worked
together harmoniously. George Wythe Randolph belonged to all three,
in addition to having been a prewar military officer. When he became
secretary of war, he superimposed on the existing structure and policies
of the Confederacy some goals of the elites he represented.

Members of the so-called First Families of Virginia—the F.F.V.—
formed an elite within the class of gentry or aristocracy. Like their ancestors of 1776, they expected to dominate the new nation they were

creating. In 1861 they did not see themselves as reactionaries or counter-revolutionaries. They did, however, believe that they could construct a governmental edifice more carefully than had their ancestors. They believed that a Southern republic under the leadership of F.F.V.s, cultural leaders, and technocrats could achieve a more lasting and harmonious society than the Founding Fathers of 1776 and 1789 had made. They hoped to found a Southern republic capable of avoiding the evils of both factory and slave exploitation. Such goals were by no means ignoble. Rather as De Tocqueville had studied America in order better to understand France, some Richmonders gave consideration to Thompson's review of Du Var Robert's account of French laborers in order better to understand the American South.

With some reason, the members of the F.F.V. elite believed that they were fitted to plan for and in behalf of all classes of society. Most of them were one step removed from being planters. They retained a patriarchal sense of responsibility for slaves with a minimum of the intellectual shackles that limited the planter mind. Long accustomed to the complex and frustrating institution of slavery, they were capable of planning in a detached manner for the benefit of all members of society. At the same time that they knew how dependent Southern planters were on urban shopkeepers and artisans for supplies either in quantity or of quality; they also knew how they depended on rural poor whites and free blacks for extra seasonal workers.[4]

Richmond's society had been by no means averse or unaccustomed to absorbing newly elected or appointed state servants. Now that Richmond had become a national capital with an enlarged bureaucracy, it set about establishing a subtle cultural dominance over out-of-staters. When the provisional government of the Confederate States of America accepted Virginia's invitation to locate its permanent capital at Richmond, its officials unwittingly adopted the social standards of their hosts, thus placing themselves in thrall to the F.F.V.s. From accepting superficial attitudes of the F.F.V. elite, Confederate officialdom gravitated to an acceptance of some of the F.F.V.s' goals. John R. Thompson spoke for more than himself when he declared on July 3, 1856, to the Phi Beta Kappa fraternity at the College of William and Mary that he cherished most "the F.F.V.—Aristocratic type of lofty sires, Of whom, 'tis said Virginia never tires." This F.F.V. elite, in collaboration with the cultural elite of Richmond, became most important in 1862 during Randolph's term as secretary of war, had its center in the War Office, and continued his and their policies after Randolph's departure. From enlightened motives, the cultural and F.F.V. elites endorsed or acquiesced in Secretary Randolph's policy to recruit technocrats to man the War Office and to subject Southern resources and labor to a professionalized, centralized management in the interest of the war economy. Richmond's new, technocratic bureaucracy provided at least a hope that it might transform the South's initially weaker industry into one capable of competing with that of the Union because of centralized concentration of effort. In the third quarter of 1862 the capital of the Southern republic was freer of whirl and distraction than at any other time. Thus it was while George Wythe Randolph was secretary of war that Richmond as a national capital provided the background against which posterity can discern the conceptual shift from a Confederacy to a Southern republic, from the vagaries of parochial states-righters to the planning by elites.[5]

There are few satisfactory measurements for assessing family backgrounds in the United States, unless one refers to English genealogical works such as *Burke's Landed Gentry, Knightage, and Peerage*. One remarkable American publication, however, can be singled out as an exceptional family record of almost three hundred years: Robert Isham Randolph's 1928 book, *The Randolphs of Virginia*. It tabulates about 18,000 descendants of William and Mary Isham Randolph of Turkey Island, the Randolphs' long-vanished seventeenth-century seat in James City County, Virginia. Of course, there were besides the Randolphs many prominent families of Virginia which belonged either to the aristocracy or gentry of the colonial and early Republican periods. Many or most of these families were interrelated with the Randolphs. For the purposes of this study, it is convenient and economical to utilize *The Randolphs of Virginia* as a record not just of the members of one family but, because of its large sample, of the larger F.F.V. elite.[6]

The First Families of Virginia constituted an elite in which kinship, education, accomplishments, profession, and association were considered hallmarks of either genetic or natural aristocracy. The F.F.V.s made up an informal, clubby, nepotistic, oligarchical, and snobbish network. Within this group existed a smaller cultural elite, represented by the antebellum discussion group of thirteen over whom John Reuben Thompson presided alternately at his office in *The Southern Literary Messenger* building and at George Wythe Randolph's law office. Of the thirteen Richmonders who made up the Thompson-Randolph cultural elite in 1859 (see table 1), eight (61 percent) were either fellow descendants of William Randolph of Turkey Island or were otherwise related or connected to George Randolph by marriage. One member was from north of the Mason-Dixon Line. Four (31 percent) had foreign experience in either trade or travel. All but two (85 percent) had attended college, of which seven were located north of the Potomac (54 percent); and three the University of Virginia (23 percent). It is not surprising that eight (61 percent) had enjoyed some legal, medical, or philosophic study or practice, but it is a little surprising that five (39 percent) had enjoyed engineering study or experience. Three (23 percent) had been either a naval midshipman or a military cadet, and six (46 percent) had served as regular or militia officers before 1860.[7]

George Randolph's law partner, Thomas P. August, was not a member of these three elites. His and Randolph's friendship was of a business, military, personal, and political variety, rather than of shared family, cultural, and intellectual bonds.

Some of the experts, technocrats, and bureaucrats from other parts of the South reinforced in numbers and self-confidence the preexisting cultural elite of Richmond. Among the latter, professional and business men who were also collectors, devotees, patrons, and philanthropists greatly outnumbered its few artistic and literary leaders. Because of the cultural elite's aesthetic, moral, and psychic leadership, it could be either a powerful ally or foe of the country's economic and political elites within the body politic.[8]

On the eve of the Civil War Richmond boasted a group which perceived itself as a cultural elite. Its identifiable core consisted of the dozen who made up John Reuben Thompson's discussion group, whose membership is best indicated by the list of those who attended his testimonial dinner in 1860. As it has been said, a society cannot afford to ignore its poets.[9] Men of this age remembered Byron at Missolonghi, quoted Tennyson's "The Charge of the Light Brigade," and had at least a dim appreciation of Lamartine's combination of poetic and political ideals during the French Revolution of 1848. Contemporaries recognized Thompson as a man whose importance to the body politic transcended his holding a sinecure from the commonwealth of Virginia. His discussion of George Fitzhugh's and French sociological works made him an interesting, unusual, and respected figure in Richmond. He exemplified the extent to which the F.F.V. was congruent with the Richmond cultural elite. Reflecting a Renaissance-like linkage of patrons and protégés, its members knew, and outsiders like Mary Boykin Chesnut of South Carolina learned, the traditions of Virginia's rural gentry. Following the lead of Hugh Blair Grigsby, the secretary of the Virginia Historical Society, they took more seriously the implications of natural aristocracy than those of descent from cavaliers.[10]

The Richmond cultural elite, to which John R. Thompson and

George W. Randolph belonged, delighted in discussing great problems of economics, politics, and society, as well as in conversing on local, mundane affairs. Although its members had their origins in the rural gentry and inclined naturally to replicate an Englishman's devotion to his country seat and its rural delights, they formed a group more representative of the urban cultural and creature pleasures of Virginia's capital. Even those who professed still to maintain as their principal residence agricultural estates in the counties of Virginia felt more at ease in the small, snug parlors of their houses in town than in their drafty country mansions. For one or two generations, their fathers had found that the burden of serving in administrative or legislative positions had included the virtual requirement that they at least winter at Richmond. This necessity afforded compensatory cultural and social relief from discomfort and isolation in the countryside and courthouse towns like Fredericksburg. The thirteen men of his discussion group attended a testimonial dinner to honor John Reuben Thompson on his departure from *The Southern Literary Messenger* and from Richmond formed a good sample of a literati not merely interested in provincial imitations of Tennysonian verse. Instead, it had a remarkably cosmopolitan and technological orientation.[11]

The concept of a natural aristocracy, hospitable to technocrats no matter what or where had been their origin, had been built into the F.F.V. system since its colonial beginnings. It had been reinforced by Jefferson's recruitment of the University of Virginia's faculty from British universities. These experts guided Virginians into seeing humanity through both classic and modern literature and into considering political economy in the light of modern British and European theories. Significantly, until the time of William Holmes McGuffey at the University of Virginia, Virginians set the example for other Southerners in following English models in preference to Noah Webster's dictionaries or educational books. Likewise, adherence to British and Continental practice of that day gave the Old Dominion a capacity to train civilian engineers as well as soldiers for her own benefit and for that of the South in general.[12]

Sympathy with technocratic culture was clearly in evidence during George Randolph's tenure in the War Office. Secretary Randolph redefined many of the positions in the War Office and recruited his own team to staff them. Though George W. Randolph inherited from his predecessors the greatest of Confederate technocrats, Josiah Gorgas, it was Randolph who gave Gorgas responsibilities equal to his talents. One reason that he emancipated Gorgas from general engineering and procurement was to make him a partner in recruiting into the War Office such men as Thomas L. Bayne, John A. Campbell, Jeremy F. Gilmer, R. Garlick Kean, Landon Rives, Francis G. Ruffin, Isaac M. and Robert S. St. John, and T. M. R. Talcott.

An established legal and military leader before 1862, George Randolph belonged to both the F.F.V. and cultural elites. His education at the University of Virginia, experience as a midshipman and a lawyer, and participation in cultural activities marked him as a member of Virginia's nongoverning elite. If his activities were limited before 1859, they were, nonetheless, more cosmopolitan and energetic than those of most F.F.V.s. George Randolph's position among the F.F.V. elite departed from the typical in that he displayed not less, but more, vigor than had his father. The reduced circumstances of the Jefferson-Randolph clan inspired him to virtues of frugality, self-discipline, and accomplishment. He consciously set out to renew his family's fame by excelling as a city lawyer. His success elevated him in the eyes both of people of aristocratic lineage but scanty accomplishment and of those whose accomplishment exceeded their family background.[13]

Because he did not show interest in so much of the conventional ideological cant that early Confederate leaders either did, or were thought to, believe important, Randolph's appointment and conduct as secretary of war has perplexed the literal-minded to the present day. He simply did not care about so-called big, national issues like Bleeding Kansas or slavery in the territories. Chicago or Cincinnati were less real to him than half a dozen European cities. If he thought about western America, other than New Orleans, it was almost as a kind of antipodes for Virginia. It was no accident that he employed the singular verbal form when the Confederate States of America was the subject. A special kind of nationalist, he desired a Southern republic that Virginia would dominate. He does not seem ever to have referred to the Civil War as the War between the States, which he knew from the outset would be a terrible experience and might result as easily in destruction as self-determination. In a manner characteristic of elites, Randolph did not confide such impolitic views to any but his closest intimates: his wife Mary, his confidante Molly, his brother Jeff, his friend John R. Thompson, his lieutenant, J. Thompson Brown, and Josiah Gorgas.[14]

Capable, assured, and willing to take responsibility for their actions, George Randolph and his close friends thought of themselves as natural aristocrats who rightfully exercised hegemony and who welcomed into their circle newcomers of exceptional talent. Close consideration of the two groups of Randolph's intimates, one on the eve of the Civil War and the other in the summer of 1862, demonstrates a coterie of cosmopolitan, sophisticated, and technological character not usually associated with the Confederate States government. Except for transcendent figures such as Davis, Lee, and Lincoln, both North and South had to refine their political, military, and administrative leadership during the course of the Civil War. In hurriedly cobbling together in 1861 an administrative apparatus, the Confederate States of America inadvertently perpetuated weaknesses of its federal model. In addition, the process of running the provisional Confederate government on an ad hoc basis for several months created other administrative difficulties. Mismatching of men and offices further overburdened the edifice so carelessly constructed. So long as the Confederate capital remained at Montgomery, Alabama, leaders worried about constitutional niceties. By the time they moved the capital to Richmond, Virginia, the swift march of events had left most of these behind. There became manifest an impatience with the old secessionists and with President Davis's cabinet. For different reasons, the able, if slippery, Judah P. Benjamin lacked experience and temperament to be secretary of war almost as much as had the first one, Leroy Walker. Besides advising the President generally, Benjamin served the purpose of being a kind of lightning rod for criticism. There was a widespread realization that new leaders at the secondary levels of power were needed: men fired with newer ideas than states rights, slavery in the territories, or acquiring Cuba—with ideas more relevant to winning the war for Southern independence. Since there was nothing new about replacing one governing elite with another, the transition from advocating confederation to Southern nationalism excited little or no comment.[15]

Pareto declared that revolutions call forth leaders from the higher strata of society who possess qualities of intelligence, character. and skill not enjoyed by the masses. Not infrequently, such elite, revolutionary leaders have emerged from the old governing class to join "the class that holds the future in its hands" as the "more spirited and creative" of the new rulers.[16]

Although at first imperceptible, there were revolutionary changes in the Confederate administrative structure in the spring of 1862. When George W. Randolph became secretary of war he quietly introduced into its top and middle-grade administrative positions a new and elite kind of decision makers. In doing so, he superimposed upon the older and at least partially discredited governing elite a coterie drawn from what previously had been nongoverning F.F.V., cultural and technocratic elites. These groups so shaped the department that it regulated the civilian economy as well as managing matters of a military nature. Representatives of the combination of elites whom Randolph brought to secondary levels of power exhibited a more aristocratic, cosmopolitan, educated, and innovative character than had those they politely superseded. As a consequence, significant changes of policy spread out in many directions.

Because Randolph was both a cause and an effect in this circulation of elites, his career deserves close study for its greater implications. As it turned out, President Davis and Secretary Randolph did not make a good team—as had Davis and Judah P. Benjamin and would Davis and James A. Seddon. As we have noted, Randolph complained of interminable and inconclusive conferences with Davis. Although his successor, Seddon, often won the president's support for almost the same propositions that Randolph had espoused unsuccessfully, the time for their successful application usually had slipped by. The chief concurrence of Davis and Randolph was the strategic decision to devote more resources to the campaigns west of the Allegheny Mountains. The chief difference between their views was Randolph's greater and Davis's lesser interest in logistics. Judah P. Benjamin as secretary of war had paved the way for Randolph in requesting more staff, but his optimism and technological inadequacy made Randolph's proposals for substantive changes seem alarming to Davis. Benjamin's reports concerning the numbers of troops and quantity of supplies were so optimistic that in comparison Randolph's proposals seemed to address imaginary crises. There was a difference between the temperaments of Randolph and Davis that generated a subliminal conflict between the two, unlikely of any but temporary compromise.

The War Department may have started out as a conventional niche in the Confederacy's structure, but wartime exigencies so increased its scope that it arguably became the most important administrative part of the government. Secretary Randolph devoted much of his energies to recruiting its technocratic bureaucrats from the several elites—the F.F.V.s, the smart young lawyers, the engineers—of which he was a member. Of the twenty-five persons listed in table 3, twenty-one served in the War Office during Randolph's secretaryship. Of these, thirteen (52 percent) were his appointees. Included in table 3 are four others with whom Randolph had close association but who were never part of the War Office staff. Eight of the twenty-five (32 percent) were members of the F.F.V. elite by virtue of their descent from William Randolph of Turkey Island, and one more was otherwise related to George W. Randolph. In terms of an educational or technocratic elite, nineteen (76 percent) appear to have had some college education. Only Col. Thomas P. August was definitely not a college man. He was not recruited into the War Office, but rather given a desk job after his health broke. The largest number of alumni from nonmilitary schools was the University of Virginia's six (24 percent) and Yale's four (16 percent). That fifteen (60 percent) of the twenty-five had enjoyed some education in the north (excluding nine who were midshipmen or cadets at either West Point or V.M.I.) shows that J. B. Jones's comments about too many Yankees had a factual basis, even though his pejorative interpretation was wrong. That seventeen (68 percent) enjoyed some foreign residence or travel is evidence of remarkable cosmopolitanism. Considering terms of occupation, it is important that seven (28 percent) had some engineering training or experience.[17]

Southerners were too preoccupied first with the excitement and then with the deepening gloom of the Civil War to recognize the creation of the bureaucratic hierarchy based on cultural, social, and technological elites, partly independent of and partly coincident with their constitutional position. The ideological character of this elite never became a political issue, since Confederate Richmond did not hatch political parties during the four-year revolutionary struggle. It is true that it did spawn evanescent factions, like what some recent scholars have called the Western Concentration Bloc; they formed a congregation of military and political pressure groups that included anti-Davis, anti-Bragg as well as pro-Western members.[18]

Wartime created so unparalleled a crisis that a consolidation of power was not only a natural centripetal development but also an opportunity for an elite quietly to manipulate the levers of power. The urgency of wartime encouraged the cooperation, if not the amalgamation, of elites, rather than their competition. If there was circulation within the War Office of the Confederacy, it was directed to bringing in new men of advanced ideas for handling important tasks and to assigning to old functionaries less crucial duties. Very few of the men left over from the days of secretaries Walker or Benjamin were pushed out of their places. Maj. Danville Ledbetter and Capt. Richard Morton were in the War Office before Randolph became secretary, but Benjamin had dispatched the former to rebuild portions of the Virginia and Tennessee Railroad that Tennessee Unionists had destroyed.[19] Presumably Benjamin sent Captain Morton on a similar mission.

No one ever has been sure how many read the writings of the sociologist George Fitzhugh, the economist George Tucker, or the historian Hugh Blair Grigsby. Richmond's cultural elite accepted much of these Virginia writers' social, economic, and historical views, masked by a genteel facade of blended Cavalier and natural leadership. Of all the Confederate military or civilian leaders, George Randolph possessed the closest links to such literati. He knew the ideas of George Fitzhugh at not less than secondhand. In addition to Thompson and the members of their discussion group, he must have conversed about the themes of Fitzhugh's *Sociology for the South* and *Cannibals All!* with his friends Conway Robinson, the lawyer and amateur historian, and their kinsman, John Moncure Daniel, the former U.S. minister to Sardinia who edited the wartime Richmond *Examiner.* Fitzhugh's sociological treatises were not inconsistent with what Randolph had learned from Tucker at the University of Virginia about protective tariffs. Nor were they inconsistent with the congruence of the F.F.V.s and a natural aristocracy that was embodied in the writings of Randolph's friend Hugh Blair Grigsby.[20]

As a midshipman George Wythe Randolph had shown that upon occasion he could be a charismatic leader. He combined the mental acuity of the lawyer he was with the speculation either of a man of literary pursuits or of a canny investor. He was the sort of man who could translate into reality an ideal or utopian program.

According to the Italian scholar of the American Civil War, Raimondo Luraghi, Southern leaders tried to fight the North on its own industrial terms. In order to equip and maintain an army capable of gaining Southern independence, the leaders of this precapitalist, emerging nation adopted what seems to Luraghi to have been a kind of state socialism. It is true that by November of 1862 the Southern republic had achieved in a roundabout, extralegal manner a system whereby the central government could meet the needs of the war economy by central planning. In the process, the central government enforced priorities concerning the utilization of raw materials, the access to railroads, the remuneration of the labor force, and the prices of basic foodstuffs. The War Department originated and executed these expedients with minimal authorization by the legislative branch of the central government. However, far from creating a Union of Socialist Southern Republics, the Southern republic employed a system for accumulating capital and for regulating domestic manufactures, mining, trade, and transportation in the traditional manner of the mercantilists of early modern Europe or of the enlightened despots of eighteenth-century Europe. The practice of such statist measures in Virginia and the South was by no means new to America. During the American Revolution, leaders of individual states were similarly concerned about winning a war against the superior industrial power of Great Britain. Randolph and his friends were as much concerned about the whole of society as have been leaders of most countries, but they did not profess concern for the white or black Southern proletariat. Their indebtedness to presocialist economics did not obligate them to embrace socialist cant. One is tempted to agree with Professor Luraghi that, if the South had nationalized sooner foreign trade, cotton, the conscription of slaves as well as of whites, she might have prevailed against the less concerted superiorities of the North.[21]

Few in the Southern government were as well fitted as George Randolph to concert Confederate military, economic, industrial and transportation capabilities. There were few who could select a team with the technocratic skills necessary to win the war. There were a number of Southerners who had enjoyed either an engineering or a legal education, but very few who had enjoyed both, as he had. Few had equivalents of Randolph's experiences in Boston, New York, Norfolk, and Pensacola, which had taught him much about his own country, just as his two years in the Mediterranean, visiting four capitals and a dozen fortresses, had taught him much about the Old World. There are few better vantage points than deck and dock from which to learn the diversity, strengths, and deficiencies of a national economy.

Admittedly, Randolph's acquaintance with Boston's entrepreneurial and manufacturing world was slight, being based on association from his youth onward with Ellen and Joseph Coolidge and their friends. George Randolph's appreciation of that world was enlarged by his Coolidge nephews' marriages with an Appleton, a Gardner, and a Lowell, but he never professed to having more than a little window on that world. In comparing the commonwealths of Massachusetts and Virginia, he concluded that what Virginia needed in the new Southern republic to match the Bay State's affluent prowess in the old republic was capital investment protected from Northern, British, and European competition. Then Virginia's able, industrious craftsmen might manifest their abilities and wax rich, making Virginia the North of the Southern republic.[22]

Logically, Virginia's best source for the needed capital was the commonwealth, itself. Although Virginia had in the mid-seventeenth century entertained religious views in some ways similar to those of New England, she never had subscribed to the so-called Puritan ethic. Nor had she ever disparaged the role of the state as an investor of capital, franchises, or privileges. Although her mercantilism was by no means unique among the states, in the 1850s Virginia presented a picture of mixed enterprise. The commonwealth customarily had subscribed three-fifths of the capital stock of all bridge, canal, ferry, and railroad corporations within her borders. For thirty-five years her Board of Public Works had made recommendations to the state legislature about the priority that should be accorded competing projects. From the beginning, the Virginia system acknowledged that the state might finance some works of internal improvement without help from the private sector, and other Southern states possessed equivalent systems. Virginia's long practice and the urgency of wartime necessity combined to lend support to applying the Old Dominion's mixed-enterprise system to the Southern republic.[23]

Few Civil War leaders recognized better than Randolph that warfare had become neither the exclusive preserve of the professional soldier nor the singular lot of the armed ploughboy, but an infinitely perilous situation involving all of the state's population and her economy. By personal action and through the technocrats he recruited, Randolph extended to all of the Southern republic a planned economy dominated by the F.F.V.s, the cultural elite and technocrats. Randolph himself epitomized these three overlapping elites and laid the foundation for a consolidated state that combined aspects of mercantilist and utopian socialist systems in order to win an unequal war.

George W. Randolph's career affords an opportunity to study three of the Confederate elites—the F.F.V.s, the cultural leaders of Richmond, and the technocrats. Besides being Randolph's own characteristics, they were those of his fellows and of those he recruited for the War Office.

# CHAPTER 10

# *Randolph Recruits His Staff*

Secretary of War George W. Randolph was to make a strategic contribution to the military policies of the Southern republic by giving greater emphasis to the war in the West, as we shall see in chapter 11. But it is beyond doubt that Randolph's greatest accomplishment was the reform of the War Department and the recruitment of a brilliant staff.

Without turning things upside down while he made departmental bureaus more responsive to military needs, he quietly improved the caliber of its officials by recruiting new, able men of special skills. As Susanne Keller has said in her book *Beyond the Ruling Class,* "Only through a change in the types of men at the top can new inventions, new experiences, and new ideas become part of the whole community." Secretary Randolph shaped a "new" War Office from a composite of elites, consisting often of men younger than those they replaced. To make room for them, Randolph both created new posts and moved middle-aged orators and drones away from sensitive jobs. In the process, he expanded the War Department's influence to the point of almost dominating many aspects of governmental operations which related to the war economy. This composite of elites was made up of the F.F.V.s and technocrats in a manner that was generally consistent with the outlook of the Richmond cultural elite. The parameters of the first and last of these already have been explored in chapter 7, while the individual characteristics of the technocrats will be demonstrated in this chapter, more or less in the order in which they received their appointment. These were Confederate leaders of the third rank who achieved their positions of trust and authority more because of technocratic ability than because of aristocratic antecedents. However, the means of Randolph's recruiting technocrats in an age when industrial technology was young became one mainly of acquaintance within or recommendation by elite groups.[1]

Because of George Tucker, his professor of natural philosophy at the University of Virginia, George Randolph had at least a vague appreciation of the French social philosopher Saint-Simon, who a generation earlier had dealt extensively with the organization of society. One of Saint-Simon's greatest contributions to social thought was his emphasis on the greater potential of industrial producers than of political leaders. He believed that "industry and science were to dominate social life . . . and their activities had to be carried out for the public good and under public surveillance." Randolph followed Saint-Simon in believing in the essential unity of politics and economics.

Emory Thomas is quite correct in saying in *The Confederate Nation* that "incredibly few men directed and managed Southern war industries," but he is only partly correct in suggesting that these were " 'traditional intellectuals'—schoolteachers, natural philosophers, and military scientists—as opposed to 'organic intellectuals'—industrial managers, mechanical engineers and the like." There were both. Without belaboring the fact that the profession of engineering was not then subdivided and that any engineer was a civil, mechanical, and military engineer, the well-known practical accomplishments of William Barton Rogers at the University of Virginia and of Benjamin Silliman at Yale should be sufficient to demonstrate that the European linkage between a nation's academic engineering and scientific laboratories and its industries existed to some degree in America. George Randolph's study under Rogers is bound to have inspired his appreciation of the interdependence of the academic and industrial spheres.[2] He recruited many engineers for his War Department staff. Although he also hired a number of bright young lawyers, American secretaries of war and defense have always done so.

Beyond doubt Randolph's chief qualification for becoming secretary of war was his demonstrated expertise in conscription. His personnel and logistical policies as secretary were to maintain an army with its regiments at full strength in numbers, belly, and muscle. Otherwise, defeat might be postponed, but it would come. The Conscription Act of 1862 authorized calling to the colors men between the age of eighteen and forty-five years of age. After almost a year of optimistic reports from Secretaries Walker and Benjamin, it must have surprised the president for Randolph to recommend that no one be conscripted over forty because "it is questionable whether a larger number [than about five hundred thousand] could be fed, clothed and armed."[3] On the other hand the new secretary was adamant that those conscripted actually perform their service. In arguments over men and matériel between state and national authorities, he made the decision early to avoid controversy with state governors. In correspondence with governors Joseph E. Brown of Georgia and Zebulon B. Vance of North Carolina, he sent many temporizing telegrams in the hope that the Confederate Congress would guarantee a national army and its rations. He avoided fraudulent claims by politicos, not excluding the president himself, that the Confederate armies were weak because state governors hoarded troops at home. Instead, he was irate at "the inefficiency of regimental and company officers" who condoned "the vast amount of stragglers which now paralyze our Army and defeat all attempts to reinforce it." To cure this evil, he asked Congress to authorize "travelling commissions to try officers" who granted leaves for insufficient reasons and who turned a blind eye to absenteeism that was so rampant as to imperil the war effort. After the Battle of Antietam, General Lee telegraphed Randolph that "unless something is done, the army will melt away." To have appointed such representatives on mission with summary powers resembling the policy of the First French Republic would, however, have been too radical for President Davis and for the Confederate Congress. Even though George W. Randolph deserved credit for his emphasis on exempting conscientious objectors from military service, he insisted that local authorities collect fees for providing substitutes from persons claiming exemptions as Dunkards, Menonites, Nazarines, or Quakers.[4]

George Wythe Randolph's forte as Secretary of War was not so much his varied experience as it was a clear perception of what the Southern republic needed to win: offsetting the North's superior numbers by more efficient use of manpower and offsetting the North's larger industrial facilities based on free enterprise by creating a system based on state ownership and controls which were more mercantilist than socialist. Randolph could make changes easily because his office was not elective and because his changes could go unnoticed for some while during the general preoccupation with battles. If, as never seems to have happened, he had been pressed for an explanation, he could successfully have pled wartime necessity.

Just as Randolph's entry into the top level of Confederate leadership had depended on the president's pleasure, so might (and did) his exit by the same door. The principal cause of stress between the two was the optimistic misconceptions that Judah P. Benjamin had encouraged in Davis. It was little to be wondered at that Davis, who continued to rely on Benjamin for advice as secretary of state, found Randolph's candid warnings too unconventional and revolutionary for immediate acceptance. Randolph's confidential grousing to his intimates about Davis's indecision became understandable, given Davis's continued reliance on Benjamin for advice of all sorts. Because of the appointive nature of Randolph's office, because of the covert quality of his reforms, and because silence was a part of his "factitious" resignation as secretary of war, Randolph never sought nor had his day in court. When he resigned, there was not—and could not have been—any outcry or call for an accounting. Because the Confederate composite of elites which Randolph had helped place in the tertiary positions of power was not displaced, and because most of Randolph's reforms were preserved by his successor James A. Seddon, the significance of Randolph's bold innovations was forgotten in the crash of the Confederacy.

Although Secretary Seddon's family origins were not so distinguished as Randolph's, he was a member of the F.F.V. and an able lawyer. Unlike Randolph, he had political status as a former U.S. Congressman. He and the president made a good team, but when Seddon was not pliant enough for Davis either, he, too, resigned.[5]

The most important difference between the two secretaries was subtle, but important. In the 1850s, Randolph had been a man who became more, rather than less, active, whereas Seddon had become almost a recluse. Randolph and Seddon were both cerebral; but Randolph discussed ideas with others—Thompson's circle of intellectuals and later Gorgas, Bayne, and a few compatriots—while Seddon donned his black skullcap and penned himself in his study. In short, Randolph was an intellectual activist and Seddon a passive intellectual.

It already has been noted in chapter 6 that Secretary Randolph inherited two assistant secretaries of war, Bledsoe and Ould. President Davis soon sent Bledsoe abroad. Randolph did not fill the vacancy for several months. Instead, he created a new position, the head of the Bureau of War, to which he named Garlick Kean with the rank of captain, well-satisfied that he would continue the able and loyal staff work that he had performed while on his staff at Suffolk.[6] Randolph and Ould were friendly on both official and personal levels, but the secretary gave Ould a job better suited to his talents. When in the early summer of 1862 Colonel Ould was named commissioner of exchange, he also became judge advocate general of courts martial and the senior officer of the Confederate Secret Service. As the chief officer who could give permission to pass through the Confederate lines, Colonel Ould conducted a bureaucratic war with the State Department over the issuance of passports. As one of the leading Roman Catholics in the Confederate bureaucracy, Ould was suspect to someone like the War Office Clerk J. B. Jones, but Randolph appreciated this honest and capable lawyer.[7]

When Secretary Randolph did fill the office of assistant secretary, he brought into the War Office one of the Confederacy's wisest civil servants, John Archibald Campbell of Alabama, a former associate justice of the U.S. Supreme Court. How this came about in the summer of 1862 must await its chronological and causative turn. For this position, Judge Campbell was well-fitted according to Randolph's standards of education, experience, and personal acquaintance or reference. Perhaps more significant, however, was Randolph's appointment of Alfred Landon Rives to head the Engineer Bureau of the War Department.

As the son of the statesman and diplomat William Cabell Rives of Castle Hill, Albemarle County, Virginia, Alfred Landon Rives was at the age of thirty-two an intimate of the younger Randolphs of Edgehill and the inheritor of more than a century of close friendship with the Jefferson-Randolphs. A great-grandson of the colonial land magnate and explorer Dr. Thomas Walker, he was of impeccable F.F.V. antecedents, to which he had added impressive technocratic ability. He had been born in Paris, France, when his father served his first ministry there. Landon Rives's American education was impressive. In another sense, his schoolboy associations demonstrated how tightly knit were the F.F.V. elite which did so much to manage the Confederate war effort. Rives had been tutored at home until he was fourteen, when he was sent to Frederick Coleman's Concord Academy, a classical school located between Richmond and Fredericksburg whose master held a master's from the University of Virginia. Garlick Kean had studied there a few years earlier. At the age of eighteen Rives was graduated from the Virginia Military Institute after only two years of study, the sixth in a class of twenty-four. He next attended the University of Virginia for a session, before joining his father, William Cabell Rives, when in 1848 he went to France for the second time as U.S. Minister. After a year of studying French and mathematics, the young man passed the regular entrance requirements for the celebrated École des Ponts et Chausées, from which he was graduated in 1854. He declined a position with the Chemin du Fer du Nord in order to take a similar post with the Virginia Midland Railway. Rives soon resigned that post to serve under Capt. Montgomery C. Meigs of the U.S. Corps of Engineers as assistant engineer of the United States Capitol and the Post Office Building. His greatest personal accomplishment during his Washington period was to design and build the Cabin John Bridge across the Potomac. Upon Virginia's secession, he accepted a commission as captain of engineers from the commonwealth, whose chief engineer in 1860 was Col. Andrew Talcott. Assigned to the lower peninsula between the York and James, Rives was responsible for designing much of the Yorktown fortifications. He headed the Confederate Engineer Bureau until the autumn of 1862. He moved to Lee's staff in an engineering capacity, but returned to head the Engineer Bureau in August of 1863. Ultimately, he attained the rank of colonel. From 1868 to his death in 1903, he was at various times chief engineer, vice-president, or general manager of the Chesapeake and Ohio, Birmingham and Mobile, Louisville and Nashville, Richmond and Danville, Panama, and the Vera Cruz and Pacific railroads. He declined the Khedive of Egypt's offer to become his chief engineer of all civil works.[8]

Andrew Talcott was another member of this coterie of kinsmen and friends possessed of special talents. Orginally a New Yorker, he had married George Randolph's cousin Harriet Randolph many years before, when he had been in charge of construction at Fort Monroe. He had come to think of himself as a Virginian. During the 1850s George Randolph sometimes had employed him as an expert witness in litigation involving engineering work. One may reasonably infer that in 1862 Talcott gave Randolph informal advice on planning railroads and making them serve military and industrial needs. With a presumed arms merchant named Lamballer, Talcott met with Randolph and Gorgas concerning ordnance in November of 1862 before Talcott returned to Mexico.[9]

Josiah Gorgas was already chief of the Bureau of Ordnance when Randolph became secretary of war, but Randolph so greatly expanded Gorgas's freedom, authority, and scope that he could be considered almost a new appointee. A West Pointer in the class of 1841, he had gone to Europe as a military observer early in his career. After having won distinction in the siege of Vera Cruz during the Mexican War, he had spent the 1850s at various army arsenals. This most brilliant of all Confederate technocrats came to consider Randolph his "most intimate" friend, as much for personal as for professional reasons. George's residence in Boston and New York made him appreciative of Josiah's respectable—but not genealogically dazzling—origins in Lancaster, Pennsylvania. The two men were about the same age. One had graduated from the U.S. Military Academy in 1841, and the other had been commissioned a passed midshipman in 1837 and graduated from the University of Virginia a Bachelor of Law in 1841. Because Randolph had studied in Farragut's naval school at Norfolk and under William Barton Rogers at the University of Virginia, conversation between them about engineering and scientific matters was easy and natural. Each was a conscientious model of Victorian virtue and scholarship.

Mrs. Amelia Gorgas once declared of Randolph that "Mr. Gorgas has no other friend in the city whose society he so much enjoys." When Amelia was away during the summer of 1862, Josiah often breakfasted with the Randolphs and played with their English terrier puppy for relaxation.[10]

Amelia Gayle Gorgas had even more in common with Mary Randolph. They shared the bond of having lived in the deep South and having become brides within a year of each other. Amelia's maternal ancestors, the Gayles, came originally from Virginia, where they were of more social than economic or political prominence. On the other hand, Amelia's father John Gayle of Mobile was a member of the political and judicial elites of Alabama in addition to moving on the highest level of its society. There was between the two ladies a substantial Mobile bond. Besides many mutual acquaintances like the St. Johns, the Gayles and Popes were Cotton Whigs. Mary and her first husband, William B. Pope, had gone to Washington, D.C., so that he could serve as Congressman Gayle's secretary.[11]

Secretary Randolph was happy to endorse Gorgas's request to bring into the War Office the latter's wounded brother-in-law, Thomas Levingston Bayne, a Georgian who had been the class orator at Yale in 1847 before entering upon a successful law practice in New Orleans. He was the husband of Maria Gayle, whom he had married in Mobile and had taken as a bride to live in the Crescent City. Among their close friends there were groomsman James Campbell and John Slidell. The first was a relative of Associate Justice John A. Campbell of the U.S. Supreme Court, whose circuit included Mobile as well as New Orleans. Slidell then was a distinguished attorney and U.S. senator from Louisiana; he later became a famous Confederate diplomat. As an older friend, Judge Campbell had been solicitous of the Bayne family both while Thomas was soldiering during the Shiloh campaign and during his convalescence from wounds afterwards. The two men discussed their fate if, as became likely, New Orleans would fall to Union forces. Bayne was anxious to go to Richmond "to report for active service." He persuaded the judge to accompany him, rather than remain in New Orleans where, if captured, he would be "imprisoned or subject to some indignity." The two men deposited Maria and the Bayne children with relatives in South Carolina before going to Richmond. Soon after their arrival, Josiah Gorgas secured from George Randolph a commission for Bayne as a captain of artillery to serve as his adjutant in the Bureau of Ordnance.[12]

Mrs. Bayne and the children soon joined Thomas in Richmond.

They solved the problem of where to live by sharing a rented house on Cary Street near Fifth Street with Judge Campbell, Capt. Joseph Denegre, and Maj. Stephen Chalaron, to give them ranks they attained in the War Department. Bayne, Chalaron, and Denegre had served together as enlisted men in the elite Washington Artillery of New Orleans. They were soon administering the blockade runners and Confederate imports. Chalaron was an accountant—at the time an unusual profession—and therefore so important that it won him high rank and kept him in Richmond. The house that the Louisianians rented was large enough to require three servants and to accommodate wounded soldiers during moments of crisis. The Gayles sent from Alabama salted bacon which the Baynes bartered for fresh meat. Through the Confederate purchasing agent in England, George A. Trenholm, they were able to get some sugar and tinned meats. Captain Denegre's father sent clothing from France. Food became so short that Mrs. Bayne once sold a New Orleans bonnet for $600 and traded in a diamond ring so that they could have enough to eat.[13]

George and Mary Randolph helped launch the Baynes on the social seas of Richmond, a feat made easy by the charm and ability of the Louisianians. Colonel Bayne became an especial friend of Burton Harrison, a fellow graduate of Yale who was the president's private secretary and later the husband of Randolph's cousin, Constance Cary. The Baynes were intimates of the Randolphs from the beginning of their Richmond days. Sometimes, Colonel Bayne sat on the Randolphs' doorstep with Mrs. Randolph while the general enjoyed the evening air from a partly concealed vantage point inside the doorway, where he could avoid being importuned by passing acquaintances. On one such occasion, Mrs. Randolph remarked to Colonel Bayne that "my poor husband is so tired and so much afraid of being called out that he must keep within doors. Can you not suggest some person from New Orleans or elsewhere who will relieve him?" The next morning, Bayne proposed Judge John A. Campbell's name to Colonel Gorgas to relay to the secretary. At once Randolph sent for Bayne to ask whether there were "any assurance that Campbell would accept the appointment." The young man replied that, although neither had mentioned the subject, he believed that the judge "was willing to do anything he could." After eliciting from several Alabama congressmen what proved to be adverse opinion, Randolph asked Bayne to arrange a time for him and Campbell to meet, if the latter were agreeably disposed. He was. Randolph called on Campbell. The judge agreed to accept the work of an assistant secretary of war provided it be without its title.

Some were skeptical about Judge Campbell's loyalty to the South. He had enjoyed eight years as Associate Justice of the U.S. Supreme Court. His family had been pleased to exchange for Alabama the greater sophistication of Washington. As Mrs. Chesnut remarked, he had resigned "for a cause that he [was] hardly more than half in sympathy with," being so lukewarm a secessionist as to deserve being called a "Laodicean." She felt much empathy for Campbell, whose face she thought "the saddest . . . I ever saw."[14]

For all that Campbell's coming into the War Office was a lucky coup, it demonstrated that George Randolph was quick to grasp an opportunity. It was obvious that besides his eminence, Judge Campbell's experience would help in developing wartime regulations and in providing dispassionate, confidential advice. Because one might have supposed that for professional reasons Campbell would have preferred the Confederate Attorney General's Office as a place for his wartime service, it was a tribute to Randolph and his team that the judge chose the War Office. It was also indicative of the informal, clubby way that Randolph and his subordinates in the War Office tended to ignore traditional boundaries in recruiting.

When Landon Rives got a transfer to the front, there were many reasons why Secretary Randolph appointed to the position of chief engineer of the Confederate armies Lt. Col. Jeremy F. Gilmer (1819–83) of Guilford, North Carolina. He had been the third-ranking graduate of the U.S. Military Academy in 1839, had seen service in the Mexican War, and had resigned from the U.S. Army in 1861. He next had served on the staff of Albert Sidney Johnston until incapacitated by a wound at Shiloh. Such good credentials were not diminished by the prominence of his father, John A. Gilmer, then in the Confederate States House of Representatives, but once such a strong unionist that President Lincoln had offered him a cabinet post. Remembering the complaint of the War Office Clerk Jones that too many in high places were insufficiently devoted to the Southern cause, it is amusing to note that a genealogical error may have helped Randolph save Gilmer from shortsighted superpatriots. Because Randolph's friends, the Gilmers of Albemarle, thought that they and the North Carolina Gilmers were distantly related, the secretary could vouch to his constituency in the F.F.V. elite that the North Carolinian's appointment satisfied social as well as technocratic standards.[15]

When Congress authorized the assignment of fifty ordnance officers to the War Office, there were so many applicants that Secretary Randolph ordered that these appointments were to be on merit after competitive examination.[16] He named William LeRoy Broun, later president of what is now Auburn University, as president of a three-man Board of Examiners. For Confederate artillery use and also as a basis for examination, Broun abridged a U.S. Army Ordnance Manual containing the elements of algebra, chemistry, physics, and some trig-onometry. The result of the examination was unexpected: so many of those who passed were Virginians that "the President declined to ap-point them until an equal opportunity was given to the young men of the different armies of the Confederacy in other States."[17]

Secretary Randolph's expansion of the Nitre and Mining Bureau was a good demonstration of how he was able to translate into practical accomplishment concepts which he had studied. When William Barton Rogers had taught Randolph natural philosophy at the University of Virginia, that scientific professor was simultaneously inventing a prac-tical method of producing chlorine, mapping the historical geology of the Appalachians and identifying mineral deposits in Virginia that were capable of profitable exploitation. George Randolph had interested himself in the production of nitre and of minerals early in 1861, when he was a member of the Virginia Convention. On the one hand, he wished to encourage householders to propagate nitre, a component of gun-powder, in their cellars. On the other, he wanted to requisition or na-tionalize large caves either where there already were such deposits or where the substance could be spawned successfully. Nor did he hesitate to requisition "Negro laborers of the Army" to provide manpower for a survey of coal and iron deposits in Virginia. To head the Nitre and Mining Bureau Randolph summoned Maj. Isaac M. St. John, whose main job was to supervise the manufacture of gunpowder. It was he who caused the construction of the largest and most modern gun-powder factory in the world, using British methods, at Augusta, Geor-gia. A Yale graduate at the age of eighteen of the class of 1845, the Georgian had been between 1848 and 1861 a civil engineer, first with the Baltimore and Ohio Railroad and then with the Blue Ridge Railroad of Georgia. He had kinfolk in Mobile who were Mrs. Randolph's friends. This member of the technocratic elite had first joined Magruder's com-mand as a private in the Corps of Engineers before Randolph plucked him out of the ranks. St. John acquitted himself well on Randolph's staff at Suffolk. In February of 1865 he married at St. Paul's Church, Richmond, Mary Randolph's niece, Ella J. Carrington, thus becoming by marriage a member of the F.F.V. elite.[18]

The two officials of the War Department who caused Randolph the greatest difficulties were Col. Abraham C. Myers and Col. Lucius B.

Northrop. Both had originated in Charleston, South Carolina and had been graduated low in their classes at West Point in the early 1830s. Both held thankless jobs respectively as quartermaster general and commissary general of subsistence. Each attracted increasing criticism as the war grew longer—especially Northrop. In August of 1863 President Davis humiliated Myers by demoting him. No matter how much they may have deserved it, few Confederate officials suffered this fate. Certainly Myers's questionable demotion was unpopular with the Confederate Senate. In contrast, although most senators castigated the president's "friend" Northrop, Davis stubbornly propped him up in office until February of 1865. The problems of logistics and manpower that the quartermaster general and commissary general faced probably were not capable of a solution. Fully appreciating their gravity, Randolph was in a delicate position. Whether Myers and Northrop were right or wrong, some concession had to be made to placate public opinion. Without approving or disapproving of either man, the secretary pretended to ignore complaints about Northrop's "peevish, obstinate, condescending and fault-finding" character at the same time that he tried to improve the quantity and quality of subsistence in the least upsetting way.[19]

Randolph brought Francis Gildart Ruffin into the War Office nominally as Northrop's principal assistant but in fact as watchdog of the commissariat. Ruffin's qualifications were superior, both as a F.F.V. and as an agricultural technocrat, but his greatest asset was his undoubted popularity. His was a very sensitive appointment, requiring great integrity, loyalty, a thick skin, and the ability to jest when the going got tough. George Randolph knew that he could count on "Frank" Ruffin in all respects. Ruffin had graduated from the University of Virginia at the age of sixteen, after having excelled in Latin. His and George's friendship stemmed from the marriage of Frank Ruffin to George's niece and contemporary, Caryanne Nicholas Randolph. While George was a young lawyer living at Edgehill, the Ruffins lived a mile away at Shadwell. Caryanne's death did not end Frank's and George's friendship. Frank placed his and Caryanne's Albemarle property in trust for the benefit of their children and left both in the care of Thomas Jefferson Randolph when he moved to Richmond to supervise his prosperous farms outside the city. He and his second wife, a descendant of John Marshall, resided in the Marshall House at 818 East Marshall Street, whence they exchanged social amenities with the Randolphs on Franklin Street. In addition to farming in Albemarle and Hanover counties, Ruffin served as secretary of the Virginia Agricultural Society and as editor of *The Southern Planter* farm journal. He knew personally many leading landowners throughout the commonwealth and was accounted "the best conversationalist of his day."[20]

Randolph wisely avoided controversy over the merits of and supposed preference accorded to West Pointers just because they had attended the United States Military Academy. In practice, he was quick to seek out persons possessing technical and analytical abilities, especially engineers. He did not so much fire old appointees or downgrade their jobs as he did create new positions to carry out new policies and to fill them with the new men of the technocratic elite specially trained in engineering, scientific, legal, or agricultural skills. Because in the 1860s there were no established means of identifying whom to recruit for what became the nerve center of the war effort, such appointments were highly idiosyncratic. The new composite of elites placed much store on fealty. Remarkably, Randolph's weakness as a politician became his strength as an administrator. To assure himself of loyalty, he most often turned to relatives. To find men of ability, integrity, and training, he often turned to the University of Virginia, with whose faculty the Jefferson-Randolphs always had maintained an easy rapport; Thomas Jefferson Randolph had served as rector of the University since 1842. The high incidence of bright young graduates of the University's law school at the desks of the War Office represented more than a group of F.F.V.s wearing the same old-school tie. Just as Randolph prized Gorgas for his genius and paid no attention to the latter's remote connection to the better families of Pennsylvania, he was equally happy to enlist the services of young men who were graduates of Yale. Under his auspices, the personnel of the War Office developed an esprit de corps not unlike that of the bureaus of enlightened European monarchies during the eighteenth century or of statist governments in the twentieth.

As important as Randolph's ability to reorganize the War Office along lines of technical expertise was the breadth of viewpoint which he brought to his position. After the first Manassas campaign, it was a commonplace to remark on the importance of railroads for the purposes of military mobilization, concentration, and supply. In April of 1862 he engaged in a heated discussion about railroads in wartime with his friend and kinsman, Peter Vivian Daniel, Jr., the president of the Richmond, Fredericksburg and Potomac Railroad. Both were much concerned with railroad technology, Daniel concentrating on the five-to-one superiority of double-track European lines to single-track American ones. In this discussion, their military issues were paramount. In their discussion of railroads, later claimed as the crown jewels of free enterprise, both men were so accustomed to Virginia's mixed economy that neither was disconcerted by the possibility that there might be conflicts between private and public investment in such utilities. After all, the Commonwealth of Virginia owned sixty percent of the stock in the Richmond, Fredericksburg and Potomac Railroad.[21] Behind the facade of social amenities among old friends, Randolph's War Office became an organization which not only executed its assigned duties more intelligently than before, but also expanded its authority informally to control the war economy.

George W. Randolph and Robert E. Lee worked together harmoniously from the beginning of their association in March of 1862 throughout Randolph's tenure as secretary of war. There was no reason why they should not, as they were members of two of the Confederate elites, the F.F.V.s and the military. Forgotten were the cousinly ill feelings between the Lees and the Jefferson-Randolphs arising from rival interpretations of the military events of 1782, party battles of the 1790s, and events leading to the outbreak of the War of 1812. Lee's experience as an army engineer, a brilliant subaltern in the Mexican War, and his continuous service in the U.S. Army for thirty years rightly entitled him to much greater military and popular esteem than Randolph. Yet Randolph possessed some attributes that Lee did not, which, though less obvious and less glamorous in a contest of arms, were a sound foundation for his excelling as secretary of war. Neither man could chide the other for having married a rich wife, because each had done so. General and Mrs. Lee relied upon income from her landed inheritance, Arlington Plantation, to supplement his army pay in meeting the expense of rearing a large family and maintaining an elegant style of living. General and Mrs. Randolph looked to railroad stocks, bank stocks, and factors' fees from cotton export to supplement his income as a lawyer and support their fashionable lifestyle. Because Randolph invested their surplus capital in corporate paper and Lee ploughed his back into farming, Randolph's interest in economic affairs was more sophisticated than Lee's. Both had suffered personal and family disappointments as youths, but their education and experience had led them in different directions. Except for military engineering, Lee's reading was mainly biographical, and he looked past his father, Light Horse Harry Lee, and his half-brother, Black Horse Harry Lee, to General Washington and the eighteenth century.[22]

Thanks to the example of enterprise by Joseph Coolidge, to instruction in political economy by Professor Tucker, and to bold speculation concerning the status of labor and the allocation of resources among his and John R. Thompson's discussion group, Randolph was able to look past the successes and failures of President Jefferson and Governor Randolph to the future. These differences had opened to George W. Randolph avenues undreamed of by Robert E. Lee. Randolph was not merely a willing tool in bringing technocrats into the War Office; he did so designedly. He was in no way loath to seize opportunities to aggrandize the powers of his department over such aspects of economic activity as manpower and distribution. He considered it necessary to plan an expansion of the Southern economy in unconventional ways in order to win Southern independence. In the process, Randolph's methods were secretive and perhaps even devious.

As secretary of war, Randolph was able to perceive the pertinence of past problems to the present. When he had followed on his grandfather's globe and maps the course of the Franco-Italian war against Austria in 1859, he had noted the role of the railroads, on which the Italian statesman Cavour had lavished state expenditures. Unlike Lee, he had to and did give much thought to industrial needs, as well as to strictly military ones. Where Secretary of War Benjamin had showed only concern for rebuilding bridges and railroad facilities destroyed by Tennessee unionists, Secretary of War Randolph took action to clear up the railway muddle by superimposing a War Office official over the private corporations and by having the central government build the new lines the War Office determined were needed for the war economy.

In March of 1862 he selected for an important railroad job Capt. Edmund Trowbridge Dana Myers, the young engineer whose fortification of Jamestown in 1861 delayed, although it did not deny, the use of the James River to Union forces. Myers had been reared on a farm on the north side of Richmond. Although not a college man, he was known to the Richmond cultural elite as the nephew of Samuel Mordecai, the author of *Richmond of Bye-Gone Days*. Myers's most celebrated exploit before the Civil War was to assist Claudius Crozet in the construction of railroad tunnels at Afton, Virginia. The story is still told that the two engineers commenced tunneling on opposite sides of the Blue Ridge and met with a discrepancy of less than an inch in their calculations. Myers was considered to possess an acute intellect, varied learning, civic virtues, integrity, and care in administrative detail. He was precisely the sort of man George Randolph had set out to be and whom he sought out. At the beginning of the war Myers was engaged in building a railroad line from Richmond to West Point on the York River. In the Seven Days Battle, he utilized its western portion to bring up heavy siege cannon mounted on railway trucks, much to the surprise of the Union army. In the postwar era, Major Myers rounded out his career as president of the Richmond, Fredericksburg and Potomac Railroad. In 1862 it became young Myers's responsibility to manage a novel and important undertaking in which the central government made a major intervention in the economic life of the South. This venture was to build the so-called Piedmont railroad line to link Danville, Virginia with Greensboro, North Carolina. The secretary authorized Captain Myers not only to impress slaves to construct the roadbed and lay the track, but also to impress iron rails from other railroads in less important service.[23]

Similarly, Randolph approved Col. Jeremy F. Gilmer's plan as Chief of the Engineer Bureau to build a trunk railroad line between Blue Mountain and Rome, Georgia. Later he authorized first a civilian agent and then Gen. Braxton Bragg to take charge of the government's construction of the Selma-Meridian rail link amid myriad difficulties. He even authorized an agent to supervise the westward extension of the New Orleans and Opelousas Railroad before New Orleans fell to Union forces.[24] It is more than interesting to note that Randolph's role as secretary of war was not quite the same in the first as in the second decision. The decision to proceed with the Virginia-North Carolina link was made before Lee succeeded General Johnston as commander during the Seven Days Battle for Richmond and while Lee was Davis's principal collaborator. The decision on the Georgia and Alabama links was made after Lee had taken the field and Davis and Randolph had become collaborators.

Between May and July of 1862 the secretary of war experienced frustrating difficulties with both civil and military railway officials in Virginia. It is well known that the movement of Stonewall Jackson's army from the Valley of Virginia to Richmond was an all-important feature of the successful defense of the capital. While the War Department frantically sought rolling stock to transport Jackson's army, a Lynchburg quartermaster refused to release for undesignated use by the War Department cars which he was holding in expectation of sending for an exchange of prisoners. When an official of the Southside Railroad in an explicitly worded telegraphic message reported to Randolph details of troop movements, the secretary was furious at his breach of security and tersely ordered him not to use the telegraph to inform him "of the number of troops ordered forward by myself." Because the subject of telegraphic censorship was a delicate one, not exclusively the concern of the War Department, Randolph's General Order 78 dealing with this subject in October of 1862 was adroit. Sidestepping censorship itself, he ordered military officials to advise against any mention of troop identities, movements, or numbers.[25] As often was the case, Randolph's methods lay between cajolery and the lash.

In one of his most significant acts, George Wythe Randolph, on August 12, 1862, recommended to President Davis that he seek congressional authority for the War Department "to control the operations of our railroads to some extent." Accepting this advice, the president included such a request in his annual message to Congress on August 18. Acting for Randolph, Quartermaster General Myers provided guidance to Confederate Congressmen, advising that they refrain from "taking military possession" of the railroads for the good reason that the army did not know how to operate them. Instead, Myers proposed that they appoint a civilian director of transportation. By December, Congress invested William Morrill Wadley with authority to "take supervision and control of the transportation and the government of all railroads in the Confederate States" as assistant adjutant general with rank of colonel, reporting to the secretary of war through Myers.

For a while it appeared that, in the case of Charles G. Talcott, Randolph's penchants for nepotism and elitism had led him into harboring a Yankee spy in the railroad operations of the Confederacy. Time has made it clear that, although there was indeed a railroad spy for the Union Army in the War Office, it was not Charles G. Talcott, for a while an innocent victim of conjecture. The spy turned out to be no less than the superintendent of the Richmond, Fredericksburg and Potomac Railroad, Samuel Ruth.[26]

Thirty years ago Professor Archer Jones showed that it was George W. Randolph who was the true father of Southern conscription. Using the Prussian conscription law as his model, Randolph had written most of Virginia's conscription ordinance of November, 1861. Because he had established a reputation for writing a conscription act that worked, conscription became the main topic of conversation between President Davis and Secretary of War Randolph in their first official conference. Davis accepted the general outlines of Randolph's plan and asked Congress for such a law. But it was owing almost exclusively to Randolph's efforts that the Confederate States Congress extended existing one-year terms of enlistment to three years, in spite of President Davis's balking. In personal conferences in April of 1862, Randolph shocked the senate and house committees to which the conscription bill had been referred by informing them that the country faced an immediate and devastating shortage of soldiers unless it arbitrarily (and without the suggestion of the president) extended enlistments. As Randolph wrote with some exaggeration to his Howitzer friend J. Thompson Brown, "We are fear-fully weak; all the able bodied men seem to have gone home, leaving a mere remnant of the great army that took the field a year ago." Congress on April 16, 1862, speedily enacted the laws as requested by Randolph. When Davis recommended to Congress that it try to solve the manpower crisis by extending conscription to men of forty-five years of age, Randolph confided to Vice President Alexander Stephens not only his disagreement but his chagrin that Davis had not consulted him in advance. To Stephens's delight, Randolph expressed his belief that it would be more efficacious to request that governors of the states furnish more troops than to call out older men. The emendation of the Conscription Act caused the first disagreements between President Davis and Secretary Randolph.[27]

When Judah P. Benjamin had been secretary of war, he had given Col. Andrew Talcott's son an army commission and sent him to Norfolk to serve under Gen. Benjamin Huger. This was Thomas Mann Randolph Talcott. Late in April of 1862, Secretary Randolph and General Lee collaborated in reassigning the young man to be Lee's aide de camp. Since engineering billets were full, Talcott was made a major of cavalry. T. M. R. Talcott clearly had earned his promotion, but the secretary did not scruple to address him as "My dear Randolph" and to conclude with the words "Your friend and Kinsman." Talcott's case demonstrated how an elitist, old-boy coterie smoothed out many kinks, corrected many errors of organization and improved upon military and economic decisions of the hastily constructed governmental apparatus. While it was Secretary of War Benjamin who had requested authority to appoint more engineering officers, it was Secretary Randolph who persuaded the chairman of the House of Representatives Military Committee to introduce legislation to increase the size of the corps of engineers. Having accomplished this expansion, he designated young Talcott "a full-blooded Engineer of suitable rank." Indirectly shaping Confederate policy at Hampton Roads, he used young Talcott to influence General Huger to obstruct the Elizabeth River by hulks and booms, "leaving a gate open for our own vessels to be closed on the approach of the enemy."[28] Thus Randolph frequently employed informal organizational patterns of the Confederate elite to reinforce the formal organization of the military and civil hierarchy. Lee, Randolph, and Talcott knew perfectly one another's relationship and trustworthiness. The young man was their confidant, not their minion. By such informal, unobtrusive methods, Lee and Randolph could work to implement their ideas.

Another instance where Randolph's penchant for accomplishing his goals through informal means concerned the procurement of supplies which were either already in short supply or were soon to become so. On the eve of the evacuation of Norfolk, Secretary Randolph authorized individuals such as Capt. William Roane Aylett to go there to buy scarce supplies for the infantry company he had raised two years earlier. In doing so, he favored a lawyer and owner of a large cotton, corn and tobacco estate in King William County at the same time that he reduced the booty Union forces would win. So scarce were army boots that the secretary of war in September of 1862 had to beg leather from whoever would give it so that inmates of the Virginia penitentiary could make of it "rawhide moccasins" to satisfy the immediate needs of General Lee's army.[29]

At the same time that Secretary Randolph and his team worked on short-term palliatives, he fashioned a scheme, which, if successful, would go far toward satisfying the Confederacy's alarming shortages: an exchange of Confederate cotton for Yankee food and clothing, which is treated in detail in chapter 11.

To summarize Randolph's recruitment for the War Department, one must see that he did not look upon his job merely as a housekeeping one, although he did consider it important to improve the administration of national conscription and the national procurement and distribution of supplies—subjects dealt with in the next chapter. In reshaping the War Office he brought in men whose education and professional experience in law, engineering, and agriculture were of an extremely high quality, justifying the word technocrat. Although Randolph demanded great competence, he also demanded a degree of loyalty and esprit de corps while at the same time keeping his own counsel. Finding these men was not entirely happenstance, and the composite of the F.F.V. and technocratic elites which Randolph and his team represented was invaluable in recognizing in professional or social circumstances men of kindred talent.

# CHAPTER II

# Trade with the Enemy and Liberation of New Orleans

By April of 1862 it was evident that the Confederacy was falling behind in its ability to subsist its armies. Secretary of War George Wythe Randolph sent to President Davis with his endorsement reports prepared by the War Office saying that "supplies [are] totally inadequate" and that, unless "requisitions can be filled promptly and to an adequate amount . . . it will be almost impossible . . . to feed [the armies]." In sounding this alarm, Randolph seasonably identified one of the most important causes for Southern defeat.[1]

There had long been criticism of Col. Lucius B. Northrop of the War Department's Bureau of Subsistence. He had been blamed for failing to feed the troops, for starving the civilians, and for causing inflation. To counter such complaints, Secretary Randolph appointed as Northrop's assistant, Francis G. Ruffin, a prominent official of agricultural improvement societies in Virginia. Because "Frank" Ruffin's first wife had been Randolph's niece, the secretary knew his independence, honesty, and friendship. Although Northrop was cantankerous and Ruffin persuasive, the two got along well enough. More importantly, Ruffin satisfied Randolph that Northrop was honest and performing reasonably well under the circumstances. In November of 1862 Northrop and Ruffin reported to Randolph that, because of deficiencies in Confederate supply and transport, neither wheat nor beef enough was being received to feed the Army of Northern Virginia after January of 1863. Ever more grimly, the two men reiterated the substance of this report at regular intervals until the end of the war. Where was the sustenance to come from that would maintain the Confederates as an effective fighting force?[2]

George Wythe Randolph's instinct was to solve the army's shortages expeditiously. A former naval officer, he had supervised the stowage aboard ship of foreign supplies to replenish stores. Placing greater emphasis on actually getting supplies than on haggling over their price, he concluded that the only way he could fully provision the Confederate armies was to exchange cotton for foreign and Union supplies. An elitist, he was not shocked by depravity or greed. He was as prepared to trade with scoundrels as with idealists, with businessmen greedy for profits as with an enemy dumb or corrupt enough to sell what the Southern republic needed.

Knowing that there was plenty of fresh, salted, and "preserved meats and vegetables" available from Great Britain, George Randolph and Frank Ruffin advocated exchanging either cotton or sterling for tinned bully-beef at up to 350 percent profit to blockade runners. According to Ruffin, meat was such a bulky article that it did not pay blockade runners to bring it unless for a premium. Although there was a shortage of skippers able to run the Union blockade, George A. Trenholm, the Confederate purchasing agent in England, often appeared to attach more importance to resisting usurious rates than to insuring delivery. In addition, President Davis's refusal to admit that there was a genuine food shortage in the Confederate States only added to the strain on Secretary Randolph's high-strung nerves.[3]

Because of the obstacles in turning to Europe to relieve Southern shortages, Randolph proposed trading with the enemy by exchanging cotton for beef and other provisions which antebellum Southerners had been accustomed to buy from the American West. After Union forces captured New Orleans in April and Memphis in June of 1862, some on both sides of the lines desired to reopen such a trade.[4] The most notorious Union official engaged in this trade was Maj. Gen. Benjamin F. Butler, the military governor of New Orleans. Soon after beginning his controversial nine-month rule over the Crescent City, Butler solved his problem of how to feed its sullen population of 90,000 whites and 75,000 blacks and mulattoes by authorizing trade with the enemy. There was a genuine necessity for Butler's action; but there also has always been an aura of general corruption about the Union occupation of New Orleans and charges of Butler's part in it. It has been alleged that, thanks to Ben Butler's influence, his brother Andrew J. Butler, a civilian merchant, made a million dollar profit from one cattle transaction.[5]

Except for a single action by Gen. P. T. Beauregard, the principal Confederate leader to trade with the enemy was George Wythe Randolph. In the early summer of 1862 the secretary of war endorsed a series of proposals which culminated in the exchange (after Randolph's resignation) of cotton for five thousand each of blankets, cavalry boots, and hats provided by the New Orleans branch of the Parisian import-export company Barrière et Frères. At about the same time that concern refused to sell another consignment of blankets to General Butler. Claiming that he had offered "a fair price," the General confiscated the blankets.[6]

On October 30, 1862, Randolph initiated formal discussion with President Davis of a double-headed plan to exchange cotton for war goods and to trade with the enemy. Citing European practice as precedent, he declared that the Act of the Confederate States Congress prohibiting trade with the enemy should "not apply to the government." Professing that "nothing less than the danger of sacrificing our armies would induce me to acquiesce in such a departure from our established policy," the secretary predicted "ruin" if the exchange of cotton for flour, bacon, salt, blankets, and shoes were not permitted. On the surface of things, Davis approved Randolph's plan in principle. J. B. Jones took note of this matter in his *Diary Of A Rebel War Clerk*, saying that the president first told Randolph that any such scheme must be postponed until January, but later informed him that he had given Governor Pettus of Mississippi "the requisite authority" to make such transactions. At about the same time that Randolph resigned as secretary of war, President Davis approved a specific proposal by Randolph to exchange cotton with a man named Stevenson "for such things as our army are suffering for." Stevenson had important New Orleans connections with officials of the Bank of Louisiana. Because his proposal was written in Richmond for the War Department, the hand of the New Orleans coterie in the War Office is apparent both in composing it and in persuading George Randolph to forward it to the president with favorable comment.[7] Davis back dated his endorsement of the Stevenson deal several weeks to November 10, 1862, presumably to cover his own tracks. It would appear that Davis killed the proposal by delay.[8] The Stevenson proposal is important not only because it was the second instance of Randolph's efforts to trade with the enemy, but also because it shows that Davis was capable of misrepresentation.

It is likely that George W. Randolph would have persisted in similar efforts if he had remained. His successor in the War Office, James A. Seddon, thought it was "fatuous" that President Davis and Secretary of the Treasury Memminger did not "get cotton abroad . . . as a relief to the currency." Like Randolph, he was overruled when he proposed getting supplies from the enemy. Besides Davis's obstinacy, there were other reasons for the Confederacy's failure to persevere in attempts to trade for supplies with Yankees along the Mississippi River near New Orleans. Hoping to break free of scandals attributed to "Beast" Butler, the next U.S. Military Governor of New Orleans, Maj. Gen. Nathaniel P. Banks, forbade "trade or travel" beyond the Union lines in southern Louisiana. On the Southern side, enemy trade which Randolph had commenced via Butler's New Orleans ended when the Confederates pronounced anathema on the "Beast" after his General Order Number 28, which categorized ladies of New Orleans as "women of the town, plying their avocation," unless they were more polite to Union soldiers occupying the city.[9]

In advance of express authority to do so, Secretary of War Randolph had begun trading with the enemy in a limited, surreptitious fashion. Not only did the New Orleans men in the War Office encourage adoption of this policy, but they became instruments in its accomplishment. Simultaneously, their role in blockade-running led them to influence him to try to regain New Orleans by hook or by crook, by a combination of conventional and unconventional means.

George Randolph reposed great trust in five members of his staff who had important associations in New Orleans. Fate had sent Thomas L. Bayne to the War Office as the first of the quintet when Randolph appointed him adjutant to Col. Josiah Gorgas in the Bureau of Ordnance. Although merely accommodating Gorgas by giving this appointment to his son-in-law, who was recuperating from a wound received at Shiloh, Randolph quickly came to appreciate Bayne on his own merits. Not long afterwards, Gorgas secured the secretary's consent to buy two ships to serve as blockade-runners in procuring European ordnance. Their success caused Randolph to create the Bureau of Foreign Supplies to manage an enlarged operation. In doing so, he made a conscious departure from his predecessors' conventional placement of war contracts, which had sought to avoid "conflict and competition" among government agencies. To direct this Bureau, he needed someone of great integrity and special skill. Bayne was just this sort of man—a kind Randolph admired and whose career he liked to advance.[10]

Bayne was an able young lawyer from New Orleans who had neither smoked "segars" nor drunk alcoholic liquors while at Yale, where he had been not only a member of the Skull and Bones Society but also the valedictorian of his class. After reading law under John Slidell, he became a partner in Slidell's New Orleans law firm, where he soon became expert on foreign trade. Randolph first promoted Bayne to lieutenant colonel and then named him chief of the Bureau of Confederate Foreign Trade, in charge of the War Department's purchase and shipment of cotton, "of all ships employed by the government" and of the transportation of "all foreign supplies." The secretary also authorized him to establish depots at Wilmington, Charleston, and Mobile. Bayne staffed them with men he could rely upon: at Charleston, his brother-in-law, J. D. Aiken of Winnsboro and Charleston; at Mobile, his friend N. Harleston Brown of New Orleans; and at Wilmington, still another fellow citizen of New Orleans, James Madison Seixas, with whom he had served as an enlisted man in the Washington Artillery at Shiloh.

Of distinguished rabbinical antecedents, Seixas was a native of Charleston, who, in the eight years before the war, had made the cotton brokerage firm Gladden and Seixas "one of the leading cotton houses" of New Orleans. Like his older contemporary, Judah P. Benjamin, he was a relapsed Jew. On the battlefield of Shiloh, Seixas had been promoted "for gallantry" to the rank of lieutenant. His social status is apparent from his marriage after the war with a Miss DeConde, the sister of Mrs. Judah P. Benjamin, Mrs. P. G. T. Beauregard, and Mrs. Robert Adams.[11]

Bayne also persuaded Secretary of War Randolph to bring into the War Office itself two other scions of New Orleans: Joseph Denegre as a captain and Stephen Chalaron as a major. Their associations were very important in Randolph's plans. Joseph Denegre had been a commission merchant in the import-export business. At the age of twenty-three he was considered conscientious and worthy, but he was overshadowed by his father, James Denis Denegre, the president of the Citizens Bank of Louisiana. Stephen Chalaron had the unusual distinction of being listed as an "accountant" by profession in the New Orleans city directories of the 1850s. If Randolph had recruited them only because of their ordinary, respectable pursuits, they at least would have strengthened his interest in taking an initiative about New Orleans. Because their temperament was adjusted to the hypocritical disguises of Latin carnival, they strengthened his propensity to act with some deviousness. The five formed what amounted to a New Orleans coterie. Of this quintet, Bayne, Chalaron, Denegre and Seixas as enlisted men in the city's celebrated Washington Artillery already had won the status of minor heroes in the Battle of Shiloh.[12]

The fall of New Orleans at the end of April was one of a series of Southern catastrophes in the first half of 1862. There was nothing constructive the Confederate leaders could do about it at once. Not only did Union forces invest the rail hub of Corinth in northern Mississippi at the end of May, take Memphis by gunboats and troops at the end of June, but they also occupied Baton Rouge from June to August. These events delayed the Southern government from making a considered response to the loss of its chief port until midsummer. These disasters required a revamping of the Confederate command structure between the Alleghenies and the Gulf of Mexico. When in June of 1862 Gen. Robert E. Lee assumed command of the Army of Northern Virginia, he no longer had time to be chief presidential military advisor. The preceding months had laid the basis for a working relationship between Secretary Randolph and President Davis. Because Randolph now did not always have to give ground to Lee or to share the president's ear with another military leader, his scope was enhanced. The way was open for Davis and Randolph to collaborate in the evolution of policy for other portions of the Southern republic, especially those which lay west and south of the Appalachian mountain ranges.

It was in harmonious collaboration that at the same time they also set the stage and assigned roles for a campaign to rewin New Orleans. Reshuffling Confederate commanders and redefining theaters of war, the two leaders created two departments: the Department of Mississippi and Western Tennessee under Lt. Gen. John C. Pemberton and the Trans-Mississippi Department to be commanded by Lt. Gen. Theophilus Holmes. Within the latter was the District of Southwestern Louisiana under Maj. Gen. Richard Taylor. Davis and Randolph were in general agreement concerning strategic goals for the West and on Taylor as its new supreme commander in fact, if not in name. Taylor's clear metes and bounds were the Mississippi River north of New Orleans, the Red River on the north, the Sabine River on the west and the Gulf on the south. From the so-called Isle of Orleans to the Gulf, there was marshy land on all sides of the several estuarial mouths of the Mississippi, which later caused confusion of boundaries. On the east bank of the Mississippi a tangle of military jurisdictions, rank, and precedence persisted until mid-October, when Davis and Randolph consolidated the geographical commands previously held by Maj. Gen. Earl Van Dorn in the District of Mississippi, Maj. Gen. Sterling Price at Vicksburg, and Brig. Gen. Daniel Ruggles in the District of Eastern Louisiana, by sending John C. Pemberton to Vicksburg to command the Army of the West with his new rank of lieutenant general to insure his supremacy of rank in the Mississippi-Tennessee department.

To alleviate tensions which could result from too strict a definition of departmental boundaries or the strict supremacy of rank, Secretary Randolph issued on October 27, 1862, an order to Holmes, giving him conditional authority to cross to the east bank and to direct combined operations. There the matter rested until mid-November.[13]

In the summer of 1862 Davis and Randolph were friendly collaborators. Advocating social efficiency through centralized planning, Secretary Randolph already had influenced Davis to adopt new ways both of raising troops and of making the war economy work. In their planning to rewin New Orleans, they agreed on broad, general, preliminary moves. George Randolph assumed much authority and showed much persistence in advocating what may be called the Randolph-Davis Plan. The president, however, never agreed to details interpolated by the secretary, and he effectively ended any real implementation of it in the autumn of 1862. The fact that very few Civil War historians have given serious consideration to the possibility of a Confederate effort to recapture New Orleans enhances the reasons to examine the Randolph-Davis Plan. It is important to show that Secretary Randolph and President Davis formed an incomplete plan to liberate its greatest port, that they considered utilizing both conventional armed forces and unconventional fifth-columnists, that they made an unprecedented effort to keep their plan secret, and, finally, that the shortage of Confederate troops ultimately compelled its abandonment.[14]

Beyond doubt Randolph's interest in New Orleans had been whetted by his Creole recruits in the War Office. His proposals to open up trade with the enemy were both a prelude to and part of the Randolph-Davis Plan to recover New Orleans. Although during the third quarter of 1862, New Orleans proper had a Union garrison of only 250 men within an irregular circle of defenses inherited from the Confederates, the city's Union conquerors could call on 15,000 troops stationed elsewhere in Louisiana and a squadron of the United States Navy. This was so substantial a defensive force that the Confederates would need much more than surprise to overcome Butler.[15]

There is ample record for the beginnings of the Randolph-Davis Plan by the end of June, 1862, when the secretary of war issued orders to Maj. Gen. Richard Taylor after the latter's conference with President Davis. These orders contained the magic phrase "to begin preparations for an attack on New Orleans." Furthermore, Randolph ordered three other commanders to send detachments to assist Taylor. In doing this, he showed his own support and that of President Davis for fluidity in concentrating troops, irrespective of geographical boundaries, political or military. As it turned out, the pressure of other events prevented any strengthening of the four columns of conventional forces intended for

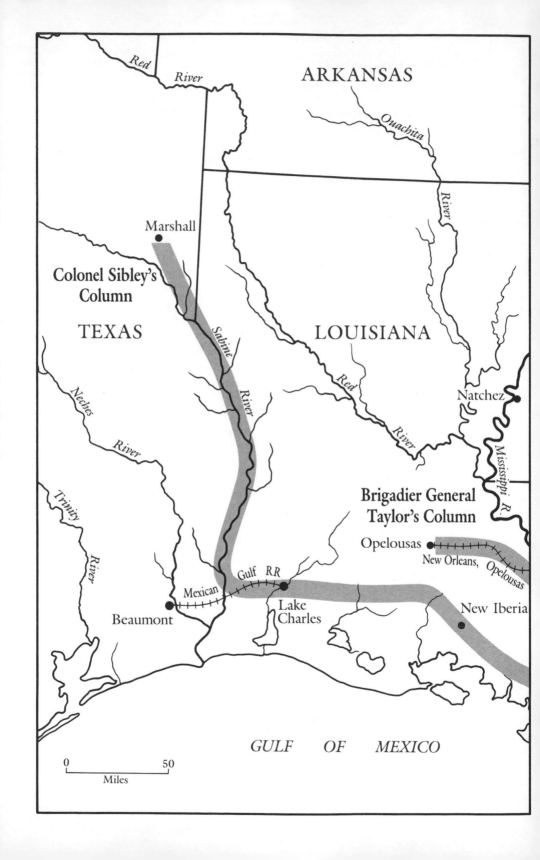

# Putative Designation of Columns to Liberate
# New Orleans (Randolph-Davis Plan, 1862)

*Mississippi*

*River*

Vicksburg

MISSISSIPPI

ALABAMA

RR

Jackson

**Brigadier General
Ruggles's Column**

New Orleans, Jackson & Great Northern

*Pearl*

*Alabama R.*

Baton
Rouge

*River*

Mobile

Biloxi

Lake
*Pontchartrain*

**Colonel Forney's
Column**

*& Great Western RR*

New
Orleans

*Verret
Canal*

*GULF*

*OF*

*MEXICO*

*Barataria
Bay*

the march on New Orleans. Chief of these events that came first to overshadow and then to obviate the proposed New Orleans campaign was the Confederacy's need to use available troops to protect its railroad net—especially its crucial junctions where Mississippi, Tennessee, and Alabama met. That there were not also enough troops available for the Confederates to have made an assault on New Orleans in the early autumn of 1862 has dissuaded military historians from appreciating how Secretary Randolph expected to compensate for conventional deficiencies. In this instance—as well as in the larger goal of winning the war— Randolph was willing to consider resort to unconventional, conspiratorial, revolutionary means. In addition to authorizing Taylor to lead his own and to direct three other columns against New Orleans, Randolph hoped to use the pretext of trading with the enemy to cloak the organization within New Orleans of a fifth column that would seize the city. As Gerald M. Capers pointed out in his *Occupied City: New Orleans Under the Federals, 1862–1865,* perhaps the best reason for giving credence to such a conspiratorial scheme was the fact that General Butler in August of 1862 withdrew Union troops to New Orleans from elsewhere in Louisiana because he feared "a counterattack supported by internal revolt."[16]

Geographically, Louisiana can be considered as a state of five parts. Eastern Louisiana is the one-fifth situated east of the Mississippi and north of Lake Pontchartrain, comprising, besides the cities of New Orleans and Baton Rouge, the "Florida" parishes of the state. The northern two-fifths of the state lies west of the Mississippi and north of the Red River. Southwestern Louisiana lies west of the Mississippi and south of the Red River to the Texas border on the Sabine River—an area including the Trans-Mississippi faubourgs of New Orleans, prosperous farms and towns along the Red River. It also comprises the bayous, fenlands, and marshes adjoining the mouth of the Mississippi south of New Orleans. How can one divide an estuarial delta? It has a unity of its own. The euphemism "the Isle of Orleans" has an undeniable rationality to even the casual visitor, as George Randolph had been in the 1850s. The fictive isle, that stretch of uncertain ground between the Mississippi and Lake Pontchartrain, has vague, terraqueous, undefined boundaries. The personal interviews between President Davis, Secretary Randolph and General Taylor were so unusual that it is obvious that one of their motives was to maintain secrecy. In giving him verbal instructions, they "specially charged [him] with the command of the troops serving in the southern part of the state," and they generally ordered him to maintain communications with militia, partisan rangers, and the nearby commands of Van Dorn east of the Mississippi and Holmes near the Arkansas-Louisiana border. Clearly, the president and secretary of war worked together to clear the Confederate administrative path for the recapture of New Orleans. The War Department also augmented Taylor's forces by ordering General Forney to send two regiments of Louisiana troops from Mobile and General Sibley to send troops from Marshall, Texas. That Holmes was nominally Taylor's superior was offset by the facts that Holmes was neither close by, able, nor aggressive. President Davis personally enjoined Van Dorn to confer with and aid Taylor and Holmes. In ordering the concentration of these conventional forces for the coming campaign to recover New Orleans, Davis and Randolph set no timetable. After events substituted Major General Ruggles for Van Dorn, neither Davis nor Randolph expected any Confederate opposition to Taylor's supremacy. In designating Taylor commander for all of southern Louisiana, they unofficially designated him liberator-to-be of New Orleans. Remarkably, Taylor omitted from his *Memoirs* mentioning this mission, even though it might have given him claim to great fame.[17]

From this point the views of the president and secretary diverged. The urgent need for the Confederacy to strengthen its forces on the Tennessee-Mississippi-Alabama border dictated a temporary suspension of the Randolph-Davis Plan. At the same time General Lee's advance into Maryland reduced the president's interest in pursuing a more active military policy in the West. When the urgency of these events dissipated, Randolph was ready to resume plans to liberate New Orleans. When General Ruggles briefly succeeded Van Dorn in command of the Mississippi Department, Taylor's western force and Ruggles's east-bank regulars and militia were in their places.[18]

Although these forces were small, there was the hope that an uprising in New Orleans might sustain the Randolph-Davis Plan. The effort to generate fifth-column activity within New Orleans had begun with Randolph's efforts to trade with businessmen there. The short-run benefit of "Beast" Butler's authorization of illicit trade might provide in the longer run a cover for the basis for an urban uprising to coincide with a conventional attack on New Orleans.

George Wythe Randolph had the mentality, the motive, and the power to lay the foundations for such a plan. Since childhood he had been made a dreamer of dreams and a schemer of schemes by having suffered a loss of status. That he had won wealth and honors before becoming secretary of war at the age of forty-four was an indication of further, rather than satiated, ambition. Younger than any other member of either the Davis or Lincoln cabinet, he saw the opportunity to take a leading role in achieving the national unification of an independent Southern republic. The model of Italy, Cavour, and Garibaldi was constantly before Randolph, who had followed closely the course of Italian liberation. He knew that dramatic calculation was almost as important as a hard fight in winning a difficult objective.[19]

While secretary, he had set in motion the acquisition of war goods in ways that were melodramatic, but for which the American Revolution had supplied a partial model in the form of Beaumarchais's dummy trading company. George and Mary Randolph were noted for getting their guests to play at charades. Having used dummy, Quaker guns to defend Yorktown and delay McClellan's advance on Richmond, it was not illogical that he believe that trade with greedy Union scoundrels could mitigate the effect of a powerful blockade and that a Creole uprising could help restore New Orleans to the South. The Confederate secretary of war was capable of serious use of what others may have thought merely theatrical tricks.[20]

Was it possible that Randolph might lead President Davis into taking unconventional steps to regain New Orleans? As it turned out, Davis balked. One can appreciate his caution. After all, the citizens of New Orleans had not shown in April of 1862 that they desired to risk their lives and property against Admiral Farragut's ships and marines. If the Confederacy were unsuccessful in a premature attempt to recapture the city, the domestic and foreign repercussions would be terrible. Yet, one must also recognize that to postpone too long such an attempt could place its success forever beyond accomplishment. The Southern loyalty of many men and women in New Orleans could not alone make a successful revolt. Although we will never know whether there was any real chance that Randolph and the New Orleans coterie in the War Office could have converted merchants of contraband into fifth-column allies, they were never put to the test. We must recognize, however, that the Randolph-Davis Plan to liberate the South's greatest port, although never carried out, was the boldest, most daring stratagem of George W. Randolph as secretary of war.

In assessing the importance of New Orleans to the Southern republic, George Randolph may have profited from comparing Jefferson's pre-1790s globe to contemporary maps. In looking at Italy, he must have observed how the House of Savoy's possession of Genoa after 1815 made possible what, during the ancien régime, the combined Piedmontese ports of Nice, Bordighera, and Ventimiglia had not—the ability to receive or dispatch logistical supplies in sufficient quantity to maintain an army. Similarities between the geopolitics of Piedmont-Sardinia and of the Confederacy must have struck him forcibly. No number of minor ports could equal the possession of a major port. If the South could recover New Orleans, it might be able to obtain from abroad what it needed in foodstuffs and munitions not merely to survive, but to win its independence.[21]

Circumstances were never more propitious for liberating New Orleans than in the autumn of 1862. To attempt by only conventional means to recapture the city would have been a daring and formidable mission, nearly impossible of accomplishment. The fewer troops the Confederacy could concentrate against New Orleans in a conventional military campaign, the more vital became the need for and the extent of an insurrection within the city. Any plan to retake New Orleans, however, had to depend on conventional troops to do the heaviest fighting. But neither an outside nor inside force could do the job alone. To orchestrate these contingencies required secretive planning. Randolph's disappointing experience in attempting secrecy when Stonewall Jackson moved from the Valley of Virginia to Richmond in the spring of 1862 had hardened his already secretive disposition. He and the president shared with the smallest number of persons possible their joint, preliminary plan to liberate New Orleans. Without specifically authorizing the organization of a fifth column, Randolph on his own went far in structuring details of the preliminary plan.[22] Bayne and the other New Orleans men in the War Office had the potential for making a much greater contribution to the War Office than getting war supplies from foreigners and Yankees. By employing New Orleans merchants in a contraband trade, they might forge links with persons inside the city to join in its liberation from the Union occupation. If there were a plot to free the excitable Creoles of New Orleans, if Davis were to be its Victor Emmanuel and Randolph its Cavour, who would be its Garibaldi?

Maj. Gen. Richard Taylor was well suited for this role. As President Zachary Taylor's son, his name commanded respectful recognition. After having grown up on army posts and been tutored in Massachusetts, "Dick" Taylor had studied briefly at Edinburgh, in France, and at Harvard before taking a B.A. at Yale in 1845. He had managed Mississippi cotton and Louisiana sugar plantations between 1850 and 1861. Originally a Whig, he had become a Democrat in the 1850s. He was a late convert to secession. As colonel of the Ninth Louisiana Infantry he had come in July of 1861 to Virginia to fight under Stonewall Jackson in the Valley Campaign. Ill during the Seven Days Battle before Richmond, he had directed his troops from an ambulance.[23]

Davis and Randolph took advantage of Taylor's presence in Richmond to give him explicit, verbal instructions whose secrecy gave them added import. Rather than risk interception or a leak of orders, President Davis ordered Taylor's colleague Van Dorn to get information from Taylor when he passed through Vicksburg. Having transmitted to him the president's orders, Taylor proceeded to Opelousas, Louisiana, whither the Confederate governor, Thomas O. Moore, had retired when Farragut approached New Orleans. He found that Moore could give him "little" help other than to place "several small bodies of state troops" under his command. Taylor sent word of his arrival at Opelousas to his nominal superior, General Holmes, with the statement that he hoped for mutual cooperation. After "many days" for the passage of communications, Holmes replied from Arkansas that he could provide Taylor "no assistance." Although Taylor was encouraged by the arrival from the east of some of the troops that had been promised him, he lamented that they were only two "skeleton" regiments and four batteries of artillery. When Maj. J. L. Brent, who had served together with George Randolph on Magruder's staff at Yorktown, arrived, bringing additional arms, Taylor quickly appointed him chief of artillery. Undismayed by his lack of regulars, Taylor addressed himself "to the heavy task of arousing public sentiment." Fortunately, there was some base upon which to build. In May of 1862 Maj. Gen. Mansfield Lovell had proposed to Governor Moore that they organize a force of five thousand men to aid a corps of partisan rangers in confining Union forces to New Orleans, with hopes of sparing the countryside from depredation and of exposing the northern soldiers to deadly summer fevers. Meanwhile, General Butler withdrew his troops from Baton Rouge in order to strengthen New Orleans and to send a four-thousand-man expedition against Donaldsonville and its vicinity.[24]

On August 20, 1862, Taylor wrote Ruggles, who had succeeded Van Dorn as commander of the Mississippi Department, that he was "about to undertake an expedition which I anticipate will place me in possession of the Opelousas Railroad up to the vicinity of Algiers." It is clear that from the start Taylor was entrusted with the chief responsibility for restoring New Orleans to the Southern republic. The terrain of the Mississippi River's west bank offered better opportunity to attack the city. Not only was Taylor given a virtually independent command, but Secretary Randolph ordered Brig. Gen. J. H. Forney at Mobile to send Taylor two Louisiana regiments by shallow-draft steamboats across Lake Pontchartrain. At the same time Richmond ordered Brig. Gen. Henry Sibley to send to Taylor troops from his brigade at

Marshall, Texas. In good time Sibley reported that he was preparing to march "towards New Iberia," the point about halfway between New Orleans and the Gulf of Mexico specified by General Taylor.[25]

Taylor's explicit authority over "southern Louisiana" gave him such broad scope that he might be excused if he construed it to include the city as part of the Isle of Orleans. Thus, he could bypass the technical superiority in rank of generals Pemberton or Holmes. Of the many preconditions for retaking New Orleans, Davis and Randolph had provided the conventional, essential foundations: "sending troops . . . [without] delay"; creating a diversion to draw off part of the New Orleans garrison; and finding a capable, charismatic military leader to whom Louisianians might rally in a campaign that would be as much one of self-determination as of liberation by an army.[26]

Self-determination was the unconventional part of George Randolph's melodramatic scheme to liberate New Orleans. Because President Davis never intended such a goal, Randolph's distinctive contribution to the plan was never perfected, much less executed. Possible models for Confederate instigation of riots in New Orleans were the Parisian riots that had introduced the French revolutions of 1830 and 1848. The French army's preoccupation in Algeria, more than the riots, had made revolutionary success possible. Although we do not know whether George Randolph had studied Aaron Burr's conspiracy closely,[27] we may surmise that he knew something about it. Could planning a Creole conspiracy be kept secret enough to achieve surprise in New Orleans?

The secretary of war exploded in anger when in the late summer of 1862 Maj. Gen. Daniel Ruggles, the commander of the District of Eastern Louisiana, sent him an uncoded telegram seeking authority to lead the way into New Orleans. Not only had neither the secretary nor the president ever confided in Ruggles, but they now could not be sure that their interest in retaking the city was still secret. Randolph furiously reprimanded the brigadier and arranged for Lieutenant General Pemberton to supersede him and establish his headquarters at Vicksburg.[28] Randolph gave Pemberton specific orders: "If a favorable opportunity [should] offer for an attack on New Orleans, you will avail yourself of it, and act in concert with Major General Richard Taylor, who commands the District of Louisiana west of the Mississippi. You will communicate with him as speedily as possible and concert with him a joint plan of operation for the defense of the river and the capture of New Orleans."[29]

When Ruggles compounded his disgrace by sending to Richmond by messenger his own detailed plan to retake New Orleans, Randolph reprimanded him for this uninvited initiative. In the first place, the universal demand for troops was exceeded only by their legitimate need everywhere. When Ruggles requested that General Forney send him Louisiana regiments from Mobile, he was asking for the same troops whom Randolph had just ordered to assist Taylor. Similarly, the luckless brigadier's request for troops from Van Dorn's troops in northern Mississippi ignored the fact that they were desperately needed there. Worse than Ruggles's asking to command the campaign secretly promised to Taylor and for troops secretly promised elsewhere was the possibility of scaring Davis away from the Randolph-Davis Plan. To raise questions about military boundaries or to entertain a move that might risk the safety of civilians might divert the president from proceeding with the Randolph-Davis Plan. Worst of all was the risk that the enemy learn of Ruggles's claim that inside New Orleans were "loyal men in large numbers under arms [who] will cooperate with our troops." Faced with such a potential breach of security by Ruggles, Randolph and his subalterns from New Orleans could take little comfort in Creole reports that, not only was the Federal occupation force in disarray, but that "Butler's spies are all asleep."[30]

As with the Burr Conspiracy half a century before, there could be no uprising by civilians in New Orleans until a part of the garrison was lured out of the city. Burr's coconspirator, Gen. James Wilkinson, had marched his troops to the frontier in 1806.[31] Algiers was the first faubourg of New Orleans on the west bank of the Mississippi. Although it contained the U.S. Navy Yard and the northern entrance of Vernet Canal to Barataria, its main importance was as the westward railroad terminus for New Orleans in a day when there was no bridge across the lower Mississippi. In the 1870s the Opelousas and Great Western would evolve into the Texas Pacific Railway, which with the Southern Pacific spanned half a continent. When General Taylor did move toward Algiers in the third quarter of 1862, troops were drawn out of New Orleans. The precondition for a combined attack and a civilian coup d'etat had been met. As had been the case in the Burr Conspiracy, support by merchants and by youths of Creole families was essential to the capture of the city. Nonetheless, the military force had to be strong enough to embolden the disarmed civilians to take up their cudgels and paving stones.[32]

Thanks to Secretary Randolph's elite recruitment, the New Orleans coterie provided the War Office with planners experienced with blockade runners, unscrupulous merchants, and soldiers of fortune who might help a self-determination effort from selfish, rather than patriotic, motives. Randolph's proposal to trade with the enemy had opened up the possibility of not only enlisting pro-Southern merchants, but also of enticing or blackmailing unwary Northern merchants to take part in a liberation movement. Although unlikely, it was not inconceivable that some Yankee merchants might even welcome an uprising against General Butler in order to punish him for giving his brother Andrew J. Butler a near monopoly of the city's trade.[33]

The most important New Orleans businessman likely to conspire to restore New Orleans to the Southern republic was James Denis Denegre (1812–65), the father of Capt. Joseph Denegre in the War Office at Richmond. The Denegres had emigrated in the eighteenth century from France, first to Saint Domingue and then to Southampton County, Virginia. After the Nat Turner Insurrection, James Denis Denegre had removed to New Orleans in 1838. He had been welcomed into Creole society in the 1840s upon his marriage with Louise Sylvanie Blanc, whose father Evariste Blanc was a prominent businessman. James Denis Denegre had been a commission merchant until 1853 when he became president of the Citizens Bank of Louisiana. His oldest son James gradually had assumed direction of the family business. As president of the Citizens Bank of Louisiana, James Denis Denegre was "one of the best-known financiers of the South." He had achieved a form of immortality by issuing his bank's ten-dollar bills with the French word "Dix" on one side, thus providing the best explanation for the designation of the South as the land of "Dixie."[34] The Denegre family represented the best of nineteenth-century New Orleans, which took pride in the openness of a white society that embraced an English-speaking majority of Southerners, a considerable Creole population of Frenchmen, Spaniards, Irishmen, and Germans, and resident foreigners; Roman Catholics, Protestants, and Jews; both old and new money; French opera and bilingual newspapers and courts of law.

A second cause for James Denis Denegre's claim to fame rested upon the story that General Butler ordered his banishment from New Orleans.[35] Butler caused a furor by seizing the silver bullion of Denegre's bank, which had important foreign correspondent banks, such as Anthony Hope and Company of Amsterdam and London and Dupossier et Compagnie of Paris. It always had been concerned with foreign exchange. Professing to fear a "run upon the banks by the rabble," President Denegre in February of 1862 deposited in the custody of the Dutch Consul, a Frenchman named Amadée Conturie, $800,000 of silver bullion, a number of New Orleans and Mobile bonds, and the steel plates for printing bank notes. General Butler respected neither The Netherlands' flag nor the consul's person in taking possession of these valuables. Denegre also attempted to secure another large amount of specie by the expedient of selling for his own and other New Orleans banks $716,196 worth of coin to the Parisian bank, Dupossier et Compagnie, payable in draughts on Paris or Le Havre. In actuality, the coin did not move further from the New Orleans banks than the French consulate, whence Butler soon seized it.

Embarrassed by Butler's unauthorized reversal of the United States' historic principle that a neutral flag provides protection for property, the Lincoln administration relieved Butler of his command, restored the specie to its owners and apologized to the governments of France and The Netherlands. On December 16, 1862, Butler was superseded by Gen. Nathaniel P. Banks, who undertook to prohibit profiteering and trade with the enemy on the one hand and to conciliate Creole society on the other. He released more than a hundred political prisoners and allowed "registered enemies" to leave the city. In the process, he quashed Butler's banishment of Denegre. When the latter reported to Banks that Butler had arbitrarily forbidden specie redemption of banknotes, he won from the unwary new commander permission for New Orleans banks to pay specie to their clients upon demand. Before Banks could change his mind, Denegre departed for France, carrying with him his friends' as well as his own specie.[36]

Randolph's resignation as secretary of war marked an end to plans to liberate New Orleans. Although his successors did not dismantle Taylor's force, they did not call upon it to execute any but limited, conventional goals. Nor did they authorize the New Orleans coterie in the War Office to expand its management of blockade-running to include trading with the enemy.

In harmonious concert Secretary Randolph and President Davis had begun plans to recover New Orleans. From beginning to end, Davis contemplated a conventional military advance on the city. Their plans were interrupted first by events on the Tennessee-Mississippi border, which siphoned off troops on the east bank of the Mississippi, and then by the Sharpsburg campaign. Although Randolph energetically resumed his planning for the liberation of New Orleans, Davis did not. Probably influenced by the New Orleans coterie, Randolph from beginning to end placed importance on unconventional factors. President Davis seems to have had no part in Randolph's scheme to nurture a fifth column in New Orleans on trade in contraband cotton.

Although Randolph had been distressed by the scorched earth

policy at Hampton in 1861, he had recognized its military necessity. We cannot know whether he would have countenanced a Confederate bombardment of New Orleans from Algiers. Perhaps only a threat to do so would have thrown Butler's occupation troops into a frenzy to throw Taylor back. Such boldness by the Confederates might have compensated partially for the lack of troops by offering a chance of success to an urban uprising like those of Paris in 1830 and 1848. Caught between a Creole uprising and Taylor's army near Algiers, Benjamin F. Butler would have been faced with the choice of fighting in the streets or abandoning the city.[37] George Wythe Randolph's scheme demonstrates how far, in order to win the war, he and his elite advisors were willing to flirt with unconventional, daring means. Had they been successful, it is conceivable that the Southern republic might have got from the United States and abroad enough food, clothing and arms to protract the war.

Even if the Southern republic had not regained New Orleans, Union distress and reprisals there would have been an important propaganda victory—especially so far as France was concerned. French cultural and economic interest in New Orleans had been enhanced by France's intervention in Mexican affairs. Indeed, at this time Mexican officials feared a Franco-Confederate conspiracy. If the Union forces did not act with restraint in dealing with a Creole uprising within the francophone city, what would the French warships in the Caribbean and Gulf of Mexico do? To demonstrate that it might be suicidal for the French to try to emulate Farragut's ascent of the Mississippi to New Orleans, General Butler ostentatiously showed to the commander of a French warship how he had strengthened the river's forts.[38]

Secretary of War Randolph's plan to retake New Orleans also demonstrates how a bureaucratic elite, unlike more cautious elected officials, can secretively manipulate levers of power and break rules in the hope of attaining a dangerous goal. Few would deny that there were high stakes to be won in a complicated and desperate gamble to liberate New Orleans. Before November of 1862 it had not become clear that the secretary of war's and the president's views concerning New Orleans diverged and that Randolph's way would not be Davis's way. The requirements of the Army of Northern Virginia and the shortage of troops needed to hold Tennessee had combined to postpone completing any plan by Randolph and Davis. Randolph did not resign as secretary of war because the uncompleted Randolph-Davis Plan was put aside, even though he believed that the president's temporizing was a fair indication that Davis did not intend to carry the plan through to completion. A more serious cause for his resignation was his concern about Davis's prolonged, indecisive responses to his proposals to trade cotton for food and to deal forcefully with the problem of permissive desertion by soldiers. It was logical that the ailing Randolph questioned whether he as Confederate secretary of war had any substantial discretionary authority.

# CHAPTER 12

## Randolph's "Factitious" Resignation

There is some truth in Samuel Eliot Morison's remark that President Jefferson Davis had a "perverse knack of infuriating the gentlemen who tried to work for him,"[1] but George Wythe Randolph's collaboration with him long seemed to be so amicable that it would have been unlikely that Randolph consider resigning as secretary of war. If there were subliminal differences between them, it seemed that neither would have professed more than mild irritation at the other. Each was so private a man that he turned an uncommunicative face to the world. Appearances of Davis's and Randolph's compatability proved to be misleading.

When Secretary Randolph proposed to the president unconventional plans concerning foreign sales of cotton to obtain capital, trading cotton to the enemy for bacon and other supplies, and sponsoring fifth-column activities, Davis was so unaccustomed to hearing such disturbing, perplexing matters that he must have been confounded. Less than six months earlier, Secretary of War Benjamin formally had reported to him in diametrically opposite, optimistic terms. Even though Davis eventually accepted from Randolph's successor some of what Randolph had proposed, he temporized in the summer of 1862 in frequent, protracted, decisionless conferences at the White House or the president's office. Most of these conferences were devoted to the president's review of detailed, routine business that exhausted Randolph's mind and body.[2] Ultimately the ill and overworked Randolph cracked, not having strong enough "nerves"[3] to stand the tension which developed between him and the president. As we shall see, he contrived a way to resign without being a weakling, a poor loser, or a spoiler.

As Randolph mastered the routine of the War Office, President Davis had granted, and the secretary assumed, increasing authority. Even the secretary's critical clerk J. B. Jones conceded that Randolph influenced Davis to devote more attention to evolving a new Confederate policy for the Mississippi valley.[4] With consternation, Randolph realized that his and the president's agreements were only tentative, that his rapport with Davis was on a strategic rather than a logistical level, that Davis was not really interested in logistics, and that their agreements were in principle only. Randolph and Davis simply did not make a good team because of their different temperaments. Randolph was not a man of much patience, having, as his mother had said, "weak nerves." Although suffering from a wasting disease, he maintained for at least three months an outer calm that belied his rising irritation with President Davis. To him it appeared that the president drew back at the last minute from decisions as frequently as giving a concurrence so belated as to lose many of the potential advantages.[5]

George W. Randolph came to question how far for his own sake and for the sake of the country he ought to go in repressing his exasperation with the president's "arrogance" or haggling over details. If he were ever going to establish a rapport better than that of master and servant, might not November of 1862 be the best time to do so? If Randolph considered such a step, he might have sought the advice of his confidantes. There is no surviving letter between him and his niece Molly on this subject. We cannot know what he told his wife, because of the absence of her papers before 1864. Two of Randolph's intimates, Josiah Gorgas and Judge Campbell, left no record either of his having complained or of having sought their advice before his resignation. But four others did leave records of Randolph's exasperation with Davis and of his decision to leave his office: Ned Anderson, Thompson Brown, Garlick Kean, and Jeff Randolph.

In late September of 1862 George Randolph told his old messmate Ned Anderson why he intended to resign. To Ned he voiced his sharpest criticism of Davis. When Anderson visited Richmond in the late summer of 1862, Randolph extended to him the president's offer to appoint him assistant secretary of war. Ned's request for George's advice was not denied. He recorded in his diary: "I had no wish from what Randolph told me to assume an office where I should be constantly interfered with by the Executive. Besides which, Randolph assured me that he himself intended to resign the secretaryship very soon, because of the arrogance to which he was constantly subjected by the President."[6]

Three others of Randolph's intimates received his frank opinions: his kinsman and chief of the Bureau of War, Garlick Kean; his brother Jeff; and his companion in arms in the Howitzers, Thompson Brown.

Soon after he resigned, he wrote the last two similar letters which may have been composed for oral circulation, and to whose contents Kean was surely privy. To those two George Randolph explained, "[President Davis] wished to impose restrictions which in my judgment were derogatory to the office and hurtful to the public service and to which I could not submit without sacrificing my self respect and the public interests. I deemed it my duty therefore to decline acquiescence in a misuse of the office and to retire from it. My continuance would have done the Country more harm than my resignation."[7] Kean declared that Randolph did not resign because of "any quarrel with the President, but by a difference of opinions." Not only did Randolph tell Kean that the president became so absorbed in details that he could not devote time to important matters, but he gave his opinion that Davis was "stubborn" and neither "a comprehensive man" nor one with an ability of "broad policy . . . of finance, strategy or supply."[8]

As late summer gave way to early autumn in 1862, Randolph lacked only a good pretext for resigning—a pretext that would make it appear that, in doing so, he challenged no person and no important principle. When he and Davis drifted into a contretemps in the Holmes Affair, the secretary determined to make it the occasion, if not exactly the cause, of his quitting his post.

On October 27, 1862, Secretary Randolph issued an order to Gen. Theophilus Holmes, giving him conditional authority to cross to the east bank of the Mississippi River from his own Trans-Mississippi Department in order to reinforce General Pemberton, commander of the Department of Mississippi, if the latter found himself hard pressed on the Alabama-Mississippi border with Tennessee. The secretary also sent an information copy of this order to Davis's office. When the president read it on November 12th, he immediately wrote Randolph a sharp letter of disapprobation for having "suggest[ed] the propriety" of Holmes's crossing the Mississippi River and taking command in General Pemberton's department. Such a violation of the boundaries of army departments, Davis wrote, "was not contemplated by me." Randolph replied calmly, saying that he was rescinding that portion of his order by sending Holmes a copy of Davis's letter. This was not enough for the Confederate president, who expostulated that "all orders and directions in relation to the movements and stations of troops and officers . . . and selection of persons to be appointed commissioned officers" must be sent via the president's staff "before action is taken." To this Randolph at once wrote a brief reply, stating that Davis's meaning was not clear to him and asking for elaboration. The secretary could have said, but did not say, that he and the president recently had established the principle not to confine commanders within geographic compartments, when they sent orders to Major General Taylor which expanded upon the strict definition of his Military District of Southwestern Louisiana to include "southern Louisiana" as well. With equal dispatch Davis responded. Without alluding to Taylor's orders, he said that the importance of moving an army and transferring a general should have "suggest[ed] the propriety of reference" to the president or the president's staff. Even in so routine an administrative function as commissioning officers, Davis asserted that he had "neither the power nor will to delegate" their appointment without "consultation in the first stage of selection."

Randolph's response was to submit his resignation on November 13, 1862. It is noteworthy that neither man waited for their biweekly meetings to discuss their differences.[9]

It does not seem that either the president or the secretary considered the Holmes Affair important in itself. It was evident to everyone by November of 1862 that liberation of New Orleans was a hopeless cause and that nothing much could be expected from Confederate forces on the lower Mississippi. Even to discuss the Holmes affair would have been pointless. Neither Randolph nor Davis availed himself of the opportunity to compromise. Whatever subliminal differences there were between them remained unidentified. If Davis's communications to Randolph seem sharp and testy, it was probably because he could not understand why the secretary seemed still to pursue the New Orleans plan that they tacitly had abandoned. It appears that Davis unwittingly paved the way for what Kean called Randolph's "factitious" resignation. In Randolph's case, the Holmes Affair was not the straw that broke the camel's back. It was not a case of Randolph's having the choice of eating crow or resigning, but he had been sharply and decisively overruled. For all of Randolph's elite qualities, he was only an appointee of the elected chief of state. He did what he already had told Ned Anderson he planned to do—resign.

It would be wrong to imply that Davis withdrew his confidence from Randolph because he determined that the secretary was too tricky. Davis appears to have been not only willing for Randolph to continue to serve in that capacity, but annoyed at having to select and break in a successor. From the vantage point of more than a century, it is clear that it was Randolph's contrivance that used the Holmes Affair to free both him and Davis from further attempts to make a mismatched pair work as a team. Randolph justified using the Holmes Affair as a pretext by saying that "my continuance would have done the Country more harm than my resignation." By the time that President Davis received Randolph's resignation, he knew that the cause was not very serious, that Randolph's mind was made up, and that "nothing remain[ed] but notice of the acceptance of your resignation."[10]

Although George Randolph had become disheartened by his inability to implement his policies and felt demeaned by Davis's "arrogance," this proud man did not resign in a huff. Only by recalling that Randolph was a criminal lawyer who possessed a conspiratorial nature can one perceive that he contrived his "factitious" resignation by using the Holmes Affair to produce a safe case for departing from the War Office.

The Richmond press was unanimous in lamenting George Wythe Randolph's resignation. The *Enquirer* wrote that he had "enjoyed the esteem of all" and that "his courtesy was unfailing, [that] his attention to duty [was] absorbing, and [that] he discharged his trust with much ability." The Richmond *Dispatch* was fuller of praise and speculation: Whatever

> may have been the cause or causes of his resignation, we are unable to say, but from all we know of the affairs of that department, we are induced to believe that the public has lost an able, upright, and most successful officer. No man can be blind to the fact that since his administration the affairs of the Confederacy have assumed an aspect that they never wore before. The army has obtained successes, and the resources of the country have been developed in a manner which attract the astonishment while they command the admiration of the world. That a large portion of these successes were due to the War Department, we hold to be incontestable. At least, it is certain that before he took charge of it, affairs wore a very different aspect. Mr. Randolph's name will go down in history in connection with one of its most splendid epochs.

The *Examiner* had less to say about Randolph than to condemn Davis: "Indeed, if cabinet ministers are to continue as mere automatons, it matters little by what names those machines are called."[11]

Even though the historian Burton J. Hendrick was wide of the mark when he said that George Randolph's resignation was the most exciting thing that occurred during his administration of the War Office, there is no doubt that it did produce a "profound sensation" in Richmond. So unexpected was it, that people were quick to look for hidden meanings. Already peevish with Davis, "most of the people seemed inclined to denounce the President." Believing that Randolph had acted either from foolishness or desperation, War Clerk Jones denied the assertion of Randolph's "friends [who] make it appear that he resigned in consequence of his being restricted in his action." Accepting at face value Jones's views, some historians mistakenly have concluded that Randolph was not equal to his job, a frail and dyspeptic Hercules who skulked in his tent.[12]

By placing the blame on misunderstood procedure, Randolph contrived that no person or policy be denegrated. Although his resignation removed the most zealous advocate of trading with the enemy and of liberating New Orleans, the time when those policies might have been viable was past.

It is hard to comprehend how John B. Jones in his *Rebel War Clerk's Diary* could have concluded that Randolph's resignation was either a "silly caprice" or a "deliberate purpose to escape a cloud of odium which he knew must sooner or later burst around him." Wisely Randolph had not made a confidant of Jones. The noncombatant clerk mistook Randolph the expert and charismatic leader for a grandee and dilettante. Uncomprehending of Randolph's elite recruitment of technocrats, the Jacksonian zealot in Jones sniffed odors of aristocratic nepotism. It is true that Randolph did take pride in fostering the careers of relatives such as Kean, Ruffin, and Talcott—but only because they lived up to his high standards. To Jones's disgust, he recruited, advanced, and defended men of Northern origin such as Josiah Gorgas, the Talcotts, and William M. Wadley, whose accomplishments as engineers placed them among the ablest Confederate leaders on the home front, despite their lack of patriotic gore.

It would be at least a half truth to say that George W. Randolph resigned because he was ill and overworked. As early as the autumn of 1861 he had realized that his condition was becoming serious enough to require transferring from a field command to a sedentary staff billet, but he believed his tuberculosis was arrested. It is true that in September of 1862 he had complained to the president of overwork. Even the unsympathetic J. B. Jones recognized from Randolph's "mass of wrinkles" that he was very frail.[13] Randolph had not bargained on endless presidential conferences. After his resignation, he told his friends that he had "grunted and sweated" so much as secretary that he was delighted to resume "the gentlemanly ease of private life." In retrospect it is easy to say that Randolph should have announced that illness was his reason for resigning as secretary of war, but to have done so would have ended a military career which he mistakenly expected to continue. He hardly can be criticized for accepting the best medical advice available in Virginia that he could stabilize his tubercular condition by limiting activities and avoiding chills and damps.[14]

If George Wythe Randolph had not resigned in the wake of the Holmes affair, it would have been only a question of time before some other incident became the pretext. Although he was a discreet man who did not join in Frank Ruffin's humorous appraisal of Davis, he doubtless was amused by the latter's quip that at first he had thought "Jefferson Davis was a *mule*, but a good *mule*." Randolph may have agreed with Kean that Davis was "jealous" of his "independent character," but it is almost certain that he would not have agreed with Anderson that Davis was a "*jackass*."[15]

Personal relations between George Wythe Randolph and Jefferson Davis were formal and correct without intimacy or friendship. Looking past the Victorian convention of formality in manner of addressing others, one can safely deduce that George Wythe Randolph would have gone to great lengths to avoid speaking or writing the Confederate president's first name. However, though Mrs. Varina Davis offended some F.F.V.s of her sex, she and Mary Randolph were friendly.[16]

Despite the brevity of his service as secretary of war, Randolph transformed the Department of War into the War Office, a technocratic bureaucracy of elites which presided over what amounted to a military-industrial complex. The fact that his successor, James A. Seddon, retained the organization and staff of Randolph's War Department proved that Randolph was correct in his prophecy that "the Army organization is so far perfected as to require little more than assiduous supervision." He believed that "Seddon's appointment [was] manifestly a declaration that the President intend[ed] to be his own Secretary, for Mr. Seddon's want of familiarity with military matters must make him dependent on the Presid[en]t." Similarly judicious was George Randolph's appraisal of Jefferson Davis:

> The President has not the time to discharge the duties of the [War] Office, nor is he well qualified to do so efficiently. He lacks system, is very slow, does not discriminate between important and unimportant matters, has no practical knowledge of the working of our military system in the field, and frequently mars it by theories which he has no opportunity to correct by personal observation, and in which he will not permit amendment from the experience of others. On the other hand he means well and understands the abstract principles of military organization. I do not therefore apprehend disaster from his absorption of the Office of Secretary of War.[17]

General Randolph does not appear ever to have commented on his successor, James A. Seddon. They possessed some similarities of background—social status, wealth, legal training at the University of Virginia, and capacity for modest scholarship. Lacking Randolph's military experience, engineering education, or experience with craftsmen and mechanics, the new secretary was fortunate to inherit Randolph's staff of technocrats. Seddon's deficiencies ended bold schemes from the War Office. He was content to do his duty as "his friend" President Davis defined it.[18]

To summarize Randolph's service as secretary of war, one must recall that he did not look upon his job merely as a housekeeping one. He created the Confederacy's national conscription. He instituted basic training for volunteers and conscripts. In conventional military matters, he became an able collaborator with President Davis in strategic planning warfare in the West. In reshaping the War Office to effect these goals, he brought in men whose education and professional experience in law, engineering and agriculture were of such high quality as to justify the word technocrat. To identify such recruits, he relied upon the F.F.V. and technocratic elites of which he was himself an outstanding example. Most important of all, he was willing to employ the consolidationist, technocratic means preferred by his constituent elites as the means best calculated to win Southern independence. No scruple prevented him from requisitioning goods or manpower in a program of national procurement and distribution of supplies that approximated nationalization. In a purposeful way he increased governmental intervention in economic affairs by construction and control of railroads. To relieve shortages, he fostered belated governmental control of foreign trade and attempted to trade with the enemy. His resignation as secretary of war was the combined result of his physical and mental exhaustion and of the frustration he felt in being badgered by a president who did not give serious consideration to his unconventional proposals to address the manpower and material needs in order to win Southern independence. Perhaps Edward A. Pollard regretted that Randolph and his recruits had not taken their places sooner, when he wrote in the earliest southern history of the Civil War: "the Confederates, with an abler Government and more resolute spirit, might have accomplished their independence."[19]

## CHAPTER 13

# *Wrecked in Health and Fortune,*
# *1864–1866*

Although the weather in Richmond during the early months of 1864 was not so severe as in 1863, when the temperature had fallen to ten degrees below zero and food shortages and overcrowding had contributed to a smallpox epidemic, it was, nonetheless, a hard winter. In February of 1864 there was a 20 percent increase in prices, the gas works suspended operations, and "Charcoal! Charcoal!" was the city's most often heard street cry.[1]

Ever since the summer of 1859, the Randolphs had been concerned about George Wythe Randolph's bronchial trouble. Its remissions had their peaks at Charlestown in 1859, at Big Bethel in the summer of 1861, at the War Office in the summer of 1862, and at Culpeper in the summer of 1863. His exchange of officialdom for the life of a private gentleman brought no lasting improvement in health to the forty-eight-year-old Randolph. Between the late summer of 1863 and that of 1864, his condition became so "wretched" that he consulted professors James L. Cabell and John Staige Davis of the University of Virginia Medical School. Diagnosing his to be a case of "chronic tubercule," they found that his right lung had partly solidified. Neither doctor speculated on how long Randolph had had the disease, nor did they know of its high incidence on the USS *Constitution,* on which he had served as a youth. They advised him to seek a better climate, take a sea voyage, and consult lung specialists in London. George Randolph procrastinated in acting on their advice. If he were pessimistic about the Southern republic, perhaps he could still help Virginia.[2]

He remained on close social and professional terms with his neighbors, the Gorgas and Bayne families. Although the Gorgases believed that "General Randolph [was] a most valuable man and the country

George Wythe Randolph in Ireland, 1865. (Courtesy of the Manuscript
Department, University of Virginia Library, Charlottesville, Va.)

[could] illy spare his resources at this critical time," they helped persuade him to accept a mission to England as a representative of the Bureau of Ordnance. He and Mrs. Randolph booked passage on a blockade runner out of Wilmington, North Carolina. On their departure from Richmond, Amelia Gorgas noted that he looked so "wretchedly" that she felt he "will never return to this country." Until the blockade runner could depart from Wilmington, the Randolphs visited there a former member of the Richmond Howitzers, James Burwell Ficklin, and his wife Fanny.[3] In running the blockade, the Randolphs' ship absorbed over a hundred shots. Fortunately the two were able to rest for several days at Nassau before taking passage, November 11, 1864, on the British steamer *Crusader* for Liverpool. It was so "rough" and "fatiguing" a crossing that Mary was seasick and George caught cold. On arriving at Liverpool, his voice and cough were "worse than when we left home." After he rested there for five days, General Randolph spent almost an equal length of time at Sheffield in attending to war goods for the Bureau of Nitre and Mining.[4]

Among the friends who welcomed the Randolphs to England, the foremost was John R. Thompson, who was now on the editorial staff of *The Index,* the Southern propaganda organ in England. He engaged quarters for them at London in the Burlington, where they remained for about a fortnight because of George's exhaustion. To repay kindnesses, the Randolphs entertained at a small dinner party the Confederate diplomatic commissioner, James M. Mason, and Capt. Fitzhugh Carter, both of Virginia; Capt. James D. Bulloch of Georgia, the naval procurement agent; William W. Corcoran, the pro-Southern banker and philanthropist; Allan Young, a British naval officer; and Thompson. Besides these and his doctors, George Randolph met with the Confederate commercial agents, Frazier Trenholm and Duncan F. McRae.[5]

Randolph could not shake off his cold. He lost his voice for a while, and he and Mary "rested" much. His medical history misled Doctors Ancill and Bagnell calmly to report that his bronchitis was a more serious threat than his tuberculosis, which they declared was arrested. Unfortunately, they gave him too great encouragement by advising that his lungs were "in a better state than last year," that the disease had "left the right lung entirely," and that the left one was "much less acutely attacked." They then "ordered" General Randolph to winter in the south of France, either at Cannes on the Mediterranean coast or at Pau in the Pyrenees, and to return for a checkup in the late spring of 1865. Before departing London, George wrote to Ellen and Joseph Coolidge greater "particulars" of their son Sydney's death in the Battle of Chickamauga on September 19, 1863, than he had been able to do when he had sent Sydney's pocketbook to her.[6]

Accompanied by John R. Thompson, the Randolphs left London on December 22, 1864, for Paris, via Dover and Calais. Together they inspected the Hotel Dessein at Calais where Thomas Jefferson and many celebrated people once had lodged. From the train shed at Paris they went immediately to their second-floor apartment in the Grand Hotel on the Boulevard des Capuchines and the Place du Nouvel Opera. Then enjoying its first flush of success, this hostelry was one of the brightest ornaments of the City of Light created by the Second Empire, even though the new opera house would not be completed for another six years. Although New Year's Day was dark and icy, George and Mary Randolph attended a Confederate dinner party at the house of Mr. F. P. Corbin on the Rue de Varennes in the Faubourg Saint Germain. Other guests were Como. James Barron, John R. Thompson, the Confederate diplomatic commissioner John Slidell, and, as special guest, Charles Stewart, a friend of the Randolph family and the uncle of the Irish patriot Charles Stewart Parnell. Well aware that the fortunes of the South gave no cause for confidence, the dejected company joined in Thompson's somber toast: "The New Year opens for us in sorrow. God grant it may close in joy." The Randolphs rested a week or ten days after their arrival before proceeding to Pau by easy stages. Foreswearing sightseeing, they deposited £500 sterling in the Paris branch of Charles Joyce and Company, the London merchant bankers whom Frazier Trenholm recommended as favored by the Confederate government.[7]

They left the city on January 3, 1865, spent the night at Angoulême, and proceeded to Bordeaux, where Randolph placed orders for Bessemer-process steel to be shipped via Liverpool, Halifax and Bermuda to Charleston, South Carolina. Reaching Pau on January 8, 1865, the Randolphs took lodgings at 4 Rue Montpensier.[8]

They were enthusiastic about Pau's natural beauty, finding in the Black Mountains and the foothills of the Pyrenees reminders of Albemarle and in the distant high Pyrenees "far more picturesque" scenery than in the Alleghenies. The historic countryside interested them. The Chateau of Pau had been the home of the youthful Henry of Navarre; it was then being restored by Violet-le-Duc; and the imperial court came there occasionally. The region possessed a tortuous and bloody history of wars between Romans and Goths, Moors and Christians, Albigensians and Catholics, English and French, Huguenots and Roman Catholics. Visiting English convalescents, foxhunters, and remittance men lent life to Pau's promenades, parks, Anglican Church, and casino, providing diversion for George and Mary Randolph during what they expected would be only a three-month stay. Conquering occasional "regret that shot and shell spared" him, George looked forward to returning to England for medical review at the end of May. He and Mary then hoped to see "something of the island and [to] visit . . . a friend in Ireland" before going home to Virginia. Still a Southern patriot, he declared: "It is intolerable to be absent at such a time, and sick or well I must tread again 'my native heath.'" George also often took occasion to acknowledge his love for and debt to Mary, saying that "by her incessant and intelligent nursing [she] keeps me afloat." Mary Randolph even wrote that, because she had heard so much about tuberculosis being arrested, "my reason bids me hope very much for an almost entire recovery."[9]

In early February of 1865, George Randolph wrote General McRae at London that he would inspect the Bessemer steel he had ordered at Bordeaux before its shipment. Soon after doing so, he suffered "the largest hemmorhage he ever had," followed by others that left him completely debilitated. Although still very feeble a month later, George still hoped to return to Virginia around September 1, 1865, unless it were clear that Union authorities considered him so "obnoxious" that he must be "arrested." Homesick as they were for "hot breads" and "an old Virginia breakfast," they resolved to make no firm plans until they consulted with compatriots at London and Paris. They also looked forward to spending "some time" at the French metropolis and becoming reconciled with his Coolidge relatives—Ellen, Joseph, and their son Thomas Jefferson Coolidge and his wife, the former Mehitable Appleton.[10]

While the news of the fall of Richmond had not been unexpected, the first, garbled report that Grant had burned the Confederate capital caused George unneeded excitement. Unexpected and more calamitous for the Randolphs was news of the bankruptcy of Charles Joyce and Company, with whom they had deposited most of their funds. George and Mary lingered at Pau, worrying about their precarious finances, while she fed him beef essence and wine whey. When they journeyed to London in June, the doctors advised that George was so much worse that he must postpone his return to Virginia until after another winter in the "bracing climate" of the Pyrenees, preferably at Bagnère de Bigonne, a spa forty miles east of Pau. It was a disconsolate and homesick George Wythe Randolph who wrote to his niece Molly that for him France had become so "flat, stale and unprofitable" that he would "rather be in a cabin on your mountainside . . . than the finest palace in Europe." Anxious for news of Albemarle, he begged Molly to "tell us what Sheridan did to you and to your Uncle Ben. We have heard it only in scraps. What Negroes went off and who behaved well. What injury did he do the canal? Is it reparable? What is the condition of the University? . . . What care I for the Black Prince or Henry IV or Roman or Goth, wrecked [as I am] in health and fortune, and without a country?"[11]

The Randolphs were not consoled when Ellen Coolidge wrote that her friend Samuel Hooper, a Boston abolitionist and member of the House of Representatives, advised that George Randolph spend another winter abroad, rather than face almost certain arrest in America. Awaiting Mrs. Coolidge herself at Paris, George Randolph's spirits rose to appreciate that "most magnificent of cities" and "metropolis of the civilized world." The onetime planner admired how "broad and magnificent boulevards" had been

> carried right through the heart of old Paris, sweeping away narrow, filthy streets and old fashioned houses to replace them with beautiful promenades lined with palaces. This operation has cost a mint of money and of course there has been a great rise of rents and an increase in the cost of living, but the French are consoled for this inconvenience, not only by the increased beauty of their darling city, but by the crowds of strangers attracted by her splendor and pouring a golden flood into Johnny Caporal's pocket. . . . Paris presents attractions to all ages; but if a man be poor in purse and sick at heart and in body, there is no enjoyment for him anywhere.

George Randolph believed that he would play at least a small part in rebuilding the Old Dominion. He wrote to Molly:

> Poor old Virginia in her chains occupies much more of my time and attention than the brilliant scene around me. I love to think . . . that she will rise to greater power and prosperity than she could have reached under the old regime. The necessity for increased exertion will nerve the rising generation and give them far more energy and enterprise than we possessed. Adversity either crushes or elevates a people, and I trust that we have too much strained to be crushed. We old folks have much suffering to encounter, but we mustn't discourage you young ones and kill your hopes by mourning the past. . . . Slavery, whether good or bad, is dead. Let us forget it and not be eternally haunted by its ghost. Free black labor is probably a mere transition to free white labor . . . in Virginia. Now that Cuffee is free to go where he likes, he will obey the law of supply and demand and go where his labor will be best paid; and I take it that the cotton and sugar and hot sun of the more Southern states will eventually draw him out of Virginia. Let us ease him off quietly, striving

to make the best use of him while he stays and wishing him a pleasant journey when he goes.

In vain did George Randolph attempt to recapture his sunny disposition and optimism. Sadly, he admitted that "my budget, like that of most of the Continental Powers, refuses even to balance. But all this would be nothing. I could make another [pile of wealth], if fortune had not literally taken me by the throat and thus paralyzed the very organ with which I work. . . . My individual prospects are gloomy and therefore I try to think as little about them as possible and trust to 'something turning up.'"[12]

The meeting of the Coolidges and Randolphs at Paris on August 4, 1865, was "quite a family reunion." George was pleased by his nephew Jefferson's kind welcome. He and Mary pretended not to notice that Joseph Coolidge was "absurdly stiff." For the time being, George proudly declined the ever-generous Joseph's offer of financial aid, saying he would need it more when he got home. "My fortune," he wrote Molly, "is pretty well swept."

> I had thirty thousand dollars in C. S. bonds. That of course is nil. . . . Mary lost six thousand in Mobile by the death and insolvency of a debtor. . . . She has as much left out there and I have some nine or ten thousand dollars of stocks in Richmond . . . in the stock of banking or insurance companies and in railroad bonds, [all of which] is probably gone. A lot in Richmond—worth a couple of thousand and a trifle in the shape of furniture are all we can count on. . . . Per contra, I owe about five thousand dollars borrowed for this trip, one half of which I lost by the bankruptcy of the merchant banker in whose hands it was.

George and Mary Randolph's British excursion in August and September of 1865 during a surcease from his illness was the time of their last happiness. They found Warwickshire "beautiful" and reveled in the glories of Stratford, Kenilworth, and Warwick Castle. They went to Liverpool, where they stayed with Morgan P. Robertson at Rumford Court, before crossing over to Ireland. The Randolphs visited two very different people in Ireland. One was John Stewart Parnell, the son of Septimia Randolph Meikleham's friend of Washington days, Delia Stewart. The other was the Duke of Devonshire, whose acquaintance George Randolph had made six years earlier when the nobleman visited Richmond in the retinue of the Prince of Wales. A few months after their Irish excursion, Mary Randolph suggested to a niece that she name her new home "Lismore . . . , the name of a beautiful castle in Ireland, the seat of the Duke of Devonshire[, situated near Cork on the

Black Water river and in the midst of a fox-hunting section where] the gentlemen are in red coats and top boots [and present] a gay scene." One of the pleasures of their British trip was seeing fellow Southerners, with whom they speculated on how much Confederate gold former Confederate foreign agents like Randolph had kept for themselves. Gladly Mary wrote: "No one knows" how much money was in their hands and hotly she denied that the former agents were dishonest, saying that "everyone thinks he might as well keep it as to give it to anyone else. They might be generous *and some are*. It is said [Judah P.] Benjamin has secured a good sum and Slidell through his son-in-law Erlanger who had, and kept, a million or two of francs."[13]

The one of the Randolphs' friends at London who had fallen from heroic to pathetic stature was Heros Von Borcke. He was no longer a young, dashing soldier of fortune. Rejected in 1864 for a Confederate cavalry command on account of lung trouble, he had gone to England, admitting that "the ball which I carry in my lungs . . . has broken my once so robust health." Disinherited by his Prussian father, he had lived on a small Confederate stipend for a vaguely defined military mission and on proceeds from his article entitled "The Principles and Issues of the American Struggle" published in *Blackwood's Magazine*. Not hopeful that Von Borcke could find any employment, Mary Randolph feared that he would drink himself to death.[14]

When the Randolphs went back to Pau, George for a while went on daily horseback rides, but he became lethargic. Mary was brave, but she exclaimed: "Oh, I am wretched about the future. I can see nothing ahead for us." It was a great boon to them both that Joseph and Ellen Coolidge came to Pau for the winter. Ellen and George were tonic for one another. Although Joseph's attitude thawed, and all four were silent or diplomatic about the events of the past five years, Mary confided to a relative in Virginia that there remained "a great gulf between me and every Northern-born person. Mrs. Coolidge has all the feelings and sympathies of the South one could wish for; but Mr. C. is bitter, as bitter as I am to the North, and I do assure you I feel more than I did a year ago. I [try] never say one word to him about North or South."[15]

In ruminating on "the abhorrence" with which Europeans regarded slavery, the general concluded that "it poisoned all sympathy for our cause and made even our friends find consolation in our downfall. We had friends in England, but on the Continent they might have been numbered on your fingers." He endorsed Von Borcke's essay in *Blackwood's Magazine,* which, in tracing causes of the American Civil War, emphasized the differences between the classes of immigrants that peopled the northern and southern states of the U.S.A. as the reason for New England's puritanism and blue laws and for southern cavaliers.[16]

Ellen Coolidge and George Randolph conversed with one another almost daily for the seven months of the winter and spring of 1865–66 about family, old times, and "our faith, our hopes, our religious aspirations." Their renewed closeness was one of both spirit and shared experience. She reminisced how she had carried him as a babe in arms and exclaimed how "honorable, noble and manly" his career had been. "As a boy, I never knew him to tell a falsehood or do a mean thing. He was always true and brave and good. Then his fine talents which he employed so well were done with such simplicity that he never seemed aware of his own superiority."[17]

Whether, how, and when to seek a pardon dominated George Randolph's mind. Molly Randolph from Virginia and Ellen Coolidge on the spot warned him not to think of returning to the United States before 1866, unless he was willing to be arrested. Ellen assured him that, if he waited, her abolitionist friend, Congressman Samuel Hooper, would present Randolph's petition for pardon. Although Randolph was daunted by the fact that there was no precedent for pardoning a U.S. citizen in absentia, he set about compiling reasons why his punishment deserved mitigation. He hoped for endorsements by Virginia unionists such as John Minor Botts and Alexander Rives because he had "discharged the former from prison and steadily resisted all importunities for the arrest of the latter."[18]

By February of 1866, Randolph decided to take the oath of allegiance during the summer before seeking pardon. He believed that, if he were arrested on landing in New York, his friends would be able to secure his parole on grounds of ill health. He hoped that his record of "no ill-treatment of prisoners" and of kindnesses to three specific ones from Massachusetts would help him return "without apprehension," to use the words of Congressman Hooper. George Randolph's former law partner, Thomas P. August, wrote that Virginia's provisional governor, Francis H. Pierpoint, had signed a petition that Randolph be allowed to return to the Old Dominion and had delivered it in person to U.S. Attorney General Henry Stanberry. Randolph declared that because he was in "absolute want," he wished to go home where he might "save something from the wreck of my fortune and m[ight] possibly make provision for my wife in case of my death. By remaining here, I shall condemn both her and myself to utter destitution." Bravely he asserted: "If I recover my voice, I shall have no difficulty."[19]

It is probable that the Coolidges took a hand in getting a U.S.

consular agent to visit Pau on April 19, 1866. He administered the oath of allegiance to George Wythe Randolph and promised to transmit Randolph's request for a presidential pardon. As it turned out, no action was ever taken on this petition. With the beginning of summer, the Randolphs went to Paris where they secured for less than $1.75 a day a "tiny" apartment on the Rue d'Alger so that he could spend mornings in the Tuilleries gardens. Every afternoon, he rode in Jefferson Coolidge's carriage in the Bois de Boulonge, where they amused themselves by observing discrepancies between the physical splendor and moral squalor of Napoleon III's Paris.[20] On August 16 Ellen and Joseph Coolidge saw George and Mary Randolph off from the Gare du Nord on their journey to England and America. The lithe girl that Ellen had been at Monticello was now a bent and bespectacled old lady, but she was still proud of her brother, whose infirmity rather than infancy now required her care:

> I have never seen anyone who had more than George the art of making friends, if that can be called an art which is pure nature. A simple, noble, manly character—an intellect of high order; manners calm, gentlemanly and distinguished; a temper at once firm and patient; considerable power of conversation; and an unmistakable stamp of integrity, truth and honour in every word, look and action. The dignified submission with which he has borne ill health, ill fortune, suffering and sorrow has produced a great impression on all who have seen and known him. He has been treated uniformly with an amount of respect and consideration which few people find. Wherever he has been, he has found warm and true friends and has received the most friendly and flattering attention.[21]

George and Mary Randolph stayed in England no longer than necessary for him to recoup a little strength for their voyage to New York in the first week of September 1866. Thence they went to Philadelphia, where three of George's sisters came to help Mary get him to Albemarle County. At first he was glad to get to Edgehill, where he enjoyed sitting out of doors and planning to resume his law practice at Richmond. Mary gave instructions that their house on Franklin Street be readied.

In October, however, George had a relapse, lost his voice, and never spoke again above a whisper. Mary had to wash and "almost dress" him. George's chief diversion was to read the Bible. The rector of Christ Episcopal Church drove out from Charlottesville to administer communion to him in bed. It was not until April 3, 1867, that George Wythe Randolph died. Surrounded by his wife and relatives, he recovered his voice enough to lament on his deathbed his former agnosticism and to admonish his relatives to profess Christianity. With his last breath, he exclaimed that he had seen Christ.[22]

Not long after General Randolph was buried at Monticello, his friend John Reuben Thompson, now an editor of the New York *Evening Post,* wrote the poem printed at the end of this book. A few days after George Wythe Randolph was interred, his widow wrote to Robert E. Lee, conveying the dying Randolph's friendly esteem and remarking on the similarities of their opinions about Virginia and Virginians. General Lee replied that he lamented that Randolph had died before Lee could pay his former colleague an intended visit. He concluded by writing: "The recollection of his esteem and friendship will always be dear to me, and his kind remembrance in his long and painful illness will be gratefully cherished. His worth and truth, his unselfish devotion to right, and exalted patriotism will cause all good men to mourn the country's loss in his death; while his gentle, manly courtesy, dignified conduct, and Christian charity must intensely endear him to those who knew him."[23]

There was little newspaper comment on George Wythe Randolph's death. A. M. Keiley, the editor of the Richmond *Examiner,* wrote a laudatory obituary that has disappeared. For the Richmond *Whig* John C. Shields wrote a long editorial praising George Randolph's "purest and most exalted character . . . great abilities and superior attainments." Identifying him as Thomas Jefferson's grandson, Shields gave him credit for organizing the Richmond Howitzers and for firing the first shot in the Battle of Big Bethel. He praised Randolph for performing "onerous and trying duties . . . in a manner more satisfactory to the public than any one before or after him who [was Secretary of War]. The exhausting labors he underwent at that time broke down a constitution never vigorous and developed the disease that carried him to the grave. . . . Few men have been so respected by the public or so beloved by friends as he."[24]

George Wythe and Mary Randolph had reconciled themselves to the fact that the wreck of the Confederacy was also the wreck of their own wealth.[25] Like his mother thirty years before, George had little to bequeath. In December of 1866 he prepared a last will and testament, dividing his estate into two parts—"the silver plate given me by my brother Jefferson and my sister Mrs. Coolidge" and "the residue." He left Mary both parts for her lifetime. After her death, he bequeathed the silver to Thomas Jefferson Randolph, Jr., or to his eldest surviving son and the residue to "Molly" Randolph with remainder to "such of my blood relations as may stand most in need of it and may best deserve the same."[26]

Mary Randolph survived her husband four years, describing herself as "the childless widow, who had everything taken from her since she was a little baby." She did not join the other Randolph ladies in reviving the Edgehill School. She moved to a small residence at 406 East Franklin Street, Richmond, where she was cared for by a single servant, Lucy Randolph. Apparently, she salvaged some of her property in Mobile and got something for George's railroad bonds. One of her husband's great-nephews, Stevens Mason Taylor, lived in her house, providing company, protection, and some cash. Having been a leader of Richmond society during the 1850s and 1860s, Mary Randolph found little to admire in the postwar city, saying: "Richmond is changing so, as regards society, that it will be hard to find any of the old families soon." Nonetheless, she declared: "I feel like clinging to the old place." Mary Randolph often visited in Baltimore her friends, the Philip Haxalls and the William Dobbinses. She spoke of going to mountain spas and probably did so; she spent much time visiting the Randolphs at Edgehill. When she suffered periodic attacks of neuralgia that were so severe that she "could not move without screaming," George's niece Sarah was particularly kind in nursing her. In the summer of 1870 Mary Randolph suffered a long illness in her Richmond house, but the following spring she was well enough to visit Baltimore. In the fall of 1871, she was at Edgehill when she had a heart attack that prostrated her until her death on December 31, 1871, at the age of forty-seven. She was buried beside George at Monticello. Aside from her position as the mistress of Richmond's most intellectually stimulating salon during the war, Mary Randolph's leadership in the city's volunteer hospital work entitles her to memory.[27]

By lineage and by his own accomplishment, George Wythe Randolph was a member of the F.F.V. elite. His prewar record as a young lawyer and founder of educational, philanthrophic, and military institutions marked him as a man who would command prominence in Virginia. His role in John Reuben Thompson's discussion group was second only to that of the editor of *The Southern Literary Messenger*. It was not Tennysonian poetry, but George Fitzhugh's conception of Southern life and labor that came to fascinate Thompson and his literary elite. George Randolph's experience as a schoolboy in Massachusetts and as a midshipman had made him cosmopolitan. His schooling under Farragut, Barton, Tucker, and Davis had made him both an engineering and legal technocrat, desirous of creating a Southern republic under Virginia's leadership.

George W. Randolph's military services for three years after the John Brown Raid saw him acclaimed a hero of the Battle of Big Bethel, voted a golden sword, and gazetted a brigadier general at the age of forty-five. His service as secretary of war lasted only nine months, but his reform of the War Office lasted the remainder of the war. This reform was of an elitist and technocratic variety, which required state planning on a vast and, perhaps, undemocratic scale. His persistent advocacy of improvement in the Confederacy's system of mobilizing manpower and supplies of food and other supplies improved, but did not cure, malfunction; it lengthened, but did not win, the war. Because the main reason for Randolph's resignation was his bad health, it would have been forthcoming irrespective of his and President Davis's agreement or disagreement.

# Conclusion

Whether because or in spite of his illustrious antecedents, George Wythe Randolph was a self-made man. His grandfather, Thomas Jefferson, died when George was eight years old; his father, Thomas Mann Randolph, Jr., died when the boy was fourteen. Neither man was George's father image. His father's sad history of altercations, loss of fortune, and touch of madness could have scarred George forever, but, fortunately, it did not. Of the tangle of emotions and debts that involved his grandfather, mother, father, and eldest brother, George followed his mother in never attempting a solution or apportioning blame. He tried to avoid Governor Randolph's uncertain quests. For him the specter of Monticello was an exhortation, not a reproach.

His brothers did not exercise great influence upon him. Jeff Randolph was too much the good county squire to be a successful emancipator and too much an emancipator to be a successful politician in antebellum Virginia. If Meriwether Lewis Randolph had not died young, George might have followed him to the West. His sister Ellen, who had been his second mother, was a powerful moral and settling influence on George, who also deferred to her husband Joseph Coolidge. Seeing that Joseph provided comforts, rewards, and the excitement of foreign travel, George made him a role model. To avoid the debts and agricultural decline that bedevilled his grandfather and father was one of George Randolph's main goals. He did not seek to emulate either, although both he and Thomas Jefferson were free-thinking lawyers who married rich widows. He pondered more on what Coolidge's opinion might be than on what his grandfather Jefferson's might have been. For a long time George emulated Coolidge's example of shunning public life in order to make a fortune with which to enjoy the contemplative comforts of family life. Even though he declined Joseph's invitation to enter the China trade under his tutelage, the younger man was a go-getter who never forgot the bustling enterprise of Boston.

George Wythe Randolph attended prep schools in Boston, Cambridge, and Washington. As a midshipman between the ages of thirteen to nineteen, he sailed on the USS *John Adams* and USS *Constitution* to the Mediterranean, where he tasted of culture and sophistication. Unknowingly, he also contracted tuberculosis. Adversity gave him self-discipline. Education gave him power of concentration. Trained in the naval school Farragut had established at Norfolk, he passed rigorous examinations to become a regular naval officer. Assignment to sea duty was the key to advancement, but assignment was so slow that he resigned his commission. At the University of Virginia, George Tucker taught him economics, history, and political science; William Barton Rogers taught him engineering, geology, and science, and A.G. Davis taught him law. He learned there something about Saint-Simon, the Virginia and Kentucky Resolutions, and Henry Clay's American System, about practical application of science as well as about the geology and mineral wealth of Virginia and the world. His excellence in these intellectual pursuits made him the ablest of Thomas Jefferson's grandsons. While George Randolph continued his family's dedication to the scientific and technical goals of the Enlightenment against the currents of the Romantic era's preoccupation with emotional religion and oratory, he later proved to be a persuasive public speaker, became a convert to the Episcopal church, and enjoyed a deathbed vision of Jesus Christ.

George Randolph seems to have decided to recoup the family fortune by becoming an urbanite, not a countryman, a high-priced lawyer, not a farmer short of cash, an aristocrat even more by cultivation of talent than by birth. Proud of what he had accomplished by his own hard work in the 1850s, he was impatient of those who did not measure up to his high standards. By removing to the city of Richmond in 1851, he freed himself of familial liabilities and was able to enjoy the expanding prospects of the state capital. His legal practice prospered. He gained prominent as well as obscure clients in cases involving commerce as well as estates. He was best known, however, as a criminal lawyer, whose impassioned pleas seem to have sprung from his sympathy for the victims of harsh naval justice.

Until 1859, Randolph was more a private than a public figure. He gained a modest fortune, a wealthy beauty for his wife, professional and cultivated men for his friends, and a cozy home. His problems of goals and identity seemed solved. He now could feel secure, enjoy privacy or the company of a select few, and indulge in books, contemplation, music, pictures, and the theater. He displayed his commitment to education, good craftsmanship and the aristocracy of talent as a founder of the Richmond Mechanics Institute. He was accepted as a thoughtful man by his fellow officers of the Virginia Historical Society. George Randolph was a city lawyer with diversified investments, desirous of a protective tariff to make his commonwealth great, and a military man who liked to make the whip snap. He was the most prominent member of a discussion group, after its leader, John Reuben Thompson, the editor of *The Southern Literary Messenger*. Meeting alternately at Thompson's and Randolph's offices, it embraced some officers of the Virginia Historical Society, some manufacturers, and some professional men. Apparently they discussed current issues treated by *The Southern Literary Messenger* that were of an economic, historical, philosophical, political, and sociological nature. Randolph's breadth of study, experience, and travel made him a local authority about foreign places, peoples, and ways of life. Without being faddish, he was open to new ideas brought before the discussion group, such as the views concerning labor and society held by the American sociologist, George Fitzhugh, and the French socialist, Du Var Robert.

George Randolph's marriage with Mary Adams was happy, whether at the peak of his career in the summer of 1862 or when he was an invalid after 1864. They were leaders of Richmond society. Sorry not to have children of their own, they took vicarious interest in the education and careers of his nieces, nephews, and their families. Much of what we know of Mary Randolph comes from Civil War diarists like Mary Boykin Chesnut. Her daguerreotype shows her to have been fully as beautiful as Mrs. Chesnut described her. Her salon on Franklin Street was said to have been the most outstanding in wartime Richmond, depending on John Reuben Thompson for its literary strength, William D. Washington for its artistic strength, and upon Constance and Hetty Cary for its beauty. J. E. B. Stuart, John B. Hood, and Heros Von Borcke provided the military heroism. Mrs. Randolph's salon was famous for its charades, the diversion of official and social Richmond while the fortunes of the Confederacy dwindled. More importantly, Mrs. Randolph devoted herself to supervising Richmond's volunteer hospital aid between 1861 and 1864.

George Randolph had no use for leaders who did not lead. He subscribed to the concept of a natural aristocracy of talent. Like Edgar Allan Poe, he shunned the folksy political shenanigans celebrated by Jacksonian democracy. He was a Whiggish Democrat whose approach to politics was lofty. He represented a revivified aristocracy, not an aristocracy in decline. Randolph's conversion from American to Southern nationalism was well under way before the John Brown Raid caused him to castigate the pernicious influence of low-class Yankee abolitionists on even the Coolidges.

With prescience, he founded in 1859 a company of light artillery which he outfitted with small naval cannon called howitzers. Making the Richmond Howitzers a crack unit, he led it to Harpers Ferry after the John Brown Raid. The Virginia General Assembly named him to a three-man commission to recommend and buy arms in the autumn of 1860. In addition to his military duties, the city of Richmond elected him as a secessionist to the Virginia Convention of 1861, which debated between February and mid-April whether or not to secede. He was one of that Convention's three-man peace commission whom the convention sent to dissuade President Lincoln from using force. Delayed by storms, the commission met with Secretary of State Seward and the president, only to learn the next day from the newspapers that Lincoln was reinforcing Fort Sumter. When they returned to Richmond, the three recommended secession.

The Howitzers expanded to a battalion of three companies under Colonel Randolph's command. He and his men were among the first Confederate heroes because of their part in the Battle of Big Bethel near Hampton, Virginia, in the late spring of 1861. While serving as chief of artillery for Gen. John Bankhead Magruder, the commanding officer of the Army of the Peninsula, Randolph helped fortify Yorktown as the bastion of the Confederate defense line. In the early winter of 1862 when he was forty-three years old, Randolph was promoted to the rank of brigadier general, commanding a force stationed at Suffolk, Virginia. In March of 1862, he accepted President Jefferson Davis's invitation to join his cabinet as secretary of war.

One can best understand Randolph's meteoric ascent from obscurity to prominence in 1861–62 by recognizing that, besides being a military officer, he represented three elite constituencies: the F.F.V.s, the Richmond literati, and the technocrats. Otherwise, one fails to appreciate the harmony of his interests and might consider him a dilettante. Although he was a secessionist, he was neither a strict constructionist nor a states-righter. Although he was a Southern nationalist and a centralizer, he wanted Virginia to rule the Southern nation through the three elites he represented. He was both a lawyer and an engineer. He was a Southern soldier who insisted on decent food for Union prisoners and who defended conscientious objectors. He was a wealthy man who encouraged Richmond artisans to go on strike in order to correct the wartime hardship caused by fixed salaries and wages and by inflation of foodstuffs. He was a professional man who respected craftsmanship, whether of the Monticello cabinetmaker John Hemings, navy petty officers, or Richmond gunsmiths.

George Wythe Randolph's actions as Confederate secretary of war form the basis for his claim to remembrance. To him, the goal of secession was independence of a Southern republic, not the extension or perpetuation of slavery, whose evil he did not comprehend until 1864. At first, his concern about slavery was about how its inefficiencies caused a loss of manpower, but he came to realize that the opposition of European leaders was the chief obstacle to foreign recognition of Southern independence. Because of his education and experience, he was interested in the revolutionary forces of his time that produced Cavour, Garibaldi, Marx, and Napoleon III. Influenced by the writings of Tucker and Fitzhugh, he was the only member of the Confederate high command with knowledge of pre-Marxist socialism. Through a combination of social and technocratic elites, he expanded the activities of the War Department to encompass most aspects of the wartime economy. To the degree to which Randolph's proposals for neomercantilist or socialist planning and control were permitted, they were effective. He perceived that only by centralized planning could food, industry, and transport support the army. Others before him had used the railroads to integrate Confederate forces into a strategic unity and to concentrate troops. His naval service in the Mediterranean and his study of maps during the Franco-Sardinian War in 1859 enabled Randolph to understand the strategic and logistical importance of Sardinia's rail net and port of Genoa. In applying these lessons to the Southern republic, he became the chief advocate of regaining New Orleans, the South's greatest port. The prewar mixed economy of Virginia had accustomed him to centralized state planning and use of state money to construct new, vital links in its rail system, but, as secretary of war, his assignment of priorities for rail traffic became a device for channeling private production into support of the war effort. Randolph anticipated Woodrow Wilson's goal of satisfying wartime needs instead of civilian fancies. Eventually, the War Office requisitioned goods and laborers, particularly for railroad construction. Such central planning was as much neomercantilist as socialist, for all of George Randolph's exposure to the writings of George Fitzhugh and Du Var Robert. The efficiencies achieved by the War Office's exercise of economic powers were sufficient to enable the Confederacy for a while to compete with its numerically and industrially superior foe. If all that George W. Randolph proposed had been adopted, it might have protracted, but probably would not have won the war.

Before Union conscription was established and with more liberal terms for occupational and conscientious exemptions, Randolph was the principal author first of Virginia's and then of the Confederacy's conscription acts, which he based on French and Prussian models. Unable to achieve the full mobilization of Southern manpower without which he knew that defeat was sure, he blamed Confederate army commanders who permitted absenteeism, instead of blaming state governors for hoarding troops. To remedy the shortage of troops, he unsuccessfully proposed, somewhat in the manner of the First French Republic, sending out representatives on mission to remove or punish guilty commanders.

In friendly and close collaboration with Josiah Gorgas and without apology for elitism or nepotism, George W. Randolph recruited representatives of the elites of the F.F.V.s and the technocrats into the War Office, not only to provide for the administration of the armies, but to stimulate and satisfy technical needs. These recruits were engineering, legal, or agricultural experts by dint of education and experience. Most of Randolph's recruits had attended either the University of Virginia or Yale College. Their advantages of family, fortune, and association were to Randolph desirable because they bespoke harmonious cooperation, honesty, and loyalty. Many of them were related to him, to one of his intimates, or to one another by blood or marriage. There was virtually no one who came into the War Office in Randolph's day who could not be vouched for by someone who was already a F.F.V. or technocrat. Under Randolph's leadership, they not only reformed the administration of the army for the rest of the war, but also molded a war economy regulating imports and exports, sales of cotton, blockade-running and trading with the enemy.

General Randolph achieved so great a degree of simple reform of military administration during his nine months as secretary of war that the War Office under his recruits continued on his course after he himself had departed. Subsequent events showed that Randolph was correct in saying that his reorganization of the War Department was "so far perfected as to require little more than assiduous supervision."

Although there were subliminal differences between Randolph and Davis arising from their membership in rival elites, they were harmonious in day-to-day affairs and, after General Lee assumed command of the Army of Northern Virginia, devoted strategic attention to the

West. Although Randolph was only an appointee of the elected chief of state, he persuaded Congress to enact his, not Davis's, proposals for conscription. Abandoning reliance on free-enterprise capitalism to fill the needs of a nation at war, Randolph in the summer of 1862 tried to develop a program of exchanging with the enemy cotton for food and other supplies for the Confederate army.

For a while, he and Davis collaborated on a plan to recover New Orleans. The Randolph-Davis Plan called for the combination of four conventional forces, whose main column was under the capable and charismatic Brig. Gen. Richard Taylor. Success would have had such important logistical and diplomatic results that Randolph believed that the Southern republic would have been justified in fostering an uprising by a fifth column within the city in concert with Taylor's advance along the railroad from Opelousas to Algiers. Other pressing needs of the Confederacy drew President Davis's attention elsewhere, but Secretary Randolph persisted, even though there was mounting evidence that the first four columns could not be brought up to the strength required. Randolph's resignation as secretary of war ended not only the possibility of fifth-column activities within New Orleans, but also new efforts to trade with the enemy. Even though these projects were never consummated, they are the best evidence of the inventiveness of Randolph and the elites whom he recruited into the War Office.

The conventional interpretation of Randolph's resignation as secretary of war in mid-November of 1862 is that it resulted from an inconsequential difference between him and Davis in the Holmes affair. Only a limited and literal reading of the documents can sustain this viewpoint. Chief of the Bureau of War Kean said that Randolph resigned for "factitious" reasons. That is to say, his ostensible reason— disagreement about the Holmes Affair—was contrived, trumped up to make it appear that Randolph's conditional order to General Holmes was not at all related to the New Orleans scheme, even though Davis had endorsed just such an authority for General Taylor to conduct operations in what was nominally General Daniel Ruggles's department. Randolph made it appear that he had inadvertently challenged Davis's powers as commander-in-chief and had violated their practice of prior consultation.

At forty-four years of age, George Randolph was more cosmopolitan and quicker to entertain new ideas than Davis. He was less encumbered by legalistic scruples of strict construction and states rights than the president, who frequently adopted Randolph's views later. They represented different elite constituencies. Although Davis was a wealthy and prominent westerner who antecedents had come from Virginia, he was not an F.F.V. Although he was a West Pointer, he could not be called an engineer. Davis's experience in the provincial cities of northern Mexico was no match for Randolph's in Europe. Davis's service as U.S. secretary of war and senator had made him expert in governance, not technology. Sooner than Davis, Randolph believed that the Southern republic must resort to unconventional measures in order to man and feed its armies and to organize its farms and factories in a war economy. Although he was disappointed by the abandonment of the Randolph-Davis Plan to liberate New Orleans, Randolph was frustrated by the failure of his proposals to keep the armies at full strength and to provide them enough food. He was worn out by the "stubborn" president's "arrogance" in endlessly repetitive conferences. The state of his own health had worsened, although neither he nor anyone else then knew that he was terminally ill of tuberculosis.

George Randolph would have been condemned as a wrecker, if he had given ground for the belief that the Davis administration had refused his chief alternative to starving the army and the civil population—trading with the enemy. It would have been bad for Confederate morale for Randolph to verify charges that absenteeism with or without leave was making a skeleton of the armies. Neither could the Southern republic adopt nor renounce the possibility of liberating New Orleans from the Yankee yoke. Because of his illness and the cumulative effect of having his projects tabled, Randolph had been considering resignation for at least a month. Finding in the Holmes Affair a good excuse, he resigned his position on November 14, 1862.

The earliest Southern history of the Civil War, written by the former editor of the Richmond *Enquirer,* Edward A. Pollard, declared that "the Confederates, with an abler Government and more resolute spirit, might have accomplished their independence." George Wythe Randolph was one of the few who had both the critical knowledge of military affairs and an opportunity to influence Jefferson Davis during the Civil War. In giving an emphasis to Western military operations they demonstrated that they were capable of harmonious collaboration. Thus, Randolph's reticence is as valuable as his few recorded criticisms of Davis. He lamented the president's insistence on running the War Department in person, saying that Davis lacked the required "time," "system," and "ability to discriminate" between important and unimportant matters. Garlick Kean agreed with Randolph that Davis was neither "a comprehensive man" nor one with a "broad policy, either of finance, strategy or supply." Worse yet, said Randolph, he would "not permit amendment from the experience of others." While George W. Randolph had good reasons for criticizing Davis, he decided that to publicize them would do no good and that there was no alternative to continuing under Davis's leadership. No one then or since has ever suggested how the Confederate administration might have been improved. As chief executive, Jefferson Davis demonstrated competence far exceeding such other unsuccessful heads of state as Charles I of England, Louis XVI of France, Nicholas II of Russia. George Wythe Randolph gave his tacit approval of the Davis administration when he contrived his "factitious" resignation.

Although he temporarily had been the president's collaborator in strategic planning the western theater of warfare, George Wythe Randolph despaired of his ability or patience to influence Davis. Believing that he had accomplished all he could do as secretary of war and that, by going gracefully, he did not prejudice the future of any person or policy, he concluded that he could resign with a good conscience. If, by the time he resigned, Randolph had despaired of winning Southern independence, he probably believed that he and his sort had no choice but to "die game," as Raimondo Luraghi has put it.

In an age which celebrated the simple, one-dimensional man, George Wythe Randolph was too complex, too cosmopolitan, too intellectual, too sophisticated. His accomplishments, experience and motives gave him an unmatched breadth of viewpoint among the Confederate administration. With the exceptions of Jefferson Davis and Robert E. Lee, no one played a greater role in setting the course of the Confederate war effort than he. Besides his military background, his membership in the elites of the F.F.V.s., the literati, the military and the technocrats inspired him to introduce their methods and goals into the mechanisms of the Southern republic. More than anyone else in the Confederate high command, he was a spokesman for the hardheaded, if not ruthless, social efficiencies of conscription, mobilization of white and black manpower, enforced capital investment through inflation of the currency, and strict regulation of the key sources of transportation and production. Randolph's shaping of the wartime economy owed something to pre-Marxist socialists like Du Var Robert and George Fitzhugh, but even more was it based on Virginia's mixed economy and upon timeless wartime expedients everywhere. The system of Randolph and his elite recruits did provide a desperate hope of winning independence through what General Grant called a "military despotism." It is probable that, if Randolph had remained secretary of war and been given more leeway, he might have prolonged the Civil War without changing the final result.

Randolph has not fared well with historians of the Lost Cause. The hero of the 1861 Battle of Big Bethel was too much a winner for the postwar era, whose myths were based on having lost. Gazetted a brigadier general at the age of forty-three, he never lost a battle. So many ingredients besides luckier timing were needed to make his scheme to liberate New Orleans work, that it may be idle to speculate on its potentialities. That posterity mistakenly has remembered him for resigning the post of secretary of war after a procedural disagreement with President Davis is due to his own calculated obfuscation. Although his reforms were mainly judicious adaptations, they were relatively fresh and inventive. To call them socialistic would be an exaggeration.

To the last Randolph sponsored innovation—on the Richmond City Council, in leading volunteers to defend the city, and in making European contracts to buy Bessemer steel. When he died in 1867, he was only forty-nine years old. If he had recovered his health sufficiently, he might have provided Virginia an intelligent leadership in the postwar period.

Without an army whose regiments were at full strength in numbers and in belly and muscle, Randolph's ingenious elaborations could be only cosmetic. Defeat might be postponed, but it would come.

JOHN REUBEN THOMPSON

# In Remembrance of
# George Wythe Randolph

I

And he is dead whom we have loved so well,
The sailor, soldier, scholar, statesman, dead!
And it remains that we shall rightly tell
His virtues, and the crowning grace that shed
A tender radiance over all his story—
A radiance deepening at the end to glory
And trailing light along the darksome way
By which he passed to everlasting day.
And he is gone, we shall not see him more
Nor hear him yet in that familiar strain—
Wherewith he held us captive, heart and brain—
Of gentlest fancies and of wisest lore:
We still sit listening, though the voice is hushed,
Nor ignorantly hold our loss less great,
That his is a translation to the skies,
From all the thickening sorrows of the state,
A land impoverished and a people crushed;
That, having borne the cross, he gains the prize!
Of little faith we are that we should weep
When God the Father calls His children hence
With love unmeasured by our mortal sense—
For so He giveth His Beloved sleep.

II

Our friend was of a lofty house and line
And owned as heritage an honoured name,

And with it, goodlier legacy than this,
The love of all things lovely, noble, true:
Wisdom with goodness did in him combine,
Yet such a modesty, most rare, was his,
And so apart he lived from noisy fame,
And held so cheaply, he to duty vow'd,
As ever only may the wise and few,
The plauditory clamour of the crowd,
Content to do the task, to bear the burden,
Careless to win the empty earthly guerdon,
His greatness might have blossomed all unseen,
Unrecognised save in the narrow view
Of home, had not the tumult of the time
And sore calamity of common weal
Called him to action on a stage sublime,
And to his life affixed the enduring seal:
But centred in that full intensest light,
That fiercest blaze of war across the land,
Wherein your little nature looks so mean,
Your party hero but a paltry thing,
He rose full statured to that kingly height
That we who had not known him for a king
But deemed him great, and worthy for command,
Rejoiced nor marvelled at his new renown;
Till wasted with his work he laid it down,
Worn out with petty rivalries and strife,

And, bending mostly 'neath the country's care,
Within the inner temple of his life
Withdrew himself as to a house of prayer,
And walked therein serenely to the close,
Through ever-present suffering, yet beguiled
By tenderest sympathy and fondest looks,
By sweet idolatries of art and books
And nature in far lands beyond the sea,
And by that love of hers who loved him best;
Thus gently solaced, chastened, reconciled,
In meek submission to the chastening rod,
But ever yearning for diviner rest,
Nearer he drew unto the peace of God
That passeth understanding richly blest

With earnest of an infinite repose
When death at last should kindly set him free.

### III

Virginia mourns him, and with happier fates,
Warriors and statesmen might have borne his pall,
Lamented by a league of sorrowing States,
And his had been a public funeral
With requiem and salvo, trumpet's wail
And pealing guns upon the evening breeze,
And flags had drooped half-mast in distant seas,
Where he, the sailor-boy, had braved the gale:
And we, when time all jealousies had stilled,
Had placed his marble image in a niche
Of that majestic fane, with sculptures rich
And soaring dome, that we shall never build:
But now his image in our hearts is shrined
And what was mortal of the man consigned,
In all the sanctity of private grief,
To mother earth, amid ancestral tombs,
Within those hallowed precincts which contain
The dust of Monticello's mighty dead.
There would I stray, alone, with reverent tread,
As o'er the mountain Spring her joyous reign
Renews, with all her beauteous tints and blooms,
And April's whisper stirs the tender leaf—
There softly stray, as in some minster dim
Where saints and martyrs slept beneath the nave,
To call up gentlest memories of him
And lay the earliest violets on his grave.

There is a broadside of this work in the Edgehill Randolph Papers, and it has been reprinted in the *Monticello Association Reports*. See John R. Thompson, "In Remembrance of George Wythe Randolph," *Poems,* 206–8; broadside, n.d., Edgehill Randolph Papers; and *Monticello Association Reports* 15: 16–18.

# Appendix

*Table 1. Characteristics of the Richmond Cultural Elite, 1859, the thirteen attending the Thompson Testimonial Dinner*

| | | Average age | 42 |
|---|---|---|---|
| Column a | Age in 1859 | | |
| Column b | # Descended from William Randolph of Turkey Island | 4 | (30%) |
| Column c | Otherwise connected to George Wythe Randolph by blood or marriage | 7 | (54%) |
| Column d | Born in Virginia | 11 | (85%) |
| Column e | Born in state south of Virginia | 0 | |
| Column f | Born in state north of Virginia | 1 | (8%) |
| Column g | Studied at University of Virginia | 3 | (23%) |
| Column h | Studied at other college south of Mason-Dixon Line (excluding Virginia Military Institute) | 5 | (39%) |
| Column i | Studied at Yale | 2 | (15%) |
| Column j | Studied at other college north of Mason-Dixon Line (excluding U.S. Military Academy at West Point) | 6 | (46%) |
| Column k | Cadet (West Point or VMI) or midshipman | 3 | (23%) |
| Column l | Foreign study, trade, or travel | 4 | (30%) |
| Column m | Profession or study of law, medicine, or philosophy | 8 | (61%) |
| Column n | Engineer | 5 | (39%) |
| Column o | Farmer | 0 | |
| Column p | Businessman | 8 | (61%) |
| Column q | Military or naval officer before 1860 | 6 | (46%) |

Column

(x = yes, — = no)

| | a | b | c | d | e | f | g | h | i | j | k | l | m | n | o | p | q |
|---|---|---|---|---|---|---|---|---|---|---|---|---|---|---|---|---|---|
| Joseph R. Anderson | 46 | x | — | x | — | — | — | x | — | x | x | — | — | x | — | x | x |
| Charles G. Barney | 45 | — | — | — | — | x | — | — | — | x | — | — | x | — | — | x | — |
| R. Milton Cary | 24 | x | x | x | — | — | — | x | — | — | — | — | — | — | — | x | x |
| William W. Crump | 40 | — | — | x | — | — | — | x | — | x | — | x | x | — | — | — | — |
| Robert W. Haxall | 57 | — | x | x | — | — | — | — | x | x | — | — | — | — | — | x | — |
| Richard B. Haxall | 54 | — | x | x | — | — | — | — | — | — | — | — | — | — | — | x | — |
| James Lyons | 58 | — | — | x | — | — | — | x | — | — | — | — | x | — | — | — | — |
| William H. MacFarland | 61 | — | — | x | — | — | — | x | x | — | — | x | x | x | — | x | x |
| William P. Munford | 42 | x | x | — | — | — | x | — | — | — | — | — | x | x | — | x | x |
| John M. Patton, Jr. | 33 | — | x | x | — | — | — | — | — | — | x | — | x | x | — | — | x |
| George W. Randolph | 41 | x | x | x | — | — | x | — | — | x | x | x | x | x | — | — | x |
| John R. Thompson | 36 | — | x | x | — | — | x | — | — | x | — | x | x | — | — | — | — |
| Thomas H. Wynne | 39 | — | — | x | — | — | — | — | — | — | — | — | — | — | — | x | — |
| Totals | | 4 | 7 | 11 | 0 | 1 | 3 | 5 | 2 | 6 | 3 | 4 | 8 | 5 | 0 | 8 | 6 |

*Table 2. Characteristics of Nine Officials in the War Department Before 1862*

|          |                                                                                                              | Average age |   |        |
| -------- | ------------------------------------------------------------------------------------------------------------ | ----------- | - | ------ |
| Column a | Age in 1861                                                                                                  | 44          |   |        |
| Column b | # Descended from William Randolph of Turkey Island                                                           |             | 1 | (11%)  |
| Column c | Otherwise connected to George Wythe Randolph by blood or marriage                                            |             | 2 | (22%)  |
| Column d | Born in Virginia                                                                                             |             | 0 |        |
| Column e | Born in state south of Virginia                                                                              |             | 4 | (44%)  |
| Column f | Born in state north of Virginia                                                                              |             | 4 | (44%)  |
| Column g | Studied at University of Virginia                                                                            |             | 2 | (22%)  |
| Column h | Studied at other college south of Mason-Dixon Line (excluding Virginia Military Institute)                   |             | 3 | (33%)  |
| Column i | Studied at Yale                                                                                              |             | 2 | (22%)  |
| Column j | Studied at other college north of Mason-Dixon Line (excluding U.S. Military Academy at West Point)           |             | 5 | (55%)  |
| Column k | Cadet (West Point or VMI) or midshipman                                                                      |             | 5 | (55%)  |
| Column l | Foreign study, trade, or travel                                                                              |             | 6 | (66%)  |
| Column m | Profession or study of law, medicine, or philosophy                                                          |             | 3 | (33%)  |
| Column n | Engineer                                                                                                     |             | 4 | (44%)  |
| Column o | Farmer                                                                                                       |             | 1 | (11%)  |
| Column p | Businessman                                                                                                  |             | 0 |        |
| Column q | Cultural, educational, and philanthropic interests                                                           |             | 4 | (44%)  |

Column

(x = yes, — = no)

| | a | b | c | d | e | f | g | h | i | j | k | l | m | n | o | p | q |
|---|---|---|---|---|---|---|---|---|---|---|---|---|---|---|---|---|---|
| Judah P. Benjamin | 50 | — | — | — | x | — | — | — | x | — | — | x | x | — | — | — | x |
| Josiah Gorgas | 44 | — | — | — | — | x | — | — | — | x | x | x | — | x | — | — | x |
| Abraham C. Myers | 51 | — | — | — | x | — | — | — | — | x | x | x | — | — | — | — | — |
| Danville Ledbetter | ? | — | — | — | — | x | — | — | — | — | x | ? | — | x | — | — | — |
| Lucius B. Northrop | 51 | — | — | — | x | — | — | — | x | x | x | x | — | — | — | — | — |
| Robert Ould | 42 | — | — | — | — | x | — | x | — | x | — | — | x | — | — | — | — |
| A. Landon Rives | 32 | — | x | — | — | — | x | x | — | — | — | x | — | x | — | — | x |
| Andrew Talcott | 65 | x | x | — | — | x | — | — | — | x | x | x | — | x | x | — | x |
| Leroy P. Walker | 44 | — | — | — | x | — | x | x | — | — | — | — | x | — | — | — | — |
| Totals | | 1 | 2 | 0 | 4 | 4 | 2 | 3 | 2 | 5 | 5 | 6 | 3 | 4 | 1 | 0 | 4 |

*Note:* Richard Morton was briefly in Richmond as a captain in the Bureau of Nitre in 1862 before being transferred to western Virginia as a district supervisor of production. He returned to Richmond as superintendent and acting chief of the bureau in February of 1865.

*Table 3. Characteristics of Twenty-five of Randolph's Appointees and Associates, 1862*

|          |                                                                                                      | Average age |       |
|----------|------------------------------------------------------------------------------------------------------|-------------|-------|
| Column a | Age                                                                                                  | 36          |       |
| Column b | # Descended from William Randolph of Turkey Island                                                   | 8           | (32%) |
| Column c | Otherwise connected to George Wythe Randolph by blood or by marriage                                 | 9           | (36%) |
| Column d | Born in Virginia                                                                                     | 12          | (48%) |
| Column e | Born in state south of Virginia                                                                      | 9           | (36%) |
| Column f | Born in state north of Virginia                                                                      | 2           | (8%)  |
| Column g | Studied at University of Virginia                                                                    | 6           | (24%) |
| Column h | Studied at other college south of Mason-Dixon Line (excluding Virginia Military Institute)           | 6           | (24%) |
| Column i | Studied at Yale                                                                                      | 4           | (16%) |
| Column j | Studied at other college north of Mason-Dixon Line (excluding U.S. Military Academy at West Point)   | 11          | (44%) |
| Column k | Cadet (West Point or VMI) or midshipman                                                              | 9           | (36%) |
| Column l | Foreign study, trade, or travel                                                                      | 17          | (68%) |
| Column m | Profession or study of law, medicine, or philosophy                                                  | 10          | (40%) |
| Column n | Engineer                                                                                             | 7           | (28%) |
| Column o | Farmer                                                                                               | 2           | (8%)  |
| Column p | Businessman                                                                                          | 6           | (24%) |
| Column q | Cultural, educational and philanthropic interests                                                    | 13          | (52%) |

Column

(x = yes, — = no)

| | a | b | c | d | e | f | g | h | i | j | k | l | m | n | o | p | q |
|---|---|---|---|---|---|---|---|---|---|---|---|---|---|---|---|---|---|
| Joseph R. Anderson | 49 | x | — | x | — | — | — | — | — | — | x | x | — | x | — | x | x |
| Thomas P. August | 40 | — | — | — | — | — | — | — | — | — | — | x | x | — | — | — | — |
| Thomas L. Bayne | 38 | — | — | — | x | — | — | — | x | — | — | x | x | — | — | — | x |
| J. Thompson Brown | 27 | — | x | x | — | — | x | — | — | x | — | x | — | — | — | — | — |
| John A. Campbell | 51 | — | — | — | x | — | — | x | x | x | x | — | — | — | x | — | x |
| Stephen Chalaron | ?? | — | — | — | x | — | — | — | x | — | — | — | — | — | — | x | — |
| William W. Crump | 43 | — | — | x | — | — | — | x | — | x | — | — | x | — | — | — | — |
| Joseph Denegre | 25 | — | — | — | x | — | — | — | — | — | — | x | — | — | — | x | — |
| Jeremy F. Gilmer | 44 | — | — | — | x | — | — | — | — | x | x | x | — | x | — | — | — |
| Josiah Gorgas | 44 | — | — | x | — | x | — | — | — | x | x | x | — | x | — | — | x |
| Thomas J. Jackson | 38 | — | x | x | — | — | — | — | x | x | x | x | — | x | — | — | x |
| R. G. H. Kean | 31 | x | x | x | — | — | x | x | — | x | x | x | x | — | — | x | x |
| Robert E. Lee | 55 | x | x | x | x | — | — | — | — | x | x | x | x | x | — | — | x |
| Abraham C. Myers | 51 | — | — | — | — | x | — | x | — | x | x | — | — | — | — | — | — |
| Edmund T. D. Myers | 32 | — | x | x | — | — | x | — | — | x | x | x | — | x | — | — | x |
| Lucius B. Northrop | 51 | — | — | x | x | — | x | x | x | x | x | x | — | — | — | — | x |
| Robert Ould | 42 | — | — | — | — | x | — | x | — | x | x | x | x | — | — | — | — |
| Roger A. Pryor | 34 | x | x | x | — | — | x | — | — | — | x | x | x | — | — | — | x |
| George W. Randolph | 41 | x | x | x | — | — | x | — | x | x | x | x | x | x | — | — | x |
| A. Landon Rives | 32 | — | x | — | — | — | x | x | — | — | x | x | — | x | — | — | x |
| Francis G. Ruffin | 42 | x | x | x | — | — | x | — | — | — | x | x | — | — | x | x | x |
| Isaac M. St. John | 35 | — | — | x | — | — | — | x | — | — | — | x | x | — | — | — | — |
| James M. Seixas | 50 | — | — | — | x | — | — | — | — | — | — | x | — | — | — | x | x |
| J. E. B. Stuart | 29 | x | x | x | x | — | — | x | — | x | x | — | — | — | — | — | — |
| T. M. R. Talcott | 24 | x | x | — | x | — | — | x | — | — | x | x | x | — | x | x | x |
| Totals | | 8 | 9 | 12 | 9 | 2 | 6 | 6 | 4 | 11 | 9 | 17 | 10 | 7 | 2 | 6 | 13 |

*Note:* For purposes of computing average, the age of Chalaron is estimated at 28.

185

*Sources to Table 1:* Crump Family Papers, Haxall Family Papers, Hollywood Cemetery Burial Register, Munford Family Papers, Patton Family Papers; Christian, "Reminiscences," 743–45; *Register of Former Cadets;* Ernst, "Thomas Hicks Wynne," 186–91; Harrison, *Virginia Carys;* Hesseltine and Gara, "Postwar Problems of a Virginia Historian," 193–95; *Dictionary of American Biography;* Laferty, *Sketches,* 48–49; R. I. Randolph, *Randolphs of Virginia; Students of the University of Virginia; Encyclopedia of Virginia Biography; Richmond City and Henrico County; West Point Cadets.*

*Sources to Table 2:* Family papers and memorabilia of Mrs. E. Griffith Dodson and of Mr. McDonald Wellford; "Principal Officers of the War Department and Its Bureaus from Feb. 18, 1861, to June 30, 1862," 1:1176; *Register of Former Cadets; Dictionary of American Biography,* s.v. "Benjamin, Judah P." and "Walker, Leroy P."; Randolph, *Randolphs of Virginia; Students of the University of Virginia; Encyclopedia of Virginia Biography; West Point Cadets; Richmond City and Henrico County;* Capt. Richard Morton to Col. Josiah Gorgas, May 7, 1862; *War of Rebellion,* 4th ser. 1: 1115–16; Table, ibid., 4th ser. 3: 1183; and Special Orders nos. 114 and 130, Aug. 3, 1861; *War of Rebellion,* 4th ser. 1: 531, 581, 1176.

*Sources to Table 3:* Family papers and memorabilia of Mr. Edward Thompson Brown, of Messrs. George and Thomas Bayne Denegre, Jr., of Mrs. E. Griffith Dodson, and of Mr. McDonald Wellford; Crump Family Papers, Hollywood Cemetery Papers, Patton Family Papers. *Register of Former Cadets;* Ernst, "Thomas Hicks Wynne," 186–91; Harrison, *Virginia Carys;* Hesseltine and Gara, "Postwar Problems of a Virginia Historian," 193–95; *Dictionary of American Biography;* "James Madison Seixas," New Orleans *Times-Democrat,* June 28, 1885; R. I. Randolph, *Randolphs of Virginia; Students of the University of Virginia; Press Reference Book of Prominent Virginians,* 53; *Encyclopedia of Virginia Biography; West Point Cadets.*

# Notes

## 1. Background and Youth

1. Taylor, "Descendants of Thomas Jefferson," 1: 235. Use of the Jane Bradick Petticolas watercolor as frontispiece, courtesy of the Thomas Jefferson Memorial Foundation. Notation by Susan Stein, curator at Monticello.

2. See table 1, appendix. See also R. I. Randolph, *Randolphs of Virginia*, and Daniels, *Randolphs of Virginia*.

3. Robert Carter Randolph debated this subject with Grigsby in the Norfolk, Virginia, *Argus* in 1858, and Robert Isham Randolph discussed it in his *Randolphs of Virginia*, 261–62. Thomas Jefferson neither owned nor alluded to Thomas Randolph's play *Amyntas* or his *Poems*. See Jefferson to John Daly Burk, June 21, 1801, quoted in Sowerby, *The Library of Thomas Jefferson*, 4: 465; Gaines, *Thomas Mann Randolph*, 115–18; and T. Randolph, *The Poems and Amyntas*.

4. Martha Jefferson Randolph to Ellen Wayles Randolph Coolidge, Nov. 16, 1825, Coolidge Collection. Hereafter, Martha Jefferson Randolph is cited as Mrs. Randolph, and Ellen Wayles Randolph Coolidge is cited as Mrs. Coolidge in all chapters.

5. John Hemmings to Septimia Randolph, Aug. 28, 1825, Meikleham Papers; Vance, "Thomas Jefferson Randolph."

6. The author is indebted to the late Dr. Walter Muir Whitehill for sharing his knowledge of naval affairs and of Boston. See Whitehill, *Boston: A Topographical History* and "Eleanora Wayles Randolph," 1: 89–99. See also George W. Randolph to Molly Randolph, Mar. 6, 1860, Jefferson-Randolph-Taylor-Smith-Nicholas Papers. Hereinafter this collection is cited as Jefferson-Randolph Papers and George Wythe Randolph as Randolph. See also Mrs. Coolidge to Col. and Mrs. Thomas J. Randolph, Aug. 21–22 and 30, 1841, Aug. 1, 1844, Coolidge Collection.

7. Mrs. Randolph to Mrs. Coolidge, Nov. 16, 1825, Coolidge Collection.

8. Mrs. Randolph to Jane Randolph, Feb. 5, 1828, Jefferson-Randolph Papers; Mrs. Randolph to Septimia Randolph, Jan. 4, 1828, and Aug. 1, 1830; Mrs. Coolidge to Septimia R. Meikleham, Apr. 16, 1820, Meikleham Papers;

Mrs. Coolidge to Mrs. Randolph, June 14, 1827, and Randolph to Mrs. Coolidge, July 26, 1831, Coolidge Collection; Scudder, *James Russell Lowell,* 1: 19, 22–25, 2: 135–37; Howard, *Victorian Knight Errant,* 9–10; and Duberman, *James Russell Lowell,* 14–15, 275–76.

9. Joseph Coolidge, Jr., to Thomas J. Randolph, Aug. 26, 1830, Mrs. Randolph to Mrs. Coolidge, Dec. 5, 1830, and Feb. 22, 1831, and Nicholas P. Trist to Joseph Coolidge, Jr., Oct. 27, 1831, all in the Coolidge Collection. See also Morgan, "Nicholas Philip," 1: 100–113.

10. Mrs. Randolph to Septimia Randolph, Nov. 12, 1831, Meikleham Papers; Mrs. Randolph to Mrs. Coolidge, Sept. 1833, Coolidge Collection; Randolph to Septimia Randolph, July 25, 1835, and Randolph to Margaret S. Randolph, Apr. 13, 1837, Jefferson-Randolph Papers.

11. Mrs. Randolph to Mrs. Coolidge, Feb. 22 and Apr. 1, 1831, Coolidge Collection; M. Lewis Randolph to Septimia Randolph, May 10, 1831, Meikleham Papers. William Segar Archer (1789–1855) of Amelia County, Virginia served in the Virginia House of Delegates from 1812 to 1819, in the U.S. House of Representatives from 1820 to 1835, and in the U.S. Senate from 1841 to 1847. See *Biographical Directory of the American Congress,* 788.

12. Acceptances for 1831, records group 45, Naval Records. See also Henry duPont, *Rear Admiral Samuel Francis duPont,* 6–7.

13. Lewis, *Farragut,* 1. Stewart won fame in the Barbary War and commanded the U.S. Mediterranean squadron after the War of 1812. See also George G. Shackelford, "Septimia Anne Randolph," 1: 128–33.

14. Dahlgren, *Memoir,* 42. Dahlgren served there in 1828 on the sloop *Ontario.*

15. Mrs. Randolph to Mrs. Coolidge, Apr. 1 and 23, 1831, Coolidge Collection.

16. Randolph to John Boyle, Apr. 6, 1831; Acceptances for 1831, records group 45, Naval Records.

## 2. *Midshipman Randolph*

1. Porter, *Adventures of Harry Marline,* 18–24. See also "Regulations for Uniform and Dress of the Navy," May 1, 1830, quoted in Naval History Division, *Uniforms of the United States Navy,* plate 55.

2. Mrs. Randolph to Mrs. Coolidge, Apr. 1 and 23, 1831, Coolidge Collection.

3. Randolph, Records of Naval Officers, M-330, roll 4, vol. G, no. 1653, records group 24, Naval Records. Mrs. Coolidge to Mrs. Randolph, Aug. 7, 1831, Coolidge Collection. George's letter to his mother went astray.

4. Porter, *Adventures of Harry Marline,* 18–24, 42, 239, 274–78.

5. Ibid., 364–65; Randolph to Mrs. Coolidge, July 26, 1831, Coolidge Collection.

6. Porter, *Adventures of Harry Marline,* 249, 251, 274–78, 280–82, 287;

Lewis, *Farragut,* 337. Presumably this was *Raoul Barbe Bleu,* the three-act comic opera by André Gretry, first performed at Paris, March 2, 1789, and revived at Vienna in 1821 and 1833. See *Annals of Opera.*

7. Mrs. Randolph to Mrs. Coolidge, Feb. 7, 1832, Coolidge Collection; see also Porter, *Memoir of Commodore David Porter,* 399–400.

8. Mrs. Randolph to Mrs. Coolidge, Feb. 7, 1832, Coolidge Collection. Randolph spelled Vourla phonetically with an 'F'. See also Page, Personal Log, Feb. 1825 to Dec. 1828.

9. Mrs. Randolph to Mrs. Coolidge, Feb. 7, 1832, Coolidge Collection.

10. Mrs. Randolph to Septimia Randolph, Nov. 12, 1833, Meikleham Papers.

11. Randolph, Records of Officers, M-330, roll 5, vol. H, no. 1813, records group 24, Naval Records. See also Mrs. Randolph to Mrs. Coolidge, June 24, July 15, Sept. 15, Oct. 27, and Dec. 2, 1833, Coolidge Collection.

12. Mrs. Randolph to Mrs. Coolidge, Sept. 15, 1833, Coolidge Collection; Mrs. Randolph to Mrs. Trist, Oct. 10 and 23, 1833, Thomas Jefferson Memorial Foundation Deposit; Randolph, Records of Officers, M-330, roll 5, vol. H, no. 1913, records group 24, Naval Records. See also Lewis, *Farragut,* 182–88, 191.

13. Randolph to Margaret S. Randolph, Dec. 30, 1833 and May 7, 1834, Edgehill Randolph Papers.

14. Mrs. Randolph to Thomas J. Randolph, Feb. 2, 1836, Edgehill Randolph Papers; Randolph to Septimia Randolph, May 7 and Nov. 13, 1834, Meikleham Papers; Randolph to Margaret S. Randolph, May 7, 1834, Edgehill Randolph Papers.

15. Randolph, Records of Officers, M-330, roll 5, vol. H, no. 1913, records group 24, Naval Records. See also Randolph to Septimia Randolph, Nov. 13, 1834, Meikleham Papers; Commander Tyrone P. Martin to the author, Oct. 14, 1975; and Lewis, *Farragut,* 189, 191.

16. Randolph, Records of Officers, M-330, roll 5, vol. H, no. 1913, records group 24, Naval Records. Although Alfred T. Mahan believed that Elliott should have been reprimanded for dilatoriness on Lake Erie in 1813, he thought that the Commodore deserved to be absolved of censure for his alleged misconduct in the Mediterranean. Elliott adopted Norfolk as his hometown because it was his wife's, and he helped suppress the Nat Turner Rebellion in adjacent Southampton County. See *Dictionary of American Biography,* S.V. "Elliott, Jessee Duncan."

17. Dahlgren, *Memoir,* 43.

18. Randolph to Margaret S. Randolph, July 25, 1835, Edgehill Randolph Papers.

19. Dahlgren, *Memoir,* 62–63; Paullin, *Rodgers,* 329, 333, 339, 353; Lewis, *Farragut,* 118. Vessels of the Mediterranean squadron were rotated frequently. In 1837 they were the frigates *Constitution, United States,* and *Potomac* and the sloops *John Adams* and *Shark.*

20. Randolph to Molly Randolph, Nov. 10, 1860, Edgehill Randolph

Papers; Paullin, *Rogers,* 338. In 1826 Rodgers thought Nauphlion as impregnable as Gibraltar. See also Page, Personal Log. Americans then called Nauphlion "Napoli di Romania."

21. Mrs. Randolph to Septimia Randolph, Mar. 3, 1836, Meikleham Papers; Professor Omer Yigitbasi to the author, January 1, 1974; Glenn L. Smith to the author, Aug. 9, 1973. See also Paullin, *Rodgers,* 353, 399. There were English, French, and Turkish hospitals at Smyrna.

22. Randolph to Mrs. Randolph, n.d., Edgehill Randolph Papers. See also Dakin, *The Greek Struggle,* 92, 97–98, 127–28; and Wordsworth, *Athens and Attica,* 246, 279–80, 282.

23. Randolph to Mrs. Randolph, n.d., Edgehill Randolph Papers; George T. Sinclair to ———— Dunlap, June 30, 184——, copied extract, Jefferson-Randolph Papers. See also Myers, *Children of Pride,* 1453. E. C. Anderson (1815–83) had been a pupil of George Bancroft. He was several times mayor of Savannah before and after the Civil War. A Confederate agent in England in 1861, he guided a blockade runner past the Union blockade and thereafter commanded the batteries defending the Savannah River.

Tarry's father, Captain Arthur Sinclair, had died in 1831 after a distinguished naval career. Tarry was the son of Sinclair's second wife; the captain's first wife had been the sister of Thomas Jefferson's eccentric friend, John Hartwell Cocke of Bremo. Appointed acting midshipman a month after George, Tarry had served on the *Potomac* and attended the Norfolk school before coming aboard *Constitution* in 1835. He was appointed a passed midshipman at the same time as Randolph. George T. Sinclair, Records of Officers, M-330, roll 5, vol. H, no. 1914, records group 24, Naval Records. See also *Virginia Magazine of History and Biography* (hereinafter cited as *VMHB*) 31 (1923), 310, and Callahan, *List of Officers,* 499.

24. Mrs. Randolph to Mrs. Coolidge, Aug. 22, 1836, and Randolph to Mrs. Coolidge, Aug. 23, 1836, Coolidge Collection; Randolph to Margaret Smith Randolph, Apr. 13, 1837, and Randolph to Thomas Jefferson Randolph, Oct. 17, 1836, Edgehill Randolph Papers; Martha J. Randolph, Last Will and Testament, Apr. 13, [1836], Edgehill Randolph Papers.

25. Randolph, Records of Officers, M-330, roll 4, vol. H, no. 1913, records group 24, Naval Records; Randolph to Margaret S. Randolph, Apr. 13, 1837, Jefferson-Randolph Papers.

26. Randolph, Records of Officers, M-330, roll 4, vol. H, no. 1913, records group 24, Naval Records. See also Callahan, *List of Officers,* 452.

27. Gaines, *Thomas Mann Randolph,* 7.

28. Log of USS *Vandalia,* Naval Records.

29. Randolph to Molly Randolph, Mar. 20 and Sept. 6, 1859, Edgehill Randolph Papers; Jones, "George Wythe Randolph," 45–59, and "George Wythe Randolph's Service," 299–314. For Randolph and the Italian campaign, Peter V. Daniel, Jr., to Randolph, Apr. 26, 1862, *War of The Rebellion,* 4th ser. 1: 1094.

### 3. Student and Lawyer in Albemarle

1. Randolph, Records of Officers, M-330, roll 4, vol. H, no. 1913, records group 24, Naval Records; Waring, "Sally Champe Carter," 1: 114–21, and Shackelford, "Martha Jefferson," 1: 45–66.

2. Randolph to Margaret S. Randolph, April 13, 1837, Jefferson-Randolph Papers; Mrs. Coolidge to Mrs. T. J. Randolph, Aug. 22, 1841 and Aug. 1, 1844, and Mrs. Coolidge to T. J. Randolph, Aug. 30, 1841, Edgehill Randolph Papers.

3. Faculty Minutes, July 3, 1838, University of Virginia Records; Randolph to John Hartwell Cocke, July 9, 1838, Cocke Papers; Proctor's Records, June 30, 1839, University of Virginia Records; Bruce, *University of Virginia*, 2: 105, 169, 171, 271–72, 309–11.

4. Faculty Minutes, July 3, 1839, and July 3, 1840, University of Virginia Records.

5. Snavely, *George Tucker*; MacLean, *George Tucker*, 35, 37, 229–30. See also Bruce, *University of Virginia*, 2: 18, 21–24.

6. Randolph to [Mary Buchanan] "Molly" [Randolph] (hereinafter cited as Molly), March 6, 1860, Edgehill Randolph Papers.

7. Virginia Randolph Trist to Septimia Randolph, Dec. 24, 1826, Meikleham Papers; Colin C. Clarke to William H. Woodley, Nov. 19, 1839, Proctor's Records, University of Virginia Records; and Bruce, *University of Virginia*, 2: 294, 3: 52–54.

8. Randolph to John H. Cocke, July 9, 1838, Cocke Papers; Randolph to Molly, Feb. 7, 1851, Edgehill Randolph Papers.

9. Randolph to Lewis Randolph, Jan. 1, 1859, Jefferson-Randolph Papers.

10. Order Book, 1837–41, Oct. 12, 1840, Circuit Superior Court of Law and Chancery, Albemarle County Records; Taylor, "Descendants of Thomas Jefferson," 1: 217, and Shackelford, "Mary Buchanan Randolph," 2: 64–69.

11. Peggy Nicholas to Jane Hollins Randolph, May 6, 1841, Edgehill Randolph Papers.

12. Pryor, *My Day*, 54, 74–75, 79–80, 84. There is a striking daguerreotype of Virginia Minor, who died in 1847, in the Minor Papers. See also Minor, *Minor Family*, 32, 123–24, and Mary Rawlings to Nannie S. Block, memorandum, circa 1940, xerox in collection of the author. Miss Rawlings cited as her source Miss Carolina Ramsay Randolph of Edgehill.

13. Pryor, *My Day*, 54, 74–75, 79–80, 84.

14. Randolph to Thomas J. Randolph, Sept. 5, 1840, and Thomas Green to Thomas J. Randolph, Nov. 22, 1840, Randolph Family Papers; Randolph to Peter Carr, Nov. 7, 1856, Carr Papers; Mrs. Coolidge to Thomas J. Randolph, Aug. 30, 1841, Coolidge Collection; David S. Meikleham to Nicholas P. Trist, July 10, 1841, Meikleham Papers.

15. Randolph to Molly, Feb. 7 and April 13, 1851, Edgehill Randolph Papers.

### 4. *Randolph Finds a Wife and Success*

1. Randolph to Lewis Randolph, Jan. 1, 1859, Jefferson-Randolph Papers.
2. Randolph to Molly, Jan. 22 and Feb. 7, 1851, Edgehill Randolph Papers; Randolph to Benjamin F. Randolph, Nov. 5, 1851, Randolph-Hubard Papers; Christian, "Reminiscences," 743–45; Laferty, *Sketches,* 48–49; *Richmond City and Henrico County; Montague's Richmond Directory; Butter's Richmond Directory;* Ellyson, *Richmond Directory;* and Ferslew, *Annual Directory.*
3. Manarin and Wallace, *Richmond Volunteers,* 152–54.
4. De Leon, *Belles,* 267. In identifying "hippo," the author acknowledges the assistance of Dr. Glenn Sonnedecker, acting director of the American Institute of the History of Pharmacy, Madison, Wisconsin.
5. Manarin and Wallace, *Richmond Volunteers,* 152–54. See also Standard, "Homes," 8.
6. Randolph to Molly, Jan. 22 and Feb. 20, 1851, Edgehill Randolph Papers.
7. Randolph to Molly, June 6, 1858, Jan. 17, 1859, and March 20, 1859, Edgehill Randolph Papers; Richmond *Dispatch,* Feb. n.d., 1861. See also H. H. Marshall to Septimia J. R. Meikleham, Apr. 7, 1860, Meikleham Papers. Each of Martha Jefferson's and Thomas Mann Randolph's children received $116.95. See also Shackelford, "Jane Hollins" and "Septimia Jefferson Randolph," 1: 87, 128–33.
8. Randolph to Lewis Randolph, Jan. 1, 1859, and Randolph to Molly, June 6 and Dec. 19, 1858, Aug. 8, 1859, Edgehill Randolph Papers; Christian, "Reminiscences," 745.
9. Deeds (Grantor) Index, no. 54, Deeds (Grantee) Index, no. 61, and Wills Index, no. 77, Richmond City Records.
10. Richmond *Dispatch,* Feb. n.d., 1861; Jones, *War Clerk's Diary,* 109.
11. Randolph to Molly, Feb. 20, 1851, Edgehill Randolph Papers; Chesnut, *A Diary from Dixie,* 110; Cary, *Recollections,* 172. See illustration of Mary Adams Randolph circa 1852.
12. Randolph to Molly, Jan. 22 and Feb. 7, 1851, Edgehill Randolph Papers; Richard Adams Estate, Deed and Contract between Samuel G. Adams, George M. Carrington, and Mary Adams Randolph (by her attorney George W. Randolph), Dec. 7, 1853, Deed Book, Richmond City Records; Richmond *Standard,* Dec. 18, 1880; Harrison, *Virginia Carys;* Hollywood Cemetery Burial Register; Mrs. C. C. Dodge to the author, Aug. 25, 1980; and Davenport Carrington to the author, May 30, 1981. See also Mordecai, *Richmond,* 34, 102–3; Stanard, *Richmond,* 21, 36, 121. Richard Adams' house was later the residence of Miss Elizabeth Van Lew. Mary Adams Pope Randolph was connected by family ties to the Randolphs, Daniels, Moncures, Skipwiths, and Southalls. See Stanard, ed., "Kennon Letters," 448, 450, and 120.
13. Probate Court, Will Book 133–37, 222–23, 226–30, Mobile County, Ala. Records; Randolph to Benjamin F. Randolph, Nov. 5, 1859; Randolph-Hubard Papers. Gayle (1792–1859) served one term in the U.S. House of Repre-

sentatives, 1847–49, after having been a state legislator, governor, and state supreme court justice and U.S. district judge. *Biographical Directory of the American Congress,* 1201.

14. Randolph to Molly, Aug. 2, 1851, Edgehill Randolph Papers.

15. Cabell, *Odd Volume,* 251–52.

16. *Southern Literary Messenger,* Oct. 1856, 311–12.

17. Randolph to Benjamin F. Randolph, Nov. 5, 1859, Edgehill Randolph
Papers. See also Jessie Dodge Pollard to author, July 30, 1980. Mary Adams
Randolph's "niece," Virginia Washington Adams, married William C. Nichols,
M.D. of New Orleans at St. Paul's Episcopal Church, Richmond, on Dec. 20,
1864.

18. Sarah N. Randolph to Virginia R. Trist, Aug. 15, 1855; Trist Family
Papers.

19. Randolph to Molly, July 17, 1858, Edgehill Randolph Papers; Richard
Adams Estate, Deed and Contract, Dec. 7, 1853, Deed Book, Richmond City
Records. See also *The City Intelligencer,* 3.

20. Hayden, *Virginia Genealogies,* 574–84. Richard Adams Estate, Deed
and Contract, Dec. 7, 1853, Deed Book, Richmond City Records. Mary Adams
Randolph does not appear to have written about Elizabeth Van Lew, who resided in the shuttered and faded elegance of the old Adams mansion on Church
Hill. In the 1850s, Miss Van Lew was considered merely an eccentric. In the
1860s, she was to be the notorious Union spy.

21. Pryor, *My Day,* 114–15.

22. Randolph to Molly, May 3, 1858, Edgehill Randolph Papers; Olivia A.
Taylor to the author, Feb. 15 and March 8, 1977; Randolph, Last Will and Testament, Dec. 14, 1866, Will Book, Albemarle County Records, 79.

23. Kean, "General George Wythe Randolph," 14–16.

24. Thompson, "The Jamestown Celebration, 1857," "Hexameters at
Jamestown," and "University of Virginia," *Poems,* 146–52, 155–66, 175–78, 210,
216; Garmon, *Thompson,* 16–17, 121, 172.

25. Pryor, *My Day,* 108, 126; Stanard, "Homes," 8.

26. Thompson, "In Remembrance of George Wythe Randolph," broadside, Edgehill Randolph Papers; *Poems,* 206–8; Stanard, "Catalogue of Portraits," 60; and interview with Virginia Minor Randolph Shackelford, circa
1934.

27. Randolph to Molly, May 3, 1858, Edgehill Randolph Papers. See also
Randolph to Conway Robinson, Conway Robinson Papers.

28. Richmond *Enquirer,* July 9 and 13, 1858. Rachal, "President Monroe,"
43–47.

29. Ibid.

30. Randolph to Molly, July 17, 1858; Mrs. Coolidge to Molly, June 21,
1858; Thompson, "In Remembrance," Edgehill Randolph Papers. See also
*Harper's Weekly Magazine,* July 17, 1858.

31. See discussion in Chapter 11.

32. Randolph to Septimia Meikleham, Oct. 14, 1860, and Dec. 20, 1864,

Meikleham Papers; Mary E. A. Randolph to Mrs. Benjamin F. Randolph, Nov. 14, 1865, Randolph-Hubard Papers.

33. Randolph to Benjamin F. Randolph, Nov. 5, 1851, Jefferson-Randolph Papers; Randolph to R. G. H. Kean, Nov. 26, 1856, Kean Papers.

34. Randolph to Molly, March 6, 1860, Edgehill Randolph Papers. See also Thompson, "The Window-Panes At Brandon," "The Jamestown Celebration, 1857," and "Hexameters At Jamestown," *Poems,* 79—80, 146—51, 175—78, 242; Stanard, "Harrison of James River"; and Joseph H. Harrison to the author, June 22, 1982.

35. Randolph to Molly, Jan. 17, 1858, and April 18, 1860, Edgehill Randolph Papers. In 1860 George W. Randolph began addressing his niece as Mary, but in this work, she will continue to be called "Molly."

36. Randolph to Nahun Capen, April 18, 1851, Kirk-Randolph-Nicholas Papers.

37. Randolph to Molly, June 10, 1860, Edgehill Randolph Papers. Mary Walker Randolph to the author, memorandum concerning G. W. Randolph's Bible concordance, May 15, 1970.

38. Quotation from Thompson, "In Remembrance," Edgehill Randolph Papers; *Poems,* 206—8. Andrew Johnston's proxy to Randolph, Claiborne, and Myers, 1858, Richmond Library County Records.

39. Thompson, *Poems,* 242; Garmon, *Thompson,* 172.

40. Randolph to Molly, July 17, 1858; Mrs. Coolidge to Molly, Aug. 17, 1858, Edgehill Randolph Papers.

41. Mrs. Coolidge to Isaetta C. Randolph, May 2, 1860, and Benjamin F. Randolph to [Sarah N. Randolph], Aug. 2, 1869, Randolph-Hubard Papers; Mrs. Coolidge to Cornelia J. Randolph, May 21 and July 25, 1860; Trist Family Papers.

42. Randolph to Molly, March 20, Aug. 8, and Sept. 6, 1859, Edgehill Randolph Papers.

### 5. *The Emergence of a Political Leader*

1. Pareto, *Mind and Society,* 2059; Richmond *Whig,* Nov. 9, 1859; Richmond *Examiner,* Nov. 1, 1859; and Randolph to Molly, Dec. 18, 1858, Edgehill Randolph Papers.

2. *Southern Literary Messenger,* Feb. and Mar. 1855, 127, 129—41; Randolph to Nahun Capen, April 18, 1851, Kirk-Randolph-Nicholas Letters. See also Fitzhugh, *Cannibals All!,* 119—29; Wish, *George Fitzhugh,* 98; and Faust, *Sacred Circle,* 127—31.

3. *Southern Literary Messenger,* March 1857, 239; Aug. 1857, 81—94.

4. For Bancroft, see ibid., July 1852, 442, and Aug. 1860, 82—91; for Campbell, see ibid., Mar. 1860, 209—20; for Grigsby, see ibid., Jan. and Feb. 1856, 110—17.

5. Ibid., June 1860, 468—72; Oct. 1852, 630—38.

6. Pryor, *My Day,* 124, 126; Manarin, *Richmond at War,* 631—32.

7. Richmond *Whig,* Nov. 19, 1859; Manarin, *Richmond at War,* 152–54. At about this time he secured for himself and his brothers Colt Navy revolvers.

8. Manarin and Wallace, *Richmond Volunteers,* 152–54; Hudnall, "Organization of the First Company," 1: 5–6. The works of Dennis H. Mahan include *Advanced-Guard, Out-Post, and Detachment Service of Troops with the Essential Principles of Strategy, and Grand Tactics, for the Use of the Militia and Volunteers; A Complete Treatise on Field Fortifications with the General Outline of the Principles Regulating the Arrangement, the Attack and the Defence of a Permanent Works;* (at least thirteen editions before 1862); and *Summary of the Course of Permanent Fortifications.*

9. Cooke, *Outlines from the Outpost,* 171; Manarin, *Richmond at War,* 3, 89. See also Villard, *John Brown,* 527, 556.

10. Randolph to Molly, Aug. 8 and Dec. 18, 1859, Edgehill Randolph Papers. See illustration of George W. Randolph circa 1852.

11. Randolph to John B. Floyd, Nov. 3, 1860, *War of Rebellion,* 3d ser. 1: 3, 4, 10. Randolph to [Virginia R. Trist], Apr. 28, 1860, and Alice Meikleham to Virginia R. Trist, May 9, 1860, Trist Family Papers. Richmond *Enquirer,* Oct. 17, 1861; report of proceedings of the convention on April 16, 1861. Henry du Pont (1812–89) was a son of Eleuthère Irénée du Pont (1771–1834) and the grandson of Pierre Samuel du Pont de Nemours (1739–1817).

12. Randolph to Floyd, Nov. 3 and Dec. 1, 1860, *War of Rebellion,* 3d ser. 1: 3–4, 10; *Calendar of Virginia State Papers* 11: 186. See also Couper, *One Hundred Years,* 1: n.p.; Chambers, *Stonewall Jackson,* 288–300. Quotation is from Randolph to Septimia J. R. Meikleham, October 14, 1860, Meikleham Papers.

13. Manarin and Wallace, *Richmond Volunteers,* 3–4, 154.

14. Randolph to Molly, Aug. 8, 1859, Edgehill Randolph Papers. He previously had puzzled over the chances of Gov. Henry A. Wise or Sen. R. M. T. Hunter obtaining the Democratic presidential nomination. See Curry, "James A. Seddon," 123–50.

15. Randolph to Molly, Apr. 18, 1860, Edgehill Randolph Papers.

16. Randolph to Septimia J. R. Meikleham, Oct. 14, 1860, Meikleham Papers. Randolph to Cornelia J. Randolph, Nov. 3, 1860, Trist Family Papers.

17. Randolph to Molly, Nov. 10, 1860, Edgehill Randolph Papers.

18. Thompson, "In Remembrance," *Poems,* 206–8.

19. Shanks, *Secession Movement in Virginia,* 153, 196.

20. Pareto, *Mind and Society,* 1424–26.

21. Shanks, *Secession Movement in Virginia,* 153, 196; Nichols, *Disruption of American Democracy.*

22. *Southern Literary Messenger,* March 1861, 340.

23. Richmond *Dispatch,* Feb. n.d., 1861.

24. Richmond *Enquirer,* Oct. 15, 1861; Shanks, *Secession Movement in Virginia,* 199.

25. Edward C. Anderson to Jefferson Davis, Richmond, Apr. 15, 1860, *War of Rebellion,* 1st ser., 51, pt. 2, 2; E. C. Anderson, Diary, Southern Historical Collection. Anderson's daughter-in-law was George Randolph's niece. Ander-

son came to Virginia in order to conduct her to Albemarle for her accouchement.

26. Richmond *Enquirer*, Oct. 15, 1861 (report of the proceedings of Apr. 16, 1861).

27. Ibid., Oct. 15 and 29, 1861 (report of the proceedings of Apr. 16 and 20, 1861).

28. Ibid., Oct. 17, 1861 (report of proceedings of Apr. 16, 1861).

29. Manarin and Wallace, *Richmond Volunteers*, 3–4.

### 6. *From a Captaincy to the Cabinet*

1. Hudnall, "Organization and Brown Raid," *History of the Richmond Howitzers*, 1: 5–60. The Howitzers never formed a fourth company.

2. *Encyclopedia of Virginia Biography*, s. v. "Magruder, John Bankhead"; Randolph to Asst. Sec. of War Albert T. Bledsoe, Richmond, Aug. 26, 1861, *War of Rebellion*, 1st ser., 51, pt. 2, 251. D. H. Hill wrote his wife in June of 1861 that Magruder was "always drunk." Quoted in Bridges, *Lee's Maverick General*, 28–29. Frank E. Vandiver asserts that, although Magruder was "nervous" and seemed "inadequate," he was "ill and overtired" at the time and that he later did reasonably well in Texas. See *Rebel Brass*, 31–33. See also Freeman, *Lee's Lieutenants*, 1: 14–18.

3. Randolph to Molly, Yorktown, Jan. 18, 1862, Edgehill Randolph Papers; Taylor, "Charles Lewis," 1: 67–75.

4. Brown became a captain in May of 1862, a major on June 2, 1862, and was killed in the Battle of the Wilderness in 1864. The Southalls were connected to the Jefferson-Randolphs by the marriage of Peter Randolph, Jr. and Eliza Southall. Brown was related through the Poythress family to Roger A. Pryor and connected to George W. Randolph. See Edward Trigg Brown to the author, March, 1984. See also R. I. Randolph, *Randolphs of Virginia*, 11; Malone, *Jefferson*, 1: 32, 96.

5. Randolph to H. C. Cabell at Young's Mill, Warwick County, Va., Yorktown, Oct. 23, 1861, Cabell Papers. See also Maj. Gen. J. Bankhead Magruder to Gen. Samuel Cooper, Mar. 10 and 15, 1862, *War of Rebellion*, 1st ser., 51, pt. 2, 498, 503; Randolph to J. Thompson Brown, Nov. 20, 1861, George Wythe Randolph Letters.

6. William H. Richardson to Josiah Gorgas, Jan. 3, 1863, and Randolph to J. Thompson Brown, Richmond, Jan. 14, 1863, George Wythe Randolph Letters; John B. Magruder to R. S. Garnet, June 10, 1861, D. H. Hill to Magruder, June 12, 1861, and Randolph to Magruder, June 12, 1861, *War of Rebellion*, 1st ser. 2: 91–101.

7. Randolph to Molly, July 23, 1861, Edgehill Randolph Papers; Magruder to Garnet, June, 1861, Hill to Magruder, June 12, 1861, and Randolph to Magruder, June 12, 1861; *War of Rebellion*, 1st ser. 2: 91–101.

8. Magruder to Garnet, June 10, 1861, Hill to Magruder, June 12, 1861, Randolph to Magruder, June 12, 1861; *War of Rebellion*, 1st ser. 2: 91–101; Freeman, *Lee's Lieutenants*, 1: 18–21; Richmond *Dispatch*, June 13, 1861.

9. Jefferson Davis to Gov. [John Letcher] of Virginia, Sept. 21, 1861; quoted in Christie Manson and Woods, *Americana*, 66.

10. Randolph to Molly, July 23, 1861, Edgehill Randolph Papers.

11. Randolph to J. Thompson Brown, Nov. 20, 1861, George Wythe Randolph Letters; Randolph to Alfred T. Bledsoe, Aug. 26, 1861, *War of Rebellion*, 1st ser., 51, pt. 2, 251.

12. Richmond *Enquirer,* Nov. 10, 13, 19, 22, and 23, 1861.

13. Randolph to Molly, Jan. 18, 1862, Edgehill Randolph Papers. An exceptionally good account is Dowdey and Manarin's *Wartime Papers of R. E. Lee*, 125–26.

14. Randolph to J. Thompson Brown, Nov. 20, 1861, George Wythe Randolph Letters; Randolph to Molly, Jan. 18, 1862, Edgehill Randolph Papers. See Jones, *Confederate Strategy*, 44.

15. Capt. John W. Phelps, U.S.A. to Brig. Gen. Benjamin F. Butler, U.S.A., Newport News, Aug. 11, 1861 and Brig. Gen. John B. Magruder to Col. George Deas, Adjutant General, C.S.A.; *War of Rebellion*, 1st ser. 4: 569, 571. Randolph said, "One-third of the town had been burned by the enemy when they evacuated it."

16. Johnston, *Narrative of Military Operations*, 111.

17. Randolph to Molly, Richmond, n.d.[c.1858], Edgehill Randolph Papers. See also chapter 3 concerning the St. John family. Kean, *Inside the Confederate Government*, xxii–xxiv, 115, 134.

18. Kean, *Inside the Confederate Government*, xvi–xxxvii, 26–27; Brig. Gen. R. C. Gatlin to Gen. Samuel Cooper, Goldsborough, N.C., Feb. 24, 1862, Mar. 7, 1862, and W. T. Dortch, O. R. Kenan et al. to Randolph, *War of Rebellion*, 1st ser., 51, pt. 2, 478, 492, 627–28.

19. Mrs. Cary Anne Randolph Cooper to the author, May 1, 1976.

20. *Southern Literary Messenger,* Feb.–March 1862, 127, 192–97.

21. Chesnut, *Mary Chesnut's Civil War,* 706.

22. Leroy P. Walker to Davis, Apr. 27, 1861, and Judah P. Benjamin to Davis, Feb. 14, 1862; *War of Rebellion*, 4th ser. 1: 147–53, 955, 962; Patrick, *Davis and His Cabinet*, 162–83.

23. Henry A. Wise to Gen. Samuel Cooper, Mar. 31, 1862, *War of Rebellion*, 1st ser., 51, pt. 2, 524–25, 535, 537, 539, 544–47, 553 presents the main outlines of this affair.

24. Jefferson Davis to Confederate States Senate, Mar. 17, 1862; *War of Rebellion*, 4th ser. 1: 1005.

25. D. H. Hill to Randolph, Mar. 22, 1862, and Joseph R. Anderson to Randolph, Mar. 28, 1862, *War of Rebellion*, 1st ser., 51, pt. 2, 516–17, 526.

26. Richmond *Enquirer,* Mar. 17, 1862; Richmond *Dispatch,* Mar. 19, 1862.

27. For examples, see Randolph to J. Thompson Brown and Brown to Randolph, April 15, 1862, *War of Rebellion*, 4th ser., 1: 1062–63; Randolph to Vance and Vance to Davis, Oct. 10, 1862, *War of Rebellion*, 4th ser. 2: 114–15, 146–48. Randolph to Davis, Oct. 20, 1862, and Davis to Randolph, Oct. 20, 1862, *War of Rebellion*, 4th ser., 2: 132; Randolph to Brown, Mar. 1, 1862 and Jan.

19, 1863, George Wythe Randolph Letters. For the Confederate Conscription Act, *War of Rebellion*, 4th ser. 1: 1095–97. See also chapters 4 and 5.

28. Walker to Davis, Apr. 27, 1861, and Benjamin to Davis, Feb. 14, 1862, *War of Rebellion*, 4th ser. 1: 247–53, 955–62; Patrick, *Davis and His Cabinet*, 162–83.

29. Walker to Davis, Apr. 27, 1861, *War of Rebellion*, 4th ser. 1: 247–53.

30. Act of Confederate States Congress, Apr. 11, 1862, and Richard Morton to Josiah Gorgas, *War of Rebellion*, 4th ser. 1: 1054–55, 1115–16, 1176. See also *Southern Historical Society Papers*, 1, A7; 12: 76.

31. D. H. Hill to Randolph, Mar. 22, 1862, Joseph R. Anderson to Randolph, Mar. 28 and May 15, 1862, Randolph to Anderson, Apr. 2, 1862, and Thomas H. Wynne to Randolph, Apr. 29, 1862, all in *War of Rebellion*, 1st ser., 51, pt. 2, 516–17, 526, 548–49, 557–58. Anderson left the direction of the Tredegar Iron Works in September 1861 to become a brigadier general in eastern North Carolina. Soon after Randolph came to the War Office, Anderson was posted to Fredericksburg, first to command a brigade and then a division. After receiving severe wounds in the Battle of Frayser's Farm, he resigned in July of 1862. *Encyclopedia of Virginia Biography*, s. v. "Anderson, Joseph Reid."

32. Albert T. Bledsoe to D. M. K. Campbell, Aug. 6, 1861, and Confederate States Congress to Benjamin, Dec. 10, 1861; *War of Rebellion*, 4th ser. 1: 532–34, 780; Randolph to Bledsoe, Aug. 26, 1861, *War of Rebellion*, 1st ser., 51, pt. 2, 251; Kean, *Inside the Confederate Government*, xxiv, 27; *Dictionary of American Biography*, s. v. "Bledsoe, Albert Taylor." Bledsoe had strong views about infant baptism. After the war Bledsoe was a vociferous defender of the Lost Cause.

33. *National Cyclopedia of Biography*, s.v. "Ould, Robert." For quotations, see Swanberg, *Sickles the Incredible*, 63–66. See also *Encyclopedia of Virginia Biography*, s.v. "Ould, Robert." The colonel's first wife, née Sarah Turpin, was related to Thomas Jefferson. Mattie, later Mrs. Paul, posed for one of the figures in William D. Washington's *The Burial of Latané*. After the war, Ould and Mrs. Randolph's relative, Major Isaac Carrington, practiced law together. See Dunaway, *History of the James River and Kanawha Canal Company*, 238.

34. Benjamin to Davis, Dec. 14, 1861, and Feb. 1862; *War of Rebellion*, 4th ser. 1: 796, 962; Beldsoe to ———, Aug. 6, 1861, and Confederate States Congress to Benjamin, Dec. 10, 1861, *War of Rebellion*, 4th ser. 1: 534, 780; Kean, *Inside the Confederate Government*, xxii–xxiii, 115, 134.

35. *War of Rebellion*, 4th ser. 1: 1005, 1176.

36. Benjamin to Davis, Dec. 1861, *War of Rebellion*, 4th ser. 1: 959.

### 7. *Randolph Assumes the Secretaryship*

1. Randolph to Edward Sparrow, chairman of Confederate States Senate Military Committee, Sept. 26, 1862, and Randolph to Col. Abraham C. Myers, Oct. 15, 1862, *War of Rebellion*, 4th ser. 2: 97–98, 122. See also Brinton, *Decade of Revolution*, 124 and chapter 2; *City Intelligencer*, 3.

2. Jones, *War Clerk's Diary*, 1: 120; Wise, *Long Arm of Lee*, 113–15. For Wise's ambition, see Shanks, *Secession Movement in Virginia*, 47.

3. *City Intelligencer*, 3; Fleet, *Green Mount*, 150.

4. War of Rebellion, 4th ser. 2: 177, 1115.

5. Stuart to Randolph, Apr. 29, 1862, and J. D. Imboden to Randolph, June 23, 1862, *War of Rebellion*, 1st ser., 51, pt. 2, 550–51, 578–79. Randolph to Albert R. Boteler, Richmond, Oct. 6, 1862, Nathaniel Tyler via Boteler to Randolph, Richmond, Sept. 27, 1862, C.S.A. War Department Papers; Alexander C. Jones Papers.

6. Hugh Blair Grigsby to Randolph, Charlotte Court House, Va., Nov. 10, 1862; Grigsby Papers.

7. Freeman, *Lee's Lieutenants*, 1: 148–51.

8. General Order 43, June 13, 1862, and Randolph to Col. Thomas M. Jones, May 13, 1862, *War of Rebellion*, 4th ser. 1: 6, 890, 1151; Kean, *Inside the Confederate Government*, xxii, 27; [McGuire], *Diary of a Southern Refugee*, 114. See also Jones, *Confederate Strategy*, 60.

9. Randolph to Capt. V. D. Groner, May 29, 1862, George Wythe Randolph Letters; Groner to Randolph, Scottsville, June 6, 1862, *War of Rebellion*, 1st ser., 51, pt. 2; Reagan, *Memoirs*, 140.

10. In order later to raid the Charleston and Memphis Railroad, Union forces fought at Shiloh (Pittsburgh Landing) on March 15, 1862, and at Corinth, Miss., on May 8, 1862. W. T. Sherman to U. S. Grant, June 19, 1862; *War of Rebellion*, 1st ser. 10: 22, 728.

11. Mayor John Park to Flag Officer C. H. Davis, June 6, 1862; *War of Rebellion*, 1st ser. 10: 911.

12. Jones, *Confederate Strategy*, 70–88.

13. Jones, *War Clerk's Diary*, 1: 191; Kean, *Inside the Confederate Government*, 30, 101. Kean alludes to the experience of both Randolph and James A. Seddon.

## 8. *The Randolphs in Wartime Richmond*

1. Randolph to J. Thompson Brown, Richmond, Jan. 14, 1863, George Wythe Randolph Letters. Randolph to Molly, Jan. 18, 1862, Edgehill Randolph Papers. The war office clerk John B. Jones was not correct in surmising that the president's contemporaneous assignment of Roger A. Pryor and of his own nephew to command brigades operated on the former secretary as an "emetic" and helped drive him out of the army. See Jones, *War Clerk's Diary*, 1: 209.

2. Chesnut, *Diary from Dixie*, 313; Jones, *War Clerk's Diary*, 1: 209.

3. Gorgas, *Civil War Diary*, 37. See also Vandiver, *Ploughshares into Swords*, 184; Kean, *Inside the Confederate Government*, 56; Jones, *War Clerk's Diary* (Miers ed.), 78; Jones, *War Clerk's Diary*, 1: 347–48. See also Reagan, *Memoirs*, 36; Richmond *Examiner*, May 3, 1863.

4. Von Borcke, *Memoirs*, 12–13, 16, 34, 267–68, 400–402. Although John

R. Thompson was not present at the great review, he contributed to its literary record later on by improving, if not ghost-writing, Von Borcke's memoirs. For information on the open-air ball on June 5, I am indebted to Mrs. Frank R. Blackford of Carysbrook, Montgomery County, Va., who permitted me to consult William W. Blackford's marginal notes in Von Borcke's *Memoirs*.

5. Randolph to J. Thompson Brown, Richmond, Jan. 14, 1863, George Wythe Randolph Letters. When the legislature did elect a chief executive, it was the sixty-six-year-old William Smith, who, besides having been a major general, had served as governor between 1846 and 1849.

6. Jones, *War Clerk's Diary,* 1: 347, 2: 68, 177; Manarin, *Richmond at War,* 287, 313–15, 320–21. Samuel O. Demoon and Richard O. Haskins were the other members of the Poor Relief Committee.

7. Randolph to Molly, June 27, 1865, Edgehill Randolph Papers; Randolph to Septimia Randolph Meikleham, Dec. 22, 1864, Meikleham Papers; Mrs. Randolph to Isaetta Hubard, Dec. 12, 1864, Randolph-Hubard Papers.

8. Thompson, *Poems,* 8–10.

9. Randolph to Molly, n.d. [1866], Kirk-Randolph-Nicholas Letters; *Harvard Memorial Biographies,* s.v. "Revere, Paul Joseph"; *Cyclopedia of American Biography,* s.v. "Revere"; Whitehill and Endicott, *Captain Joseph Peabody,* 184, 196.

10. Randolph to J. Thompson Brown, Jan. 14, 1863, George Wythe Randolph Letters; Richmond *Enquirer,* May 29, 1863; Jones, *War Clerk's Diary,* 1: 177, 218–20, 280. After protracted efforts, Randolph finally gained an exemption for a dentist named Benton, which especially annoyed Jones.

11. Confederate States of America to George W. Randolph, $1,000 bond, Feb. 13, 1863, George Wythe Randolph Letters; Jones, *War Clerk's Diary,* 1: 384; Thomas H. Ellis, "Edgar A. Poe: A Letter to the Editor," Richmond *Standard,* May 7, 1881. Mr. Allan never became Poe's foster father officially. Maria Caterina Rosalbina de Munck (1800–65), a soprano, performed under her mother's name, Caradori, in Italy, France, Germany, Great Britain, and the United States between 1822 and the 1850s. Stainsbury, *Dictionary of Musicians,* 133–34; Fetis, *Biographie universelle des musiciens,* 181–82; *New Grove Dictionary,* 2: 56–57. Allan, *Lay of the Sylph.* See also *Dictionary of American Biography,* s.v. "Dix, Morgan." The Reverend Mr. Dix married when he was fifty years old. Although he fostered church music in the United States, he was not related to the English lay master of hymnody, William Chatterton Dix. See also for fictional account, Dowdey, *Experiment in Rebellion,* 302–3.

12. Sarah N. Randolph to [Septimia R. Meikleham], June 16, 1861, Trist Family Papers.

13. Chesnut, *Diary from Dixie,* 115.

14. Ibid., 95–96, 115.

15. Agnes Rice Pryor, *Reminiscences,* 168, 181–82.

16. Randolph to Molly, n.d. [1866], Kirk-Randolph-Nicholas Letters; *Harvard Memorial Biographies,* s.v. "Revere, Paul Joseph"; *Cyclopedia of American Biography,* s.v. "Revere"; Whitehill and Endicott, *Captain Joseph Peabody,*

184, 196. This seems to have been the only time that Mary Adams Randolph encountered Miss Van Lew, despite their common Church Hill background.

17. Randolph to J. Thompson Brown, Jan. 14, 1863, George Wythe Randolph Letters; Randolph to Molly, July 23, 1865, Edgehill Randolph Papers; Chesnut, *Diary from Dixie*, 281. George Randolph blamed himself for his wife's financial reverse because he had not kept a closer watch over her Mobile investments.

18. Cary, *Recollections*, 61–62, 67–68, 77–78. Mrs. Monimia Fairfax Cary was the youngest daughter of Thomas, ninth Lord Fairfax. Connie's grandmother, Virginia Randolph of Tuckahoe, was raised by her brother and sister-in-law, Gov. and Mrs. Thomas Mann Randolph, Jr. The Cary girls also were related to Mary Elizabeth Adams Pope Randolph.

19. Patrick, *Davis and His Cabinet*, 333.

20. Randolph to Molly, Edgehill Randolph Papers; Chesnut, *Diary from Dixie*, 328–29, 346–47; Reagan, *Memoirs*, 60; De Leon, *Belles*, 201–2; Chesnut, *Diary from Dixie*, 281. Mary Randolph's loss resulted from the insolvency of a debtor and amounted to a prewar value of $6,000, then a princely sum.

21. Chesnut, *Diary from Dixie*, 346–47; Trent, *Southern Writers*, 351–56. See also Mason, *Southern Poems;* De Leon, *Belles*, 201–2. Besides verses on the deaths of such Confederate heroes as Latané, Ashby, Jackson, and Stuart, Thompson wrote highly considered lyrical pieces such as "The Battle Rainbow" and "Music in Camp." His 1871 poem in memory of George Wythe Randolph is included in this work on pages 175–77. See Thompson, "In Remembrance," *Poems*, 206–8; broadside, n.d., Edgehill Randolph Papers, and Kean, "General George Wythe Randolph," 15: 16–18.

22. De Leon, *Belles*, 201–2, 284–92. See also Johnson and Lipscomb, *Amelia Gayle Gorgas*, vi. Although said to have been a distant relative of the president, Washington was not. He was active from 1834 to 1870, and the Corcoran Gallery in Washington owned at least three of his works but now has none. See Belinda Barham to the author, July 2, 1985. The *Burial of Latané* was engraved in 1868, after which Washington sold the painting to L. P. Payne, a Southern banker active as a broker in Washington and New York, who is not thought to have been a kinsman of Thomas Levingston Bayne.

23. Mrs. Randolph to Sarah N. Randolph, June 5, [1865], Edgehill Randolph Papers.

24. Mrs. Randolph to Isaetta Hubard, Aug. n.d. and 20 [1861], Oct. 21, [1861], Sarah N. Randolph to Isaetta Hubard, Aug. 24, 1861, Randolph-Hubard Papers. See also De Leon, *Belles*, 228–29.

25. Randolph to J. Thompson Brown, Richmond, Jan. 14, 1863, George Wythe Randolph Letters.

26. Von Borcke, *Memoirs*, 1: 17–18, 49; 2: 67–68. See also Chesnut, *Diary from Dixie*, 332; and Reagan, *Memoirs*, 76, 140.

27. Cary, *Recollections*, 172–75. See also Chesnut, *Diary from Dixie*, 356–58; and Reagan, *Memoirs*, 76.

28. Chesnut, *Diary from Dixie*, 368–70. See also De Leon, *Belles*, 228–29.

Jennie (Virginia) Pollard was the daughter of Mary Innes Adams and George Pollard (1797–1863). Mrs. C. C. Dodge to the author, Aug. 25, 1980. There is no record of George Randolph's having sung at Richmond's wartime amateur theatricals, although his distant kinsmen Innes and John Randolph did so. Captain Joseph Denegre of the War Department had a brother named James Taylor Denegre (1848–75), but Mrs. Chesnut was mistaken in identifying the serenader of the Scythian Girl as "Captain Jimmy Denegre."

29. Chesnut, *Diary from Dixie*, 356–58.

30. Ibid., 346–47, 352. Mrs. Chesnut sent her husband first to visit Mrs. Davis, then to their fellow South Carolinian, Mrs. William Campbell Preston, then to Mrs. Randolph, and finally to seven other ladies.

31. Luraghi, *Rise and Fall*, 74–80, 150–52.

## 9. The F.F.V. and the Technocrats

1. Thomas, *Confederate Nation*, and Hattaway and Jones, *How the North Won*, are the best general studies, but even they devote little attention to Randolph and none to elites.

2. Randolph to Molly, Jan. 18, 1860, Edgehill Randolph Papers. The Department of War was ordered to move on May 25, 1861. *War of Rebellion*, 4th ser. 1: 354. Concerning cosmopolitanism, see De Leon, *Belles*, 125.

3. Pareto, *Mind and Society*, 1: 169. For American applications of the concept of elites, see Lasswell, *Study of Elites*, and Parsons, *Essays In Sociological Theory*.

4. The Cavalier theme has an immense literature, including R. I. Randolph, *Randolphs of Virginia*, 261; De Leon, *Belles*, 17, 59. See also Mannahan, "The Cavalier Remounted"; Colomy, "Stunted Differentiation"; and Baskin, "Free Blacks."

5. Quotation from Thompson, "Virginia," *Poems*, 143.

6. R. I. Randolph, *Randolphs of Virginia*. There are, of course, thousands of Randolphs, many who never amounted to much, many who died as infants, many of whom nothing good or bad is known. There is no reason to suspect that the compiler consciously omitted any name.

7. Table 1. See also chapter 3, R. I. Randolph, *Randolphs of Virginia*, and *Cyclopedia of Virginia Biography*.

8. Keller, *Beyond the Ruling Class*, 250.

9. Ibid., 290.

10. Chesnut, *Mrs. Chesnut's Civil War*, 96, 435. Shackelford, "New Letters," 322–26, 337.

11. See appendix, table 1.

12. Abernethy, *A Short Sketch*.

13. Pareto, *Mind and Society*, 1421, 1423, 1431; Keller, *Beyond the Ruling Class*, 234, 261–63. Concerning Richmond's cosmopolitan status, see De Leon, *Belles*, 125; Chesnut, *Mary Chesnut's Civil War*, 96, 435.

14. Randolph to Molly, Jan. 18, 1860, and Randolph to T. J. Randolph,

Nov. 25, 1862, Edgehill Randolph Papers; Randolph to J. Thompson Brown, Jan. 14, 1863, George Wythe Randolph Letters.

15. Pareto, *Mind and Society,* 1421. The Department of War was ordered to move to Richmond on May 25, 1861. *War of Rebellion,* 4th ser. 1: 354. For standard accounts of this transition, see Bill, *Beleaguered City;* Dowdey, *Experiment in Rebellion;* Meade, *Judah P. Benjamin;* and Thomas, *Confederate State of Richmond.*

16. Pareto, *Mind and Society,* 1431; Keller, *Beyond the Ruling Class,* 244, 257. The Marxist phrase is from Karl Marx and Frederick Engels, "Manifesto," *Collected Works,* 6: 109.

17. Appendix, table 2.

18. Beringer, *Historical Analysis,* 153–57; Jones, *Confederate Strategy,* 42–43.

19. Acting Chief of Bureau of Nitre and Mining A. Landon Rives to Benjamin, Mar. 12, 1862, *War of Rebellion,* 1st ser. 9: 61; Rives to R.E. Lee, Mar. 18, 1862; ibid., 4th ser. 1: 1176; Capt. Richard Morton to Col. Josiah Gorgas, May 7, 1862, ibid., 4th ser. 1: 1115–16; Table of Principal Officers of the War Department, ibid., 1st ser. 12: 831, 1302, and 4th ser. 1: 833.

20. Randolph to Molly, Dec. 18, 1859; Edgehill Randolph Papers and chapter 4. See also Bagby, "John M. Daniels's Latch-Key," 111–43; Wish, *George Fitzhugh;* McLean, *George Tucker;* Klingberg and Klingberg (eds.), *Correspondence;* Torrence, "Letters," 315–56; Shackelford, "New Letters," 322–26, 337; Rachal, "Hugh Blair Grigsby," and chapter 3.

21. Luraghi, *Rise and Fall,* 74–80, 89–91, 101–2, 150–52.

22. Randolph to Molly, Dec. 18, 1859, Edgehill Randolph Papers. See also Taylor, "Descendants of Thomas Jefferson," 1: 146, 223, 227.

23. Goodrich, "The Virginia System," 355–87; Dunaway, *History of the James River and Kanawha Company,* 188n.

## 10.  *Randolph Recruits His Staff*

1. *War of Rebellion,* 4th ser. 1: 1176. See also Kean, *Inside the Confederate Government,* xxiii–xxiv, 27. Keller, *Beyond the Ruling Class,* 8–9, 13–15, 250. Karl Mannheim in his *Man and Society in an Age of Reconstruction* distinguishes between an integrative elite composed of leaders working through political organizations and a sublimative elite made up of moral-religious, aesthetic, and intellectual leaders working through more informal groups, cliques, and coteries. He suggests that these elites are interdependent and that their active leaders form a "body politic" for the organization of society.

2. Chapter 3 and fn. 24 following. See also Randolph to Molly, Apr. 18, 1860, Edgehill Randolph Papers. Thomas, *Confederate Nation,* 207–14.

3. Randolph to Edward Sparrow, chairman of the Confederate States Senate Military Committee, Sept. 26, 1862, Randolph to Col. Abraham C. Myers, Oct. 15, 1862, *War of Rebellion,* 4th ser. 2: 97–98, 122. See also Brinton, *Decade of Revolution,* 124, chapter 2; and *The City Intelligencer,* 3.

4. Perry, "A Parallel for Grant's Action," 24: 114. Act of the Confederate States Congress, introduced Apr. 21, 1862, approved Oct. 11, 1862, and issued as General Order No. 82, Nov. 3, 1862, *War of Rebellion*, 4th ser. 2: 161, 166.

5. Curry, "James A. Seddon," 123–50.

6. Randolph to Bledsoe, Aug. 26, 1861, *War of Rebellion*, 1st ser., 51, pt. 2, 251; Kean, *Inside the Confederate Government*, xxiv, 27; *Dictionary of American Biography*, s.v. "Bledsoe, Albert Taylor."

7. *National Cyclopedia of American Biography*, s.v. "Ould, Robert." For quotations, see Swanberg, *Sickles the Incredible*, 63–66. See also *Encyclopedia of Virginia Biography*, s.v. "Ould, Robert." The colonel's first wife, née Sarah Turpin, was related to Thomas Jefferson. Colonel and Mrs. Ould were not so intimate with the Randolphs as was their beautiful daughter, Mattie, later Mrs. Paul, who posed for one of the figures in William D. Washington's *The Burial of Latané*. After the war, Ould and Mrs. Randolph's relative, Major Isaac Carrington, practiced law together. See Dunaway, *History of the James River and Kanawha Canal Company*, 238.

8. *Virginia Cyclopedia of Biography*, s.v. "Rives, Landon," is incorrect in maintaining that Rives was chief of the Engineer Bureau "to the end of the war." Gen. R. E. Lee was the godfather of Rives's daughter Amelie, later the Princess Troubetzkoy. Rives's father was William Cabell Rives (1793–1868) who married Judith Page Walker, the heiress of Castle Hill. He held many offices: U.S. congressman (1823–29), U.S. senator (1832–34 and 1836–39), U.S. minister to France (1829–32 and 1849–53), member of the Peace and Virginia conventions (1860–61), and Confederate States senator (1861–62). He had become a member of the Whig party in 1844. See *Dictionary of American Biography*, s.v. "Rives, William Cabell."

9. *Dictionary of American Biography*, s.v. "Talcott, Andrew"; Talcott Diary, entry for Dec. 1861 and Nov. 4, 1862, Talcott Papers; Shackelford, "Lieutenant Lee Reports," 458–87. Andrew Talcott (1797–1883), an 1818 graduate of West Point, resigned from the U.S. Army in 1836 after a fine career in the Corps of Engineers to practice civil engineering. His greatest work was locating and constructing the Vera Cruz to Mexico City Railroad, 1857 to 1867, temporarily suspended between 1860 and 1861 for financial reorganization.

10. Gorgas, *Civil War Diary*, 32; quotation from Johnston and Lipscomb, *Amelia Gayle Gorgas*, 52–57, 61, 71; *Encyclopedia of Virginia Biography*, s.v. "Gorgas, Josiah"; and Kean, *Inside the Confederate Government*, 122.

11. *Biographical Directory of the American Congress*, s.v. "Gayle, John."

12. Thomas L. Bayne, Autobiographical Sketch, 1870, Bayne-Gayle Papers. Mary Tabb Lancaster Johnston called this source to my attention and lent me its photostat.

13. In 1857 Stephen Chalaron's office was at 27 Old Levee, and his residence was on Rampart Street in New Orleans. See Gardener, *Directory for 1857*, 48. In 1864 Capt. Stephen Chalaron was listed fifteenth in the roster of twenty-one officers of the Nitre and Mining Service with the assigned duty over nitriaries and foreign correspondence. Lt. J. Adolph Chalaron (presumably his

brother) continued with the Washington Artillery, winning commendations for being "gallant and daring." For quotations, see *War of Rebellion,* 1st ser. 10: 515, 820; 52: 54, 3d ser. 3: 702.

14. *Dictionary of American Biography,* s.v. "Campbell, John A." Chesnut, *Mary Chesnut's Civil War,* 19, 92, 479, 710; the Revelation of St. John, the Divine, 3: 14—16. Campbell (1811—89) had been briefly a cadet at West Point. He moved to Mobile around 1830. When he was appointed to the U.S. Supreme Court in 1853, he emancipated his slaves. Presumably he was not related to the Campbells of Virginia.

15. Speed, *Gilmers in America,* 196—99. Courtesy of Dr. Thomas W. Gilmer of Virginia Polytechnic Institute and State University.

16. *War of Rebellion,* 4th ser. 1: 1124, 2: 143.

17. Broun, "Red Artillery," 366.

18. *Dictionary of American Biography,* "St. John, Isaac M."; Wakelyn, *Biographical Dictionary of the Confederacy,* 377—78.

19. Goff, *Confederate Supply,* mistakenly identifies Edmund Trowbridge Dana Myers as the son of Abraham C. Myers. They were not related. See MacDonald Wellford to the author, March, 1984. See also *Dictionary of American Biography,* s.v. "Myers, Abraham C.," and "Northrop, Lucius Bellinger"; Kean, *Inside the Confederate Government,* xxiii—xxiv, 89—90, 116—17, 136, 200. For Col. Chesnut's good opinion of Northrop, see Chesnut, *Mary Chesnut's Civil War,* 706.

20. Whitmore, "Caryanne Nicholas Randolph," 2: 70—80. Quotation from the obituary appearing in the Richmond *Dispatch.* Ruffin worked better with Northrop than Bayne did, especially in the autumn of 1864. Ruffin recommended that the firm of Power, Low, and Company receive a contract to deliver foreign meat at 350 percent of cost because it was so "bulky" that blockade-runners would not bring it. Bayne opposed the deal, insisting that he had enough money and power to get all the meat that was needed and that he was getting it, even though he was not able to counter Ruffin's charge that Bayne had procured only 300,000 pounds of meat in the last fifteen days of October, which the Army of Northern Virginia alone consumed in ten days time. F. G. Ruffin to L. B. Northrop, Oct. 18, Nov. 4, 1864; *War of Rebellion,* 4th ser. 3: 738—39, 781—85.

21. Peter V. Daniel, Jr. to Randolph, Apr. 26, 1862, *War of Rebellion,* 4th ser. 1: 1094; Dunaway, *James River and Kanawha Canal Company,* 188n. Johnson, "Disloyalty on Confederate Railroads," 416.

22. Jefferson, *Papers of Thomas Jefferson,* 4: 267; Randall, *Life of Jefferson,* 3: 660—64; Malone, *Jefferson,* 1: 301—69; 3: 279—83; 5: 220; 6: 15—17, 220.

23. Randolph to Gilmer, Oct. 22, 1862, *War of Rebellion,* 4th ser. 1: 139—40, 1013—14, 1048—49, 1055, 1066, 1089—91, 1107, 1108—9, 1113. See also Randolph to A. S. Gaines at Demopolis, Ala., urging the "early completion" of the Selma-Meridian rail line "without change of cars," *War of Rebellion,* 4th ser. 1: 1048—49; Black, *Railroads of the Confederacy,* 99—100, 150—60, 178—79. See also MacDonald Wellford to the author, Mar. 26, 1984; Goff, *Confederate Supply;*

Stanard, "Proceedings"; Stanard, "Kennon Letters," 187; and Stanard, "Randolph Family."

24. Randolph to D. H. Bird, June 13, 1862, Samuel Cooper for Randolph, General Orders 78, Oct. 28, 1862, *War of Rebellion*, 2d ser. 4: 772, 4th ser. 1: 149.

25. A. C. Myers to W. P. Chiltern, chairman of the Military Committee, Confederate States House of Representatives, Oct. 3, 1862. Wadley had been president of the Vicksburg and Shreveport Railroad and was considered "one of the most energetic and reliable men connected with railroad service in the Confederate States." *War of Rebellion*, 4th ser. 4: 1048.

26. Johnson, "Disloyalty on Confederate Railroads," 410–26. Charles Gratiot Talcott (1834–67) was the superintendent of the Richmond and Danville Railroad and charged with the responsibility for building and operating its Piedmont subsidiary. He resigned under heavy criticism and joined his father in Mexico.

27. Confederate Conscription Act, *War of Rebellion*, 4th ser. 1: 1095–97, 2: 177, 1115; Randolph to J. Thompson Brown, Nov. 23, 1861, and March 1, 1862, George Wythe Randolph Letters. The first of these letters contains his explanation to intimates. See Randolph to T. J. Randolph, Nov. 25, 1862, Edgehill Randolph Papers. See also Jones, "George W. Randolph's Service," 303–5; and Richardson, *Little Aleck*, 239.

28. Randolph to T. M. R. Talcott, Mar. 12, Apr. 4, Apr. 28 and July (n.d.) 1862, Talcott Papers.

29. W. R. Aylett to Randolph, Camp Randolph [Richmond?, Va.], Mar. 13, 1862, Aylett Papers. Randolph to Col. A. C. Myers, quartermaster general, Sept. 26, 1862, *War of Rebellion*, 4th ser. 2: 96.

## 11. *Trade with the Enemy*

1. A. C. Myers to Randolph, May 23, 1862; Lucius B. Northrop to Randolph, Apr. 29, 1862; *War of Rebellion*, 4th ser. 1: 1101, 1127; Goff, *Confederate Supply*, 112–15, 123, 243–45.

2. L. B. Northrop to Randolph, Nov. 3, 1862, Francis G. Ruffin to Randolph, Nov. 3, 1862, Ruffin to James A. Seddon, Feb. 8, 1864, *War of Rebellion*, 4th ser. 2: 157–59, 3: 84–88. In 1864 Ruffin stated: "There . . . is not meat enough in our limits to feed both army and people at half their customary rates, and starvation is the parent of mutiny and discontent." See also Whitmore, "Caryanne Nicholas Randolph," 2: 70–80. On Apr. 26, 1861, J. G. Crenshaw, acting commissary general of Virginia, requested that Ruffin be commissioned captain of Virginia Volunteers to serve under him (*War of Rebellion*, 1st ser. 51: 40). L. B. Northrop, commissary general of Confederate subsistence, to Sec. of War Judah P. Benjamin, Jan. 18, 1862, listed Ruffin as a major and commissary of subsistence (*War of Rebellion*, 4th ser. 1: 870–78). One of the complaints against Northrop was that he held his job only because he was a crony of President Davis.

3. Mrs. Randolph to Mrs. Coolidge, Feb. 7, 1832, Coolidge Collection. See also William G. Crenshaw to Seddon, Mar. 30 and Apr. 13, 1863, Ruffin to Seddon, Feb. 8 and Dec. 5, 1864, Ruffin to Northrop, Oct. 18, 1864, *War of Rebellion,* 4th ser. 2: 480–81, 537, 3: 84–88, 738–739, 899–901. Ruffin claimed that the Crenshaw contract brought in only "one-twelfth . . . of what we consume:" 1,013 packages of bacon, 314 barrels of pork, 126 tierces beef, and 1,664 cases of preserved meats and vegetables. He quoted General Lee's statement that "desertions are taking place in his army from short bread rations." See Crenshaw to Seddon, Dec. 5, 1864, *War of Rebellion,* 4th ser. 5: 899–901.

4. Randolph to Davis, Oct. 30, 1862, *War of Rebellion,* 4th ser. 2: 151; C. A. Barriere and Bros. of New Orleans per Charles Jones to Randolph, Nov. 7, 1862, *War of Rebellion,* 4th ser. 2: 173–75.

5. Butler, *Private and Official Correspondence,* 1: 442–43, 458; West, *Lincoln's Scapegoat General,* 136–38, 156, 161. See also Nash, *Stormy Petrel,* 171–81. See also Parton, *Butler in New Orleans;* Capers, *Occupied City,* 83–85; Dawson, *Army Generals and Reconstruction,* 6, 19; and Johnson, *Red River Campaign,* 19, 128–62. Johnson states that Banks began his campaign after defeats by the Confederates in "northern" Louisiana. Of New Orleans's 168,000 residents in 1860, about 99,000 were white, accounting for three out of seven whites in the entire state. Rhodes, *History of the United States,* 3: 629.

6. Jones, *War Clerk's Diary,* 1: 186–88. Special Agreement between Seddon and Barriere and Bros. of New Orleans, Dec. 19, 1862, *War of Rebellion,* 1st ser., 26, pt. 2, 418–19; Count Mejan to Butler, Oct. 31, 1862; Butler to Count Mejan, Nov. 1, 1862; *War of Rebellion,* 3d ser., 2: 710–12; Williams, *P. G. T. Beauregard,* 152.

7. Randolph to Davis, Oct. 30, 1862, *War of Rebellion,* 4th ser. 2: 151. See also R. H. G. Kean, Memorandum, circa 1867, Kean Papers; and Jones, *War Clerk's Diary,* 1: 191.

8. John A. Stevenson to Randolph, Nov. 10, 1862, forwarded by Randolph to Davis, endorsed by Davis; quotation by Davis, *War of Rebellion,* 1st ser. 15: 861–64.

9. Kean, *Inside the Confederate Government,* 48, 98; Parton, *Butler in New Orleans,* 322–45; Nash, *Stormy Petrel,* 158–70; Capers, *Occupied City,* 85.

10. Randolph to Davis, Oct. 30, 1862, *War of Rebellion,* 4th ser. 2: 151; Randolph to Lewis Randolph, Jan. 1, 1859, Jefferson-Randolph Papers. Especially important is Thomas L. Bayne, Autobiographical Sketch, 1870, Bayne-Gayle Papers. George M. Denegre of New Orleans generously made available to me a manuscript version (perhaps the original) of this sketch from the Denegre Family Papers. Mary Tabb Johnston of Blacksburg kindly lent me a photostat of the Chapel Hill copy.

11. "James M. Seixas," New Orleans *Times-Democrat,* June 28, 1889.

12. See Gardner's *Directory for 1857,* 48; *War of Rebellion,* 1st ser. 10: 515, 820, 52: 54, 3d ser. 3: 702.

13. Hattaway and Jones, *How the North Won,* 213; Jones, *Confederate Strategy,* 57, 72–73.

14. Jones, "George W. Randolph's Service," 305–6.

15. Capers, *Occupied City*, 113–15, 314, states that Maj. Gen. Lovell, C.S.A., built breastworks completely around the city.

16. Samuel Cooper to Richard Taylor, July 30, 1862, *War of Rebellion*, 1st ser. 15: 791; West, *Lincoln's Scapegoat General*, 169–70; Capers, *Occupied City*, 83–85, 113–15. Jones, *Confederate Strategy*, 57, in referring briefly to Randolph's "rather unrealistic project for the recapture of New Orleans," limited his discussion to basic, conventional military preparations. He and Herman Hattaway repeated these remarks in *How the North Won*, 213.

17. Cooper to Taylor, July 30, 1862, *War of Rebellion*, 1st ser. 15: 791; Davis to Van Dorn, July 30, 1862, *War of Rebellion*, 1st ser. 18: 794–95; Randolph to Maj. Gen. John C. Pemberton, Sept. 30, 1862, *War of Rebellion*, 1st ser. 17, pt. 2, 716–17. Taylor formed a low opinion of Pemberton after meeting him. Pemberton was promoted in Oct. 1862. See Jones, *Confederate Strategy*, 73 and also "George W. Randolph's Service," 308.

18. Randolph to Pemberton, Sept. 30, 1862, *War of Rebellion*, 1st ser. 17, pt. 2, 716–17.

19. Peter V. Daniel, Jr., to Randolph, Apr. 26, 1862, *War of Rebellion*, 4th ser. 1: 1094; see also chapters 1, 2, and 3.

20. For Beaumarchais's dummy trading company, Rodriguez, Hortalez, and Compagnie, see *Diplomatic Correspondence*, 2: 314, 328; and Bailey, *Diplomatic History*, 12–13, 16; Alden, *American Revolution*, 120, 180–83. Despite General and Mrs. Randolph's interest in opera and theater, it is likely that they knew Beaumarchais's dramatic works only in bowdlerized form. See chapters 2 and 3. Among the participants in tableaux was Captain Jimmy Denegre.

21. See chapter 4.

22. Curry, "James A. Seddon," 123–50; and chapter 6. Randolph never confided to Seddon any part of the New Orleans scheme.

23. Thomas J. Durant to Benjamin F. Butler, [n.d., 1862], quoted in Parton, *Butler In New Orleans*, 253–54. *Dictionary of American Biography*, s.v. "Taylor, Richard." Butler referred to "guerrillas."

24. Cooper to Taylor, July 30, 1862, Davis to Van Dorn, July 30, 1862, Taylor to Brig. Gen. Daniel S. Ruggles. Aug. 20, 1862, *War of Rebellion*, 1st ser. 15: 791, 802, 18: 794–95. See also Taylor, *Destruction and Reconstruction*, 102–3, 108, 113.

25. Randolph to Brig. Gen. J. H. Forney, Sept. 1, 1862, H. H. Sibley to Randolph, Oct. 1, 1862; *War of Rebellion*, 1st ser. 15: 806–7, 819; Taylor, *Destruction and Reconstruction*, 102–3, 108, 113. Taylor used an ambulance in Louisiana, too.

26. Cooper to Taylor, July 30, 1862, Davis to Van Dorn, July 30, 1862, Randolph to Forney, Sept. 1, 1862, Taylor to Ruggles, Sept. 30, 1862, *War of Rebellion*, 1st ser. 15: 791, 806–7, 819, 18: 794–95.

27. Abernethy, *Burr Conspiracy*.

28. Ruggles to Cooper, Sept. 30, 1862, *War of Rebellion*, 1st ser. 15: 817.

29. Randolph to Pemberton, Sept. 30, 1862, *War of Rebellion*, 1st ser. 17, pt. 2, 716—17.

30. Ruggles [telegram and letter] to Cooper, Sept. 11, 1862, Preston Pond, Jr., to Cooper, Sept. 21, 1862, Jasper S. Whiting to Ruggles, Sept. 23, 1862, *War of Rebellion*, 1st ser. 17: 806—7, 809—10.

31. West, *Lincoln's Scapegoat General*, 169—70. In early 1863, Banks, believing that Taylor might attack New Orleans, sent Brig. Gen. Godfrey Weitzel's force of 4,500 Union troops to stop him. In 1864 Taylor's little army inflicted heavy losses on Banks's larger forces in the Red River campaign. See Butler, *Autobiography and Reminiscences*, 397, 484, 496. In October 1864, Taylor's advance towards Algiers on the Opelousas and Great Western Railroad drew away from the city into the hinterland five regiments under Weitzel.

32. W.P.A. Writers Program of Louisiana, *Louisiana*, 343—44; W.P.A. Writers Program of New Orleans, *New Orleans Guide*, 358—62; Cowan et al., *New Orleans Yesterday and Today*, 85—86. Although Algiers was not formally absorbed by New Orleans until 1870, it had been in the parish of Orleans since 1803. The Opelousas Railroad was begun in 1853.

33. Chapter 8.

34. Although Capers in *Occupied City* refers to Randolph's having advisors from New Orleans, he does not name them. James Denis Denegre was a commission merchant. In 1861 he and his son Joseph had different business addresses, though in 1860 they were both at 20 Dryades Street. See Gardner, *Directory for 1859*, 87, *Directory for 1860*, 174, and *Directory for 1861*, 132. Denegre was not a member of the Boston Club, but he was a subscriber to the New Orleans Opera House Company. See Landry, *History of the Boston Club*, 265. See also *National Cyclopedia of Biography*, s.v. "Denegre." Joseph Denegre declined a Confederate States War Department mission to Europe in 1865. After Appomattox he went to Pau, France, where he died of tuberculosis on July 21, 1868. See Denegre Family Papers; New Orleans *Daily Picayune*, Aug. 6, 1868; and *National Cyclopedia of Biography*, s.v. "Denegre." In 1859, Slidell's name was not included as a partner of Clarke and Bayne. See Denegre Family Papers and Gardner, *Directory for 1859*, 32 and *Directory for 1860*, 45.

35. *National Cyclopedia of Biography*, s.v. "Denegre." See also Korn, *Early Jews*, 228. In antebellum days, Jews were admitted to "every nook and cranny of [the] social, political and cultural life [of New Orleans]." Members of the exclusive Boston Club then included Judah P. Benjamin and three of the Seixas family. See Gardner, *Directory for 1859*, 269 and Landry, *History of the Boston Club*. Social inclusiveness was demonstrated in the Washington Artillery. Bayne, Chalaron, and Seixas were commended for their "gallant actions" at Shiloh. See Capt. W. Irving Hodgson to Capt. W. G. Barth, Apr. 11, 1862, *War of Rebellion*, 1st ser. 10: 515, 52: 54.

36. Parton, *Butler in New Orleans*, 364—66, 375, 427. For J. D. Denegre's and B. F. Butler's correspondence about these matters, see *War of Rebellion*, 3d ser. 2: 117, 166—67. See also Butler, *Autobiography and Reminiscences*, 518. The

French so well appreciated Denegre's abilities that he was offered the position of minister of finance in Maximillian's Mexican empire. Whether it was because Denegre was perspicacious or because he realized the extent of his failing health, he declined. Never returning to America, he died in Brussels on June 3, 1865. See also Capers, *Occupied City,* 98, 104, 107.

37. Chapter 5.

38. Butler, *Autobiography and Reminiscences,* 469, 478; Holtzman, *Stormy Ben Butler,* 98–99.

## 12. *Randolph's "Factitious" Resignation*

1. Morrison, *Oxford History of the American People,* 617.

2. Kean, *Inside the Confederate Government,* 30.

3. Mrs. Randolph to Mrs. Coolidge, Feb. 7, 1832, Coolidge Collection.

4. Jones, *War Clerk's Diary,* 1: 191.

5. Kean, *Inside the Confederate Government,* 30.

6. Edward C. Anderson, Diary 5: 1, 173. Remaining in the Navy a decade longer than Randolph, Lieutenant Anderson resigned because of slow promotion. A prosperous businessman and sometime mayor of Savannah, he came to Richmond in the spring of 1861 for a family wedding, renewed his friendship with Randolph, and placed arms contracts with the Tredegar Company for the state of Georgia.

7. Randolph to T. J. Randolph, Nov. 25, 1862, Edgehill Randolph Papers; Randolph to J. Thompson Brown, Nov. 25, 1862, George Wythe Randolph Letters; Kean, Memorandum, circa 1867, Kean Papers. See also Kean, *Inside the Confederate Government,* 30–31.

8. Kean, Memorandum, circa 1867, Kean Papers; Randolph to Davis, Oct. 9, 1862, *War of Rebellion,* 4th ser. 4: 113; Kean, *Inside the Confederate Government,* 30–31.

9. Randolph to Holmes, Oct. 27, 1862, Davis to Randolph, Nov. 12, 1862, [Randolph to Davis, Nov. 12, 1862] referred to in Davis to Randolph, Nov. 14, 1862, Davis to Randolph, Nov. 15, 1862, *War of Rebellion,* 1st ser. 13: 906–7, 15: 914–15; and Davis, *Jefferson Davis, Constitutionalist,* 5: 369, 371–72, 374. See also Jones, "George W. Randolph's Service," 307–14.

10. Davis to Randolph, Nov. 15, 1862, *War of Rebellion,* 1st ser. 15: 914–15; Davis, *Jefferson Davis, Constitutionalist,* 5: 374; Kean, *Inside the Confederate Government,* 30.

11. Richmond *Examiner,* Nov. 17, 1862; Richmond *Enquirer,* Nov. 18, 1862; Richmond *Dispatch,* Nov. 18, 1862.

12. Hendrick, *Statesmen of the Lost Cause,* 325.

13. Jones, *War Clerk's Diary,* 1: 191. See also chapter 9. Wadley was recommended as "the most energetic and reliable man connected with railroad service in the Confederate States" because of his service as president of the Vicksburg and Shreveport Railroad. See Charles T. Pollard, Pres. of Alabama and Florida Railroad of Alabama, Apr. 4, 1862, *War of Rebellion,* 4th ser. 1: 1048. Randolph

quieted D. H. Hill's suspicions that, because Gorgas was born in the North, he was responsible for "foul play" and sabotage. See Bridges, *Lee's Maverick General,* 35.

14. Quotations from Randolph to J. Thompson Brown, Nov. 25, 1862, George Wythe Randolph Letters. See also Jones, *War Clerk's Diary,* 1: 174. From Virginia's Eastern Shore and presumably related to the Custis family, Jones was technically eligible to be counted among the F.F.V., but he did not belong to that elite. A newspaperman, he lacked the literary qualifications and sophistication to be accepted by the Richmond literati. The War Office clerk was a less fortunate version of John Moncure Daniel, United States minister to Piedmont-Sardinia and then editor of the Richmond *Examiner.* Daniel had Swift and Voltaire as his models; Jones seems to have looked no higher than the likes of Duff Green. That Daniel neither praised nor condemned Randolph may be considered a mark of respect. See Bagby, "John M. Daniel," 111–43; and *Encyclopedia of Virginia Biography,* s.v. "Daniel, John M."

15. Anderson, Diary 5: 1, 173; Kean, *Inside the Confederate Government,* 30.

16. Chapter 7.

17. Kean, *Inside the Confederate Government,* 30 and chapter 9.

18. Curry, "James A. Seddon," 123–50. Seddon's advantage over Randolph of his two terms in Congress (1845–47, 1849–51) and his prowess as a college orator were more telling in political life than in the War Office.

19. Pollard, *The Lost Cause,* 729.

## 13. *Wrecked in Health and Fortune*

1. Chesnut, *Diary from Dixie,* 381, 383; Dabney, *Richmond,* 178.

2. Randolph to Molly, June 27, 1865, Edgehill Randolph Papers; Randolph to Septimia R. Meikleham, Dec. 22, 1864, Meikleham Papers; Mrs. G. W. Randolph to Isaetta R. Hubard, Dec. 12, 1864, Randolph-Hubard Papers.

3. Randolph, Account to Bureau of Nitre and Mining, 1864–65, Kirk-Randolph-Nicholas Papers; Amelia Gorgas to Millie Crawford, Sept. 24, 1864, Gorgas Papers. Mary Tabb Lancaster Johnston, Amelia Gorgas's biographer, kindly gave me a xerox copy of this letter. James Burwell Ficklin had conducted a hardware business with Randolph's former law partner, Mr. Watkins. He served in the Howitzers, 1859–63. Presumably the Randolphs called Fanny "Cornucopia" because of the rapidity with which the Ficklin children had arrived after James and Fanny's marriage in 1860. See Ficklin, *Genealogical History,* 46, 58, 81–82; and Chesnut, *Mary Chesnut's Civil War,* 664.

4. Randolph, Account to Bureau of Nitre and Mining, 1864–65, Kirk-Randolph-Nicholas Papers; Mrs. G. W. Randolph to Isaetta R. Hubard, Dec. 12, 1864, Randolph-Hubard Papers; Chesnut, *Mrs. Chesnut's Civil War,* 675.

5. Randolph to Gen. C. J. McRae, Feb. 3, 1865, Kirk-Randolph-Nicholas Papers; Mrs. G. W. Randolph to Sarah N. Randolph, Nov. 20, 1865, Jefferson-Randolph Papers. See also De Leon, *Four Years in Rebel Capitals,* 107; Thompson, *Poems,* xliv; Garmon, *Thompson,* 111–19. The Burlington was near

Thompson's own quarters on Saville Row, where Richard Brinsley Sheridan had lived.

6. Randolph to Septimia R. Meikleham, Dec. 22, 1864, Meikleham Papers; Mrs. G. W. Randolph to Isaetta R. Hubard, Dec. 12, 1864, Mrs. G. W. Randolph to [Robert] Ould, Dec. 12, 1864, Mrs. G. W. Randolph to Mrs. B. F. Randolph, March 18, 1865, Randolph-Hubard Papers. In writing to Virginia kin, the Randolphs used as a "cover" Robert Ould, the Confederate States commissioner for the exchange of prisoners at Richmond. See also Whitehill, "Eleanora Wayles Randolph," 1: 97, 228; and Garmon, *Thompson,* 121.

7. Randolph, Account to Bureau of Nitre and Mining, Grand Hotel to M. Randolphe [*sic*], Jan. 4, 1865, Kirk-Randolph-Nicholas Papers; Mrs. G. W. Randolph to Mrs. Benjamin F. Randolph, Mar. 18, [1865], and Mrs. G. W. Randolph to Julia [Hubard?], Easter, April, [1865], Randolph-Hubard Papers. See also Thompson, *Poems,* xlv; Garmon, *Thompson,* 121; Ross; *First Lady of the South,* 208.

8. Randolph, Account to Bureau of Nitre and Mining, Grand Hotel to [Randolph], Jan. 5, 1865, and Randolph to Gen. R. L. McRae, Feb. 3, 1865, Kirk-Randolph-Nicholas Papers; Mrs. G. W. Randolph to Julia [Hubard?], Easter, April, 1865, Randolph-Hubard Papers.

9. Randolph to Septimia R. Meikleham, Dec. 22, 1864, Meikleham Papers; Randolph to Molly, June 27, 1865, Edgehill Randolph Papers; Randolph to Septimia R. Meikleham, Dec. 22, 1864, Meikleham Papers; Mrs. G. W. Randolph to Mrs. Benjamin F. Randolph, March 18, [1865], Randolph-Hubard Papers.

10. Randolph to McRae, Feb. 3, 1865, Kirk-Randolph-Nicholas Papers; Mrs. G. W. Randolph to Mrs. Benjamin F. Randolph, Mar. 18, [1865], Randolph-Hubard Papers. See also Shackelford, *Collected Papers,* 1: 228.

11. Mrs. G. W. Randolph to Julia [Hubard], Easter, April 1865, Randolph-Hubard Papers; G. W. Randolph to Sarah N. Randolph, June 5, [1865], Edgehill Randolph Papers.

12. Randolph to Molly, June 27 and July 23, 1865, Edgehill Randolph Papers. Samuel Hooper (1808–75) had been a merchant abroad and in Boston. He was elected as a Republican in 1861 to succeed William Appleton. See *Biographical Directory of the American Congress,* 1328.

13. Randolph to Molly, Aug. 11, 1865, Edgehill Randolph Papers; Randolph to Septimia R. Meikleham, Dec. 22, 1864, Meikleham Papers; Mrs. G. W. Randolph to Mrs. Benjamin F. Randolph, Mar. 18, 1866, Randolph-Hubard Papers; Mrs. G. W. Randolph to Sarah N. Randolph, Nov. 20, 1865, Edgehill Randolph Papers.

14. Mrs. G. W. Randolph to Sarah N. Randolph, Nov. 10, 1865. Jefferson-Randolph Papers. See also Von Borcke, *Memoirs,* 1: 17–18, 49, 67–68, 2: 264–65, 316–18.

15. Mrs. G. W. Randolph to Mrs. Benjamin F. Randolph, Nov. 14, 1865, and Randolph to Molly, Aug. 11, 1865, Edgehill Randolph Papers.

16. Randolph to Molly, June 27, 1866, Edgehill Randolph Papers; Sarah N. Randolph to Hugh B. Grigsby, Apr. 12, 1869, Grigsby Papers.

17. Mrs. Coolidge to Mrs. T. J. Randolph, Apr. 29, 1868, Meikleham Papers.

18. Randolph to Molly, June 27 and Aug. 11, 1865, Mrs. G. W. Randolph to Sarah N. Randolph, June 5, 1865, Edgehill Randolph Papers; Randolph to Sarah N. Randolph, July 23, 1865, Jefferson-Randolph Papers. Mary confided to Sarah that she believed Davis's life was in danger. She wrote to Mrs. Davis of George's and her concern for the imprisoned former president.

19. Randolph to niece [Molly], Feb. 3, 1866, Edgehill Randolph Papers; Randolph to Molly, n.d. [1866], and C. W. H. Lewis to T. G. Peyton, Apr. 13, 1866, Kirk-Randolph-Nicholas Papers.

20. Randolph to Carry [Randolph], June 28, 1866, Kirk-Randolph-Nicholas Papers; George W. Randolph file, Civil War Amnesty Papers, Adjutant General Records, National Archives, Washington, D.C.

21. Mrs. Coolidge to Carry Randolph, Aug. 17, 1866, Meikleham Papers.

22. Molly to _____, Sept. 8, 1860, and Jan. 19, 1867, Kirk-Randolph-Nicholas Papers; Mrs. Randolph to Isaetta R. Hubard, Dec. 5, 1866, Randolph-Hubard Papers; Sarah N. Randolph, memorandum, April 9, 1867, Edgehill Randolph Papers.

23. Robert E. Lee to Mrs. Randolph, April 11, 1867, R. E. Lee Letterbook.

24. Richmond *Whig,* Apr. 5, 1867; Richmond *Examiner,* Apr. 16, 1867, corrects the obituary, retracting statement that Randolph had gone abroad in 1864 on a Confederate mission for the treasury. See also Cappon, *Virginia Newspapers,* 192–93.

25. Mrs. G. W. Randolph to Sarah N. Randolph, Nov. 20, 1865, Jefferson-Randolph Papers; Mrs. G. W. Randolph to Carry [Randolph], Dec. 13, [1865], Mrs. Benjamin F. Randolph to Isaetta R. Hubard, Aug. 16, 1867, Mrs. G. W. Randolph to Isaetta R. Hubard, Dec. 5, [1866], Randolph-Hubard Papers. See also Taylor, "The Edgehill School," 14–25.

26. Randolph, Last Will and Testament, Dec. 14, 1866. Will Book, Albemarle County Records, Charlottesville, Va.

27. Mrs. G. W. Randolph to Mrs. Benjamin F. Randolph, Apr. 4, [1871], Mrs. Benjamin F. Randolph to Isaetta R. Hubard, Nov. 22, 1869, and Sarah N. Randolph to Mrs. Benjamin F. Randolph, July 28, 1879, Randolph-Hubard Papers. [Sarah N. Randolph], memorandum for obituary of Mary E. A. P. [Mrs. G. W.] Randolph, Dec. 31, [1871], Jefferson-Randolph Papers. See also Boyd, *Directory of Richmond City . . . 1869,* 179; Olivia Taylor, Interview, June 28, 1980, Charlottesville, Va. and Taylor, "Descendants of Thomas Jefferson," 1: 212–13. Stevens Mason Taylor (1847–1917) left his studies at the University of Virginia at the age of sixteen to serve as an army courier. He was surrendered at Appomattox.

# Bibliography

*Manuscripts*

Clerk's Office. Charlottesville, Va.
    Albemarle County, Va., Records. Order Book, 1837–41, Circuit Superior
        Court of Law and Chancery; and Will Book for 1866.
Denegre Family Papers. Private collections. New Orleans, La.
Mobile County Records. Mobile, Alabama. Will Book 2.
Museum of the Confederacy. Richmond, Va.
    George Wythe Randolph Letters.
National Archives. Washington, D. C.
    Civil War Amnesty Papers, Adjutant General Records.
    Naval Records. Acceptances for 1831, records group 45; Records of Of-
        ficers, M-330, roll 4, vol. G, no. 1653; roll 5, vol. H, no. 1913, records
        group 24; and Log of USS *Vandalia*. Microcopies, Virginia Poly-
        technic Institute and State University, Blacksburg, Va.
University of Alabama. Gorgas Library. Tuscaloosa, Alabama.
    Gorgas Papers.
University of North Carolina. Wilson Library. Chapel Hill, N.C.
    Anderson, Edward Clifford. Diary.
    Bayne, Thomas L. Autobiographical Sketch, 1870.
    Bayne-Gayle Papers.
    Trist Family Papers.
University of Virginia. Alderman Library. Charlottesville, Va.
    Carr Papers.
    Cocke Papers.
    Coolidge, Ellen Wayles Randolph. Collection.
    Edgehill Randolph Papers.
    Jefferson-Randolph Papers.
    Jefferson-Randolph-Smith-Nicholas Papers.
    Jefferson-Randolph-Taylor-Smith-Nicholas Papers.
    Kean Papers.
    Kirk-Randolph-Nicholas Papers.

Meikleham Papers.
Minor Family Papers.
Randolph Family Papers.
Randolph-Hubard Papers.
Thomas Jefferson Memorial Foundation Deposits.
University of Virginia Records: Faculty Minutes; Proctor's Records.
Virginia Historical Society. Richmond, Va.
Aylett Papers.
Cabell Papers.
Confederate States of America, War Department Papers.
Crump Family Papers.
Grigsby Papers.
Haxall Family Papers.
Hollywood Cemetery Papers.
Alexander Jones Papers.
Robert E. Lee Letterbook.
Munford Family Papers.
Midshipman Richard L. Page. Personal Log on USS *Constitution,*
    1825–28.
Patton Family Papers.
Richmond Library Company Records.
Conway Robinson Papers.
Talcott Family Papers.
Virginia State Library. Richmond, Va.
Richmond City Records. Deeds (Grantor) Index no. 54, Deeds
    (Grantee) Index no. 61; and Wills Index no. 77. Deed Book, 1853.

### Newspapers and Periodicals

*Harper's Weekly Magazine,* July 17, 1858.
New Orleans *Daily Picayune,* Aug. 6, 1868.
New Orleans *Times-Democrat,* June 28, 1889.
Richmond *Dispatch,* Feb. n.d., and June 13, 1861; Mar. 19, 1862.
Richmond *Enquirer,* July 1858; Oct. 15, 17, and 29, 1861; Nov. 10, 13, 19, 22, and 23,
    1861; Mar. 17, 1862; May 29, 1863.
Richmond *Examiner,* Nov. 1, 1859; May 3, 1863.
Richmond *Standard,* Dec. 18, 1880; May 7, 1881.
Richmond *Whig,* Nov. 9 and 19, 1859.
*Southern Literary Messenger,* July and Oct. 1852; Feb. and Mar. 1855; Jan. and Feb.
    1856; Mar. and Aug. 1857; Mar., June, and Aug. 1860; Mar. 1861; and Feb.–
    Mar. 1862.

### Books, Dissertations, and Essays

Abernethy, Thomas Perkins. *The Burr Conspiracy.* New York: Oxford, 1954.
———. *A Short Sketch of the University of Virginia.* Richmond, Va.: Dietz Press,
    1946.

Alden, John. *The American Revolution, 1775–1783*. New York: Harper, 1954.

Alexander, Thomas B. and Richard E. Beringer. *The Anatomy of the Confederate Congress*. Nashville, Tenn.: Vanderbilt University Press, 1972.

Allan, Rosalbina Caradori. *Lay of the Sylph, Il Silfo*. Boston: Oliver Ditson, c. 1845.

*Annals of Opera, 1597–1940*. 2d ed. New York, 1940.

Bagby, George W. "John M. Daniel's Latch-Key: A Memoir of the Editor of the Richmond *Examiner*." In *The Old Virginia Gentleman and Other Sketches*, edited by Ellen M. Bagby. Richmond, Va.: Dietz Press, 1938.

Bailey, Thomas A. *A Diplomatic History of the American People*. 3d ed. New York: Crofts, 1946.

Baskin, Andrew. "Free Blacks in Franklin County, Virginia." Unpublished seminar paper, Virginia Polytechnic Institute and State University, Blacksburg, Va.

Belin, J. Paul. *Commerce des livres prohibés à Paris, 1750–1789*. Paris, 1913.

Beringer, Richard E. *Historical Analysis: Contemporary Approaches to Clio's Craft*. New York: John Wiley and Sons, 1978.

Bill, Alfred H. *The Beleaguered City*. New York: Knopf, 1948.

*Biographical Directory of the American Congress, 1774–1948*. Compiled by James L. Harrison. Washington: GPO, 1950.

Borcke, Heros Von. *Memoirs of the Confederate War for Independence*. Philadelphia: Lippincott, 1871.

Boyd, William H. *Directory of Richmond City . . . 1869*. Richmond, Va.: West and Johnson, 1869.

Bridges, Hal. *Lee's Maverick General: Daniel Harvey Hill*. New York: McGraw-Hill, 1961.

Brinton, Crane. *A Decade of Revolution, 1789–1799*. New York: Harper and Brothers, 1934.

Brown, William Le Roy, "The Red Artillery." *Southern Historical Society Papers* 26: 366.

Bruce, Philip A. *History of the University of Virginia, 1818–1919*. 5 vols. New York: Macmillan, 1921.

Butler, Benjamin F. *Autobiography and Personal Reminiscences* . . . . Boston: Thayer, 1892.

———. *Private and Official Correspondence of Gen. Benjamin F. Butler During the Period of the Civil War*. 5 vols. Compiled by Jessie A. Marshall. Norwood, Mass., 1917.

*Butter's Richmond Directory*. Richmond, Va., 1855.

Cabell, Julia Mayo. *An Odd Volume of Facts and Fictions*. Richmond, Va.: Nash and Woodhouse, 1852.

*Calendar of Virginia State Papers* . . . . 11 vols. Edited by William H. Flournoy. Richmond, Va., 1875–93.

Callahan, Edward W. *List of Officers of the Navy of the United States and of the Marine Corps*. New York: Harnersley Company, 1901.

Capers, Gerald M. *Occupied City: New Orleans Under the Federals, 1862–1865*. Lexington: University of Kentucky Press, 1965.

Cappon, Lester J., ed. *Virginia Newspapers, 1821–1935.* New York: Appleton-Century, 1936.

———. *The Adams-Jefferson Letters.* 2 vols. Chapel Hill: University of North Carolina Press, 1952.

Cary, Constance. *Recollections Grave and Gay.* New York: Scribner's, 1911.

Chambers, Lenoir. *Stonewall Jackson.* 2 vols. New York: Morrow, 1959.

Chesnut, Mary Boykin. *A Diary from Dixie.* Edited by Ben Ames Williams. Boston: Houghton Mifflin, 1949.

———. *Mary Chesnut's Civil War.* Edited by C. Vann Woodward. New Haven, Conn: Yale University Press, 1981.

Christian, George L. "Reminiscences of Some of the Dead of the Bench and Bar of Richmond." *Virginia Law Register* 14 (1909): 743–45.

Christie, Manson and Woods International, Inc. *Americana: English and European Printed Books and Manuscripts, Dec. 14, 1984.* New York: 1984.

*City Intelligencer or Stranger's Guide.* Richmond, Va.: McFarland and Fergusson, 1862.

Colomy, Paul B. "Stunted Differentiation: A Sociological Examination of Virginia's Political Elite, 1720–1850." Ph.D. diss., University of California, Los Angeles, 1982.

Cooke, John Esten. *Outlines from the Outpost.* Edited by Richard Harwell. Chicago: Donnelley, 1961.

*Correspondence Between Henry Stephens Randall and Hugh Blair Grigsby, 1856–1861.* Edited by Frank J. and Frank W. Klingberg. Berkeley: University of California Press, 1952.

Couper, William. *One Hundred Years at Virginia Military Institute.* 2 vols. Richmond, Va.: Garrett and Massie, 1939.

Cowan, Walter G. et al. *New Orleans Yesterday and Today: A Guide to the City.* Baton Rouge: Louisiana State University Press, 1983.

Curry, Roy W. "James A. Seddon." *Virginia Magazine of History and Biography* 63 (1955): 123–50.

*Cyclopedia of American Biography.* 6 vols. Edited by James G. Wilson and John Fiske. New York: Appleton, 1888.

Dabney, Virginius. *Virginia: The New Dominion.* Garden City, N.Y.: Doubleday, 1971.

———. *Richmond: The Story of a City.* Garden City, N.Y.: Doubleday, 1976.

Dahlgren, John A. *Memoir of John A. Dahlgren, Rear Admiral, United States Navy.* Edited by Madeleine V. Dahlgren. New York: Webster, 1891.

Dakin, Douglas. *The Greek Struggle for Independence, 1821–1833.* London: Batsford, 1973.

Daniels, Jonathan. *The Randolphs of Virginia: America's Foremost Family.* Garden City, N.Y.: Doubleday, 1972.

Davis, Jefferson. *Jefferson Davis, Constitutionalist: His Letters, Papers and Speeches.* 10 vols. Edited by Dunbar Rowland. Jackson, Miss.: Mississippi Department of Archives and History, 1923.

Dawson, Joseph G. *Army Generals and Reconstruction: Louisiana, 1862–1877.* Baton Rouge: Louisiana State University Press, 1982.

De Leon, Thomas Cooper. *Belles, Beaux and Brains of the '60s.* New York: Dillingham, 1909.

———. *Four Years in Rebel Capitals.* 1890. Reprint edited by E. B. Long. New York: Collier, 1970.

*Dictionary of American Biography.* 20 vols. Edited by Allen Johnson and Dumas Malone. New York: Scribner's, 1928–44.

*Diplomatic Correspondence of the United States.* Edited by Francis Wharton. 6 vols. Washington, 1889.

Dowdey, Clifford. *Experiment in Rebellion.* Garden City, N.Y.: Doubleday, 1946.

Dowdey, Clifford and Louis H. Manarin. *The Wartime Papers of R. E. Lee.* Boston: Little, Brown and Company for the Richmond Civil War Centennial Committee, 1961.

Duberman, Martin. *James Russell Lowell.* Boston: Houghton Mifflin, 1966.

Dunaway, Wayland F. *History of the James River and Kanawha Company.* New York: Columbia University Press, 1922.

du Pont, Henry A. *Rear Admiral Samuel Francis du Pont: A Biography.* New York: National Americana Society, 1926.

Ellyson, M. *Richmond Directory and Business Advertiser.* Richmond, Va., 1856.

*Encyclopedia of Virginia Biography.* 5 vols. Edited by Lyon G. Tyler. New York: Lewis Publishing Company, 1915.

Ernst, William. "Thomas Hicks Wynne." *Virginia Cavalcade* 27: 186–91.

Escott, Paul D. *After Secession: Jefferson Davis and the Failure of Southern Nationalism.* Baton Rouge: Louisiana State University Press, 1978.

Faust, Drew G. *A Sacred Circle: The Dilemma of the Intellectuals in the Old South.* Baltimore: Johns Hopkins University Press, 1977.

Ferslew, W. Eugene. *Annual Directory for the City of Richmond.* Richmond, Va.: 1859 and 1860.

Fetis, Joseph, *Biographie universelle de musiciens.* 2d ed. Paris, 1875.

Ficklin, Walter H. *A Genealogical History of the Ficklin Family.* Denver: Keister, 1912.

Fitzhugh, George. *Cannibals All! or Slaves Without Masters.* Edited by C. Vann Woodward. Cambridge, Mass.: Belknap Press of Harvard University Press, 1960.

Fleet, Robert. *Green Mount: A Virginia Plantation Family During the Civil War: Being the Journal of Dr. Robert Fleet and Letters of His Family.* Edited by Betsy Fleet and John C. P. Fuller. Lexington: University of Kentucky Press, 1962.

Freeman, Douglas S. *Lee's Lieutenants.* 3 vols. New York: Scribner's, 1942–44.

———. *R. E. Lee: A Biography.* 4 vols. New York: Scribner's, 1935.

Gaines, William H., Jr. *Thomas Mann Randolph: Jefferson's Son-in-Law.* Baton Rouge: Louisiana State University Press, 1966.

*Gardner's Directory . . . .* New Orleans, 1857, 1859, 1860, and 1861.

Garmon, Gerald M. *John Reuben Thompson.* Boston: Twayne, 1979.

Goff, Richard D. *Confederate Supply.* Durham, N.C.: Duke University Press, 1968.

Goodrich, Carter. "The Virginia System of Mixed Enterprise." *Political Science Quarterly* 64: 355–87.

Gorgas, Josiah. *The Civil War Diary of General Josiah Gorgas.* Edited by Frank E. Vandiver. Tuscaloosa: University of Alabama Press, 1947.

*Grove's Dictionary of Music and Musicians.* 10 vols. Edited by Eric Blom. New York: St. Martin's Press, 1954.

Harrison, Fairfax. *The Virginia Carys.* New York: DeVinne Press, 1919.

*Harvard Memorial Biographies.* 2 vols. Edited by Thomas W. Higginson. Cambridge, Mass.: Sever and Francis, 1866.

Hattaway, Herman, and Archer Jones. *How the North Won: A Military History of the Civil War.* Urbana: University of Illinois Press, 1983.

Hayden, Horace E. *Virginia Genealogies* . . . . 1891. Reprint. Baltimore: Southern Book Company, 1959.

Hendrick, Burton J. *Statesmen of the Lost Cause: Jefferson Davis and His Cabinet.* New York: Literary Guild, 1939.

Hesseltine, William B., and Larry Garra. "Postwar Problems of a Virginia Historian." *Virginia Magazine of History and Biography* 61 (1953), 193–95.

Holtzman, Robert S. *Stormy Ben Butler.* New York: Macmillan, 1954.

Howard, Leon. *Victorian Knight Errant: A Study of the Early Literary Career of James Russell Lowell.* Berkeley: University of California Press, 1952.

Hudnall, Henry. *Contributions to a History of the Richmond Howitzer Battalion.* 4 pamphlets. Richmond, Va., 1883–1886.

Jefferson, Thomas. *The Papers of Thomas Jefferson.* Edited by Julian P. Boyd. 20 vols. to 1982. Princeton: Princeton University Press, 1950–.

Johnson, Angus J., II. "Disloyalty on Confederate Railroads in Virginia." *Virginia Magazine of History and Biography* 63 (1955): 416.

———. *Virginia Railroads in the Civil War.* Chapel Hill: University of North Carolina Press, 1961.

Johnson, Ludwell H. *The Red River Campaign: Politics and Cotton in the Civil War.* Baltimore: Johns Hopkins University Press, 1958.

Johnston, Joseph E. *Narrative of Military Operations.* New York: Appleton, 1874.

Johnston, Mary Tabb Lancaster, and Elizabeth J. Lipscomb. *Amelia Gayle Gorgas: A Biography.* Tuscaloosa: University of Alabama Press, 1978.

Jones, Archer. *Confederate Strategy from Shiloh to Vicksburg.* Baton Rouge: Louisiana State University Press, 1961.

———. "George Wythe Randolph." *Virginia Magazine of History and Biography* 61 (1953): 45–59.

———. "Some Aspects of George Wythe Randolph's Service as Confederate Secretary of War." *Journal of Southern History* 26 (1960): 299–314.

Jones, John Beauchamp. *A Rebel War Clerk's Diary.* 2 vols. Edited by Howard Swiggett. New York: Old Hickory Bookshop, 1935.

———. *A Rebel War Clerk's Diary.* Edited by Earle S. Miers. New York: Sagamore Press, 1958.

Kean, Jefferson Randolph. "General George Wythe Randolph." *Reports of the Monticello Association* 15 (1928): 14–18.

Kean, Robert Garlick Hill. *Inside the Confederate Government: The Diary of Robert Garlick Hill Kean*. Edited by Edward Younger. New York: Oxford, 1957.

Keller, Suzanne. *Beyond the Ruling Class: Strategic Elites in Modern Society*. New York: Random House, 1963.

Korn, Bertram W. *The Early Jews of New Orleans*. Waltham, Mass.: American Jewish Historical Society, 1969.

Laferty, J. J. *Sketches of the Virginia Methodist Conference*. Richmond, Va., 1880.

Landry, Stewart O. *History of the Boston Club*. New Orleans: Pelican Publishing Company, 1938.

Lasswell, Harold D. *The Comparative Study of Elites*. Palo Alto, Calif.: Stanford University Press, 1952.

Lewis, Charles L. *David Glasgow Farragut, Admiral in the Making*. Annapolis, Md.: U.S. Naval Institute, 1941.

Luraghi, Raimondo. *The Rise and Fall of the Plantation South*. New York: New Directions, 1978.

[McGuire, Judith White Brockenbrough.] *Diary of a Southern Refugee*. 1867. Reprint. New York: Arno, 1972.

McLean, Robert C. *George Tucker, Moral Philosopher and Man of Letters*. Chapel Hill: University of North Carolina Press, 1961.

Mahan, Dennis H. *Advanced-Guard, Out-Post, and Detachment Service of Troops with the Essential Principles of Strategy, and Grand Tactics, for the Use of the Militia and Volunteers*. New York: J. Wiley, 1860.

———. *A Complete Treatise on Field Fortifications with the General Outline of the Principles Regulating the Arrangement, the Attack and the Defence of a Permanent Works*. 2d ed. New York: J. Wiley, 1860.

———. *Summary of the Course of Permanent Fortifications*. West Point, N.Y.: U.S. Military Academy, 1850.

Malone, Dumas. *Jefferson and His Time*. 6 vols. Boston: Houghton Mifflin, 1948–81.

Manahan, John E. "The Cavalier Remounted: A Study of Virginia's Population, 1620–1700." Ph.D. diss., University of Virginia, 1959.

Manarin, Louis H., ed. *Richmond at War: The Minutes of the City Council, 1861–1865*. Chapel Hill: University of North Carolina Press for the Richmond Civil War Centennial Committee, 1966.

Manarin, Louis H. and Lee A. Wallace, Jr. *Richmond Volunteers . . . 1861–1865*. Richmond: Westover Press for the Richmond Civil War Centennial Committee, 1969.

Mannheim, Karl. *Man and Society in an Age of Reconstruction*. London: Kegan Paul, 1946.

Marx, Karl and Frederick Engels. *Collected Works*. 41 vols. New York: International Publishers, 1975–87.

Mason, Emily V. *Southern Poems of the War*. 5th ed. Baltimore: J. Murphy, 1867.

Meade, Robert D. *Judah P. Benjamin*. New York: Oxford University Press, 1943.

Minor, John B. *The Minor Family of Virginia*. Lynchburg, Va.: Bell, 1923.
*Montague's Richmond Directory and Business Advertiser*. Richmond, Va.: 1851 and 1852.
Mordecai, Samuel. *Richmond in By-Gone Days*. Richmond, Va.: George M. West, 1856.
Morgan, Gerald, Jr. "Nicholas Philip and Virginia Randolph Trist." In *Collected Papers of the Monticello Association*. Vol. 1. Princeton: Princeton University Press, 1950.
Morrison, Samuel E. *The Oxford History of the American People*. New York: Oxford University Press, 1965.
Myers, Robert M. *Children of Pride*. New Haven: Yale University Press, 1972.
Nash, Howard P. *Stormy Petrel: The Life and Times of General Benjamin F. Butler, 1818–1893*. Rutherford, N.J.: Fairleigh-Dickinson University Press, 1969.
*National Cyclopedia of American Biography*. 63 vols. New York: James T. White and Company, 1891–1984.
Naval History Division, U.S. Department of Defense. *Uniforms of the United States Navy, 1776–1967*, ser. 1 (1776–1898). Washington: GPO, 1966.
Nichols, Roy F. *The Disruption of American Democracy*. New York: Macmillan, 1948.
Pareto, Vilfredo. *The Mind and Society*. 4 vols. Edited by Arthur Livingston. New York: Harcourt, Brace and Company, 1935.
Parsons, Talcott. *Essays In Sociological Theory*. New York: Macmillan, 1954.
Parton, James. *General Butler in New Orleans: History of the Administration of the Department of the Gulf in the Year 1862*. 7th ed. New York: Mason Brothers, 1864.
Patrick, Rembert. *Jefferson Davis and His Cabinet*. Baton Rouge: Louisiana State University Press, 1944.
Paullin, Charles O. *Commodore John Rodgers . . . 1783–1838*. 2d ed. Annapolis, Md.: U.S. Naval Institute, 1967.
Perry, Leslie J. "A Parallel for Grant's Action." *Southern Historical Society Papers* 24: 114.
"Poem." *Southern Literary Messenger,* Oct. 1856, pp. 311–12.
Pollard, Edward A. *The Lost Cause*. New York: E. B. Treat, 1866.
Porter, David D., Jr. *The Adventures of Harry Marline, or Notes from an American Midshipman's Lucky Bag*. New York: Appleton, 1885.
————. *Memoir of Commodore David Porter*. Albany: J. Munsell, 1875.
*Press Reference Book of Prominent Virginians*. Edited by A. B. Tunis. Richmond, Va.: Richmond Newspapers, 1916.
Pryor, Sara Agnes Rice. *Reminiscences of Peace and War*. New York: Macmillan, 1905.
————. *My Day: Reminiscences of a Long Life*. New York: Macmillan, 1909.
Rachal, William M. E. "President Monroe Returns to Virginia." *Virginia Cavalcade* 3 (Summer 1953): 43–47.

Randall, Henry S. *The Life of Thomas Jefferson*. 3 vols. New York: Derby and Jackson, 1857–58.

Randolph, Robert Isham. *The Randolphs of Virginia: A Compilation of the Descendants of William Randolph of Turkey Island and of His Wife Mary Isham of Bermuda Hundred*. Chicago, [1928].

Randolph, Thomas. *The Poems and Amyntas* . . . . Edited by John Jay Parry. New Haven: Yale University Press, 1917.

Reagan, John H. *Memoirs With Special Reference to Secession and Civil War*. 1906. Reprint. Austin: University of Texas Press, 1968.

*Register of Former Cadets, Virginia Military Institute*. Edited by E. Raymond Dixon. Lexington, Va., 1970.

*The Revolutionary Diplomatic Correspondence of the United States*. 6 vols. Edited by Francis Wharton. Washington, D.C.: GPO, 1889.

Rhodes, James F. *The History of the United States from the Compromise of 1850*. 8 vols. New York: Harper, 1893–1906.

Richardson, E. Ramsay. *Little Alec: A Life of Alexander H. Stevens*. New York: Grossett and Dunlap, 1932.

*Richmond City and Henrico County, Virginia, 1850 Census*. Richmond, Va.: Virginia Genealogical Society, 1977.

Ross, Ishbell. *First Lady of the South: The Life of Mrs. Jefferson Davis*. Westport, Conn.: Greenwood, 1973.

Scudder, Horace. *James Russell Lowell: A Biography*. 2 vols. Boston: Houghton Mifflin, 1901.

Shackelford, George G. "Lieutenant Lee Reports to Captain Talcott . . . ." *Virginia Magazine of History and Biography* 60 (1952): 458–87.

———. "New Letters Between Hugh Blair Grigsby and Henry Stevens Randall, 1858–1861." *Virginia Magazine of History and Biography* 64 (1956): 322–57.

———. "Jane Hollins and Thomas Jefferson Randolph," "Martha Jefferson and Thomas Mann Randolph," and "Septimia Jefferson Randolph and David Scott Meikleham." In *Collected Papers of the Monticello Association*. Vol. 1. Princeton: Princeton University Press, 1965.

———. "Mary Buchanan Randolph, Carolina Ramsay Randolph and Sarah Nicholas Randolph." In *Collected Papers of the Monticello Association*. Vol. 2. Charlottesville: Monticello Association, 1984.

Shackelford, George G., ed. *Collected Papers of the Monticello Association*. Vol. 1. Princeton: Princeton University Press, 1965; Vol. 2. Charlottesville, Va.: Monticello Association, 1984.

Shanks, Henry T. *The Secession Movement in Virginia, 1847–1861*. Richmond: Garrett and Massie, 1934.

Snavely, Tipton R. *George Tucker as Political Economist*. Charlottesville, Va.: University Press of Virginia, 1964.

*Southern Historical Society Papers*. 52 vols. Edited by J. William Jones et al. Millwood, N.Y.: Krauss Reprint Company, 1977.

Sowerby, E. Millicent. *The Catalogue of the Library of Thomas Jefferson.* 5 vols. Washington: Library of Congress, 1952–59.

Speed, John Gilmer. *The Gilmers in America.* New York: 1897.

Stainsbury, John S. *A Dictionary of Musicians from the Earliest Times.* 2 vols. Reprint of 1825 edition. New York: Da Capo, 1966.

Stanard, Mary Newton. *Richmond: Its People and Its Story.* Philadelphia: Lippincott, 1923.

Stanard, William G. "Catalogue of Portraits in the Collection of the Virginia Historical Society." *Virginia Magazine of History and Biography* 35 (1927): 60.

———. "Harrison of James River." *Virginia Magazine of History and Biography* 30 (1922): 408–12.

———. "Homes of the Virginia Historical Society." *Virginia Magazine of History and Biography* 39 (1931): 8.

———. "Kennon Letters." *Virginia Magazine of History and Biography* 31 (1923): 187, 310.

———. "Proceedings of the Virginia Historical Society." *Virginia Magazine of History and Biography* 13 (1905–1906): xvi, xviii.

———. "Randolph Family." *William and Mary Quarterly,* 1st ser. 8:120.

*Students of the University of Virginia: A Semi-Centennial Catalogue.* Edited by Maximillian Schele de Vere. Baltimore: Harvey, 1878.

Swanburg, William A. *Sickles the Incredible.* New York: Scribner's, 1956.

Taylor, Olivia. "Charles Lewis and Anne Cary Randolph Bankhead" and "Descendants of Thomas Jefferson and His Wife Martha Wayles." In *Collected Papers of the Monticello Association.* Vol. 1: Princeton: Princeton University Press, 1965.

Taylor, Richard. *Destruction and Reconstruction: Personal Reminiscences.* New York: Appleton, 1879.

Thomas, Emory M. *The Confederate Nation, 1861–1865.* New York: Harper and Row, 1979.

———. *The Confederate State of Richmond: A Biography of the Capital.* Austin: University of Texas Press, 1971.

Thompson, John R. *The Poems of John R. Thompson.* Edited by John S. Patton. New York: Scribner's, 1920.

Torrence, Clayton. "Letters of Sarah Nicholas Randolph to Hugh Blair Grigsby." *Virginia Magazine of History and Biography* 59 (1951): 315–36.

Trent, William P., ed. *Southern Writers: Selections in Prose and Poetry.* New York: Macmillan, 1905.

Vance, Joseph. "Thomas Jefferson Randolph." Ph.D. diss., University of Virginia, 1954.

Vandiver, Frank E. *Ploughshares into Swords: Josiah Gorgas and Confederate Ordnance.* Austin: University of Texas Press, 1952.

———. *Rebel Brass: The Confederate Command System.* Westport, Conn: Greenwood Press, 1956.

Villard, Oswald G. *John Brown* . . . . Boston: Houghton Mifflin, 1910.

Wakelyn, Jon L. *Biographical Dictionary of the Confederacy*. Westport, Conn.: Greenwood Press, 1977.

Waring, Clelia P. M. "Sally Champe Carter and Benjamin Franklin Randolph." In *Collected Papers of the Monticello Association*. Vol. 1. Princeton: Princeton University Press, 1965.

*The War of the Rebellion . . . Official Records of the Union and Confederate Armies*. Edited by Russell A. Alger, Fred C. Ainsworth, and Joseph W. Kirthy. 1st ser., 10; 1st ser. 26, pt. 2; 1st ser., 51, pts. 1 and 2; 4th ser., 1–3. Washington: GPO, 1882–1900.

West, Richard S. *Lincoln's Scapegoat General: A Life of Benjamin F. Butler, 1818–1893*. Cambridge, Mass.: Houghton Mifflin, 1965.

*West Point Cadets*. West Point, N.Y.: U.S. Military Academy, 1937.

Whitehill, Walter Muir. *Boston: A Topographical History*. 2d ed. Cambridge, Mass.: Belknap Press of Harvard University Press, 1968.

————. "Eleanora Wayles Randolph and Joseph Coolidge, Jr." In *Collected Papers of the Monticello Association*. Vol. 1. Princeton: Princeton University Press, 1965.

Whitehill, Walter Muir and William C. Endicott. *Captain Joseph Peabody . . . , His Ships and . . . Family*. Salem, Mass.: Peabody Museum, 1962.

Whitmore, Madeline McMurdo. "Caryanne Nicholas Randolph and Francis Gildart Ruffin." In *Collected Papers of the Monticello Association*. Vol. 2. Charlottesville, Va.: Monticello Association, 1984.

Williams, T. Harry. *P. G. T. Beauregard: Napoleon in Gray*. Baton Rouge: Louisiana State University Press, 1954.

Wise, Jennings C. *The Long Arm of Lee*. 2 vols. Lynchburg, Va.: J. P. Bell Company, 1915.

Wish, Harvey. *George Fitzhugh: Propagandist of the Old South*. Baton Rouge: Louisiana State University Press, 1943.

Wordsworth, Christopher. *Athens and Attica*. London: John Murray, 1837.

Works Progress Administration Writers Program of Louisiana. *Louisiana*. New York: Hastings, 1941.

Works Progress Administration Writers Program of New Orleans. *New Orleans Guide*. Boston: Houghton Mifflin, 1938.

# Index